Contents

Preface

This is the second volume in the series commissioned by the Office of Population Censuses and Surveys to analyse the ethnic group question in the 1991 Census. The 1991 Census was the first in Great Britain in which such a question had been posed. The other volumes in the series are:

Volume 1 Demographic characteristics of the ethnic minority populations. Edited by David Coleman and John Salt

Volume 3 Social geography and ethnicity in Britain: geographical spread, spatial concentration and internal migration. Edited by Peter Ratcliffe

Volume 4 Employment, education and housing among the ethnic minority populations of Britain. Edited by Valerie Karn

Acknowledgements

Grateful acknowledgement is made to the Economic and Social Research Council for the purchase of the computer files of the 1991 Census and to the University of Manchester Computer Centre and to the University of Manchester Census Microdata Unit through which these files were made available to the academic community. Specifically, the work for Volume 2 was carried out with financial assistance from the OPCS and from the ESRC (Research Grant R45126412793). The editor also gratefully acknowledges the computational assistance of Dr David Rossiter of the Oxford University Computing Service.

OFFICE FOR NATIONAL STATISTICS

Ethnicity in the 1991 Census

Volume Two

The ethnic minority populations of Great Britain

Edited by Ceri Peach

London: HMSO

Notice
On 1st April 1996 the Office of Population Censuses and Surveys (OPCS) and the Central Statistical Office (CSO) merged to form the Office for National Statistics. The Office for National Statistics will be responsible for the full range of functions carried out by OPCS and CSO.

The views expressed in this publication are not necessarily those of the Office for National Statistics

Front cover photograph: © Crispin Hughes/Photofusion

Printed in the United Kingdom for HMSO
Dd 0301924 6/96 C10 65862

Notes on contributors

Madawi Al-Rasheed is a lecturer in social anthropology at the Institute of Social and Cultural Anthropology, Oxford University and Fellow of Wolfson College. Her research interests are in the anthropology of tribal societies in the Middle East, political organisation and religious experience. More recently, she has done research on Arab immigrants in London with special reference to the Iraqi community. Her publications include: *Politics in an Arabian Oasis* (London: I. B. Tauris, 1991) and a number of articles on ethnicity, migration, the myth of return and exile. She is currently preparing a monograph on the Iraqi Assyrian Christians in London.

Roger Ballard is a Lecturer in comparative religion at Manchester University, and he previously taught at Leeds. His primary research interests are in the process of South Asian migration to Britain and the associated emergence of ethnic colonies, as well as the broader dynamics of ethnic and religious polarisation. He has carried out extensive ethnographic fieldwork in India and Pakistan, as well as in urban Britain. His publications include: *Desh Pardesh: The South Asian Presence in Britain* (London: Hurst and Co., 1994); *The Ethnic Dimensions of the 1991 Census: A preliminary report* (Manchester: Manchester Census Group, 1994); 'New clothes for the emperor? The conceptual nakedness of the British race relations industry' *New Community* 1992, 18, 481—92; 'Migration and kinship: the impact of marriage rules on processes of Pakistani migration to Britain' in: Clarke, Peach and Vertovec (eds), *South Asians Overseas* (Cambridge: Cambridge University Press, 1990).

Judith Chance is a senior lecturer in geography at Oxford Brookes University. Her research interests lie in social geography, especially the study of Irish migration. Publications include: contributions to *Race and Racism* (ed. Peter Jackson, London: Unwin Hyman, 1987) and, with C. Peach et al, *British Social Trends since 1900* (ed. A. H. Halsey, London: Macmillan, 1988).

Yuan Cheng is a research fellow at the Policy Studies Institute. She received her doctorate in sociology at the University of Oxford where she was subsequently employed as a research officer. Her research interests are ethnic stratification, employment and unemployment. Books and main articles include: *Education and Class: Chinese in Britain and the United States* (Avebury Press, 1994); with Anthony Heath, 'Ethnic origins and class destinations', *Oxford Review of Education*, 1993; with Duncan Gallie, Michael White and Mark Tomlinson, 'The Employment Commitment of Unemployed People' *Unemployment and Public Policy in a Changing Labour Market* (ed. Michael Whites, PSI, 1994); with Jianzhong Dai, 'Intergenerational mobility in modern China' *European Sociological Review*, 1995.

Patricia Daley is a lecturer in geography at Oxford University and a fellow at Jesus College. She has taught at Dartmouth College, New Hampshire and at Loughborough University. Her research interests are in the processes of refugee migration, environmental change and African development. Papers include: 'Gender displacement and social reproduction: settling Barundi refugees in western Tanzania' *Journal of Refugee Studies* 1991, 4, 3, 248—66; 'The politics of the refugee crisis in Tanzania, in: Campbell, H. and H. Stein (eds), *Tanzania and the IMF: The Dynamics of Liberalization* (Boulder, CO: Westview Press, 1992, pp. 125—46); 'From the Kipande to the Kibali: the incorporation of Barundi refugees and labour migrants in western Tanzania 1900—1987, in: Black, R. and V. Robinson (eds), *Geography and Refugees: Patterns and Processes of Change* (Belhaven, 1993, pp. 17—32); 'Women, war and the environments in southern Africa' *Africa World Review*, April 1993, 14—17.

John Eade is principal lecturer in anthropology and sociology at Roehampton Institute, London. He is author of *The Politics of Community: The Bangladeshi Community in East London* (Avebury, 1989) and has published articles and chapters in edited books on issues involving Bangladeshis in Britain, especially those concerning local politics, Islam, health, identity and globalisation. He has also edited, with Michael J. Sallow, *Contesting the Sacred: The Anthropology of Christian Pilgrimage* (London: Routledge, 1992).

David Owen is a senior research fellow at the Centre for Research in Ethnic Relations, University of Warwick. His research interests are in the analysis of the social and economic circumstances of minority ethnic groups in Britain, internal migration and population change and local labour market analysis. He is joint author, with A. Champion, A. Green, D. Ellin and M. Coombes, of *Changing Places* (1987), and has recently had published a major research report for the Equal Opportunities Commission entitled *Ethnic Minority Women and the Labour Market: analysis of the 1991 Census.*

Ceri Peach is professor of social geography and head of department at Oxford University. He is a fellow of St Catherine's College. He has held visiting fellowships at ANU, Berkeley and Yale. His research interests are in patterns of migration, settlement and segregation. Books include: *West Indian Migration to Britain: A Social Geography* (Oxford: Oxford University Press, 1968); *Urban Social Segregation* (Longman, 1975); with Susan Smith and Vaughan Robinson, *Ethnic Segregation in Cities* (Croom Helm, 1981); with Colin Clarke and David Ley, *Geography and Ethnic Pluralism* (Allen and Unwin, 1984); with Colin Clarke and Steven Vertovec, *South Asians Overseas: Migration and Ethnicity* (Cambridge: Cambridge University Press, 1990).

Vaughan Robinson is director of the University of Wales Migration Unit and a senior lecturer in the geography department at the University of Wales, Swansea. His main research interests are in migration studies, ethnic relations and refugee studies. His books include: with Susan Smith and Ceri Peach, *Ethnic Segregation in Cities* (Croom Helm, 1981); *Transients, Settlers and Refugees* (Clarendon, 1986); *The International Refugee Crisis* (Macmillan, 1991); with Richard Black, *Geography and Refugees* (Belhaven, 1992); *Geography and Migration* (Elgar, 1995).

David Rossiter is a senior computing officer at Oxford University Computing Service. He received his doctorate in geography at the University of Sheffield for research into the use of census data to estimate inter-war patterns of electoral behaviour in the British coalfields. He provides advice on the use of statistical and mapping software and is responsible for supporting users of census data at Oxford. He has also published several papers on electoral redistricting and is currently working on a research project funded by the Leverhulme Trust into the operations of the Parliamentary Boundary Commissions.

Tim Vamplew is a researcher at Surrey County Council Social Services Department. His first degree was in sociology from the University of Kent in 1991. He took an MSc in social research methods from the University of Surrey in 1993.

Introduction

Ceri Peach

1 The ethnic question

Recording ethnic identity in national censuses is a politically sensitive issue. There are two schools of thought. On the one hand, there are those who argue that since, in principle, all people are equal before the law, questions of ethnic, socially constructed identities that divide the population serve to heighten divisions. They argue that the data should not be collected. On the other hand are those who argue that inequality of condition and treatment on ethnic and racial lines exists in Great Britain and that until it is quantified, the targets for correction will not exist (Anwar, 1990).

The Census of Great Britain in 1991 asked, for the first time, a question on ethnicity. The question took the form of nine labelled boxes, seven with pre-coded categories and two with space for elaborating possible responses.

Answers to the ethnic group question were assigned one of 35 codes. This full classification incorporates the seven pre-coded categories — White, Black–Caribbean, Black–African, Indian, Pakistani, Bangladeshi and Chinese — plus another 28 categories derived from multi-ticked responses

11 Ethnic group	
Please tick the appropriate box.	White ☐ 0
	Black-Caribbean ☐ 1
	Black-African ☐ 2
	Black-Other ☐
	please describe
	Indian ☐ 3
	Pakistani ☐ 4
	Bangladeshi ☐ 5
	Chinese ☐ 6
If the person is descended from more than one ethnic or racial group, please tick the group to which the person considers he/she belongs, or tick the 'Any other ethnic group' box and describe the person's ancestry in the space provided.	Any other ethnic group ☐
	please describe

Source: 1991 Census of Population, H enumeration form for private households, reproduced in Dale and Marsh (1993), p.367.

or written in descriptions under 'Black–Other' and 'Any other ethnic group'. For the purposes of most statistical output from the census, the full classification of 35 codes has been condensed into 10 categories. Many of the multi-ticked responses were merged into the 'pure' categories: White, Black–Caribbean, Black–African and Black–Other, while two further categories, Other–Asian and Other–Other were created. A full listing of the 35 codes in their disaggregated form together with their assignation to one of the macro categories are given in Table 1 (OPCS/GRO(S), 1993, Table A). The results of the mixed allocation, used in the published census tables, is compared with the results of the 'pure' allocation in Table 2.

The effect of not allocating the mixed categories is relatively small for most of the 'pure' groups. The Indian, Pakistani, Bangladeshi and Chinese groups would be unchanged. The Black–Caribbean and Black–African populations would diminish by a few thousand, the Black–Other population would increase significantly and the Other–Asian and Other–Other groups would merge into an expanded residual category of Other, numbering over half a million. Reviewing the categories in Table 1, it could be argued that the Black British (code 7) should have been part of the Black–Caribbean and that codes 10 and 11 (East African Asians or Indo–Caribbean and Indian subcontinent) should have been allocated to the Indian category.

History of the ethnic group question

In census terms, before 1991, country of birth data, used in various permutations, were the only basis for ethnic estimates. The relationship between country of birth and ethnicity was not as congruent as it appeared. 'New Commonwealth' was frequently used as a euphemism for non-White minorities in Britain, whereas in fact, one fifth of this population is shown by the 1991 Census to be White. In particular, Whites born in India, but living in Britain, complicated the interpretation of the characteristics of the Indian population when only birthplace data were available. The 1991 Census demonstrates that of the 409,022 persons born in India, 62,895 or 15 per cent were White (OPCS/GRO(S), 1993, vol 1, Table 5). The 1991 Samples of Anonymised Records (SAR) show that of the Whites born in India living in Britain in 1991, 88 per cent were aged 50 or over. Thus, in earlier censuses the White proportion is likely to have been higher. Peach and Winchester (1974) calculated that one third of the 322,670 persons born in India living in Britain in 1971, were White.

An ethnic group question had been contemplated for the 1981 Census, but abandoned after testing, because of political sensitivity and because of ethnic consumer resistance during the piloting stage (Sillitoe, 1978; 1987). In the 1971 Census, the question had been circumvented, not entirely successfully, by asking a question on the birthplace of parents. Ethnicity was implied from the total of those with both parents born in a given country. In 1951 and 1961, birthplace alone was the surrogate measure of ethnicity. As early as 1951, the census was indicating the danger of imputing ethnicity from birthplace. The 1951 Census General Report shows that 68 per cent of the 12,180 persons born in Egypt and living in England and Wales at that time, were thought to be the children of British service personnel (Registrar

Table 1 *Ethnic group, full group code and summary classifications, Great Britain, 1991*

Code	Category	Number
All	Total	54,888,844
0	White	51,810,555
1	Black–Caribbean	493,339
2	Black–African	208,110
3	Indian	840,255
4	Pakistani	476,555
5	Bangladeshi	162,835
6	Chinese	156,938
Black–Other: non-mixed origin		
Total 7–14	Total	143,667
7	British	58,106
8	Caribbean Islands, West Indies or Guyana	3,093
9	North African, Arab or Iranian	6,471
10	Other African countries	927
11	East African Asian or Indo-Caribbean	1,271
12	Indian subcontinent	4,005
13	Other–Asian	24,854
14	Other answers	44,940
Black–Other: mixed origin		
Total 15–17		75,424
15	Black/White	24,687
16	Asian/White	69
17	Other mixed	50,668
Any other ethnic group: non-mixed origin		
Total 18–30		364,310
18	British–ethnic minority indicated	16,170
19	British–non ethnic minority indicated	13,971
20	Caribbean Islands, West Indies or Guyana	3,532
21	North African, Arab or Iranian	58,720
22	Other African countries	3,325
23	East African Asian or Indo-Caribbean	6,110
24	Indian subcontinent	41,333
25	Other–Asian	119,961
26	Irish	n/a
27	Greek (including Greek Cypriot)	17,982
28	Turkish (including Turkish Cypriot)	18,876
29	Other European	22,148
30	Other answers	41,725
Any other ethnic group; mixed origin		
Total 31–34		156,856
31	Black/White	29,882
32	Asian/White	61,805
33	Mixed White	3,776
34	Other mixed	61,393

Source: OPCS/GRO(S) (1993) 1991 Census Ethnic Group and Country of Birth, Great Britain Volume 2 Appendix, Table A, pp. 830-1 and 858-9.

Table 2 *Ethnic group code output allocation for standard census tables compared with non-allocation of mixed groups*

	Codes for standard (mixed) tables	Number	Codes for 'pure' disaggregated tables	Number
White	0,26-29,33	51,873,794	0	51,810,555
Black–Caribbean	1,8,20	499,964	1	493,339
Black–African	2,10,22	212,362	2	208,110
Black–Other	7,14,15,17	178,401	7–17	219,091
Indian	3	840,255	3	840,255
Pakistani	4	476,555	4	476,555
Bangladeshi	5	162,835	5	162,835
Chinese	6	156,938	6	156,938
Other – Asian	11–13,23–25	197,534		
Other – Other	9,16,18,19,21 30–32,34	290,206		
Others			18-34	521,166

Source: OPCS/GRo(S) (1993) Volume 2, pp. 474, 496, 830-831,858,859.

General, 1958, 110). The 1991 ethnic group question therefore stands alone and there are no earlier census data with which to make direct comparisons.

The problems of using birthplace as a surrogate for ethnicity became more marked after 1961 as the proportion of second generation ethnic population, born in Britain, grew. In the case of the Black–Caribbean population, primary immigration had finished by the early 1970s (Peach, 1991; see also Figure 1). Growth since that time has been almost entirely due to natural increase. Over half (54 per cent) of the 1991 Black–Caribbean ethnic resident population of 499,964 were born in the United Kingdom. For the Indian ethnic population, 43 per cent were born in the United Kingdom; for the Pakistani population the figure was 50 per cent and for the Bangladeshi population it was 37 per cent. Of the Black–Other population, 85 per cent were born in the United Kingdom, suggesting that it was a Black British ethnicity in the making.

The 1991 ethnic group question was not uncontroversial with ethnic minority groups. At the experimental stage of designing the ethnic group question for the 1991 Census, OPCS piloted a religious question for South Asian groups. Although there was a good response, it was not included in subsequent schedules (Sillitoe, 1987). The Islamic Secretariat of the UK campaigned among Muslims to reject the ethnic group question on the 1991 Census and to write in the word 'Muslim' instead (Islamic Secretariat, 1991). As far as one can tell, this advice was not widely adopted. The history and difficulties of including an ethnic question in the census are examined by David Owen in Chapter 3 of this volume.

Accuracy of the count

The Census Validation Survey executed after the census, suggested that the 1991 count missed 2.2 per cent of the resident population of Great Britain (or about 1.2 million people). This undercount was not uniform across ethnic groups, age, gender or geographic areas. The 1991 Census (OPCS/GRO(S), 1993 vol 2, 479) published tables of adjustment figures for age, sex and ethnic group. These tables suggest that the undercount was greater for men than women and for 20–29-year-olds than for other age-groups. It is particularly marked for young ethnic minority men, where the undercount for 25–29-year-olds is in the range of 13 to 17 per cent. However, having noted the problem, this volume accepts the recorded data as given.

Problems of ethnic identity

While birthplace is an unambiguous category, ethnic identity is more mercurial. Critically, ethnicity is contextual rather than absolute. One may be Welsh in England, British in Germany, European in Thailand, White in Africa. A person may be Afro–Caribbean by descent but British by upbringing so that his or her census category might be either Black–Caribbean or Black–Other. Similarly, a person may be an East African Asian, an Indian, a Sikh or a Ramgarhia. Thus ethnicity is a situational rather than an independent category. The Census Quality Validation has indicated confusion about which category to claim, especially for those of mixed ethnic background.

The ten main ethnic categories produced by the 1991 Census are not unambiguous. The emphasis in the classification is on categorising the non-European minority groups, while aggregating the European population into a single White group. Taking the categories in the order in which they appear in the census, White is not an ethnic group but a racial designation; it conflates all European identities and more besides. Black–Caribbean is complicated by the uncertainty as to whether those who wrote themselves into the census as 'Black British' (58,106; see code 7 in Table 1) should have been included in this category rather than Black–Other. Within the Black–Caribbean group there are differences between those originating from different islands and territories within the Caribbean (see Chapter 1). Black-African is clearly a racial designation, but it hides a great range of national and ethnic identities within it and does not represent a homogeneous group (see Chapter 2). Black–Other is similarly a residual category, containing not only second generation Afro-Caribbeans, but also African-Americans (significant in the geography of military bases) and old established dockland ethnic minorities in Liverpool, Cardiff and other places (see Chapter 3). Indian as a category represents nationality as much as ethnicity. There are very significant differences within the group according to religion, language and place of origin (see Chapter 4). Pakistani is relatively unambiguous as a title, although significant differences exist within the group according to place of origin (see Chapter 5). Bangladeshi is perhaps the least ambiguous of the groups, with a high proportion originating from the Sylhet District in the north east of the country (see Chapter 6). The Chinese are drawn from Hong Kong, Singapore, Vietnam and Taiwan as well as from the People's Republic itself (see Chapter 7). Other–Asians are another residual category containing the Japanese, Malaysians and a myriad of small groups (see Chapter 8). Other–Other is perhaps the most ambiguous of all the groups, although Middle Easterners figure prominently within it (see Chapter 9). Finally, the Irish pose a significant problem of identification. There was no Irish ethnic question on the census and birthplace has additional problems of interpretation in this case as two very different traditions are involved for the 'born in Ireland' category (see Chapter 10).

Although the 1991 Census was the first to ask a direct ethnic question, two official government surveys, the Labour Force Survey (LFS) and the General Household Survey (GHS), had regularly asked such questions during the 1980s. The surveys, however, were small in relation to the 100 per cent coverage of the census and collected relatively small ethnic samples within their broader coverage. They were helpful in giving a snapshot of the country as a whole, but less helpful in pinpointing geographical differences within the country or in measuring change over time. Small numbers meant that the surveys of several years had to be amalgamated to create a sample size large enough to be robust and this militated against measuring change over time. Similar problems of sample size made anything other than coarse regional disaggregation impossible.

Although the LFS and the GHS had asked questions on ethnic identity, the 1991 Census did not follow the categorisations used by those enquiries (see Table 3).

Ethnic or 'racial' categories?

While certain categories — Indian, Pakistani, Bangladeshi, Chinese — are common to both the Census and the LFS, other groups differ in nomenclature (West Indians versus Black–Caribbean; African versus Black–African) or are not reproduced at all. In particular, there is no Arab group given in the census although there is in the Labour Force Survey. Similarly, the 'Mixed'

Table 3 *Comparison of ethnic categorisation used in 1991 Census and by the Labour Force Survey*

1991 Census	1991	Labour Force Survey	1989/91
White	51,873,794	White	51,808,000
Black–Caribbean	499,964	West Indian (including Guyanese)	455,000
Black–African	212,362	African	150,000
Black–Other	178,401		
Indian	840,255	Indian	792,000
Pakistani	476,555	Pakistani	485,000
Bangladeshi	162,835	Bangladeshi	127,000
Chinese	156,938	Chinese	137,000
Other – Asian	197,534		
Other – Other	290,206		
		Arab	67,000
		Mixed	309,000
		Other	154,000
		Not stated	495,000
Persons in households with household head born in Ireland	1,089,603		

Source: OPCS/GRO(S) (1993) Volume 2, Table 6 and Table 11, Labour Force Survey 1990 and 1991 (HMSO, 1992, p34).

group given by the LFS is dispersed over several census categories, including Black–Other and Other–Other. These problems are more severe than they may appear at first sight. As indicated above, it is not clear what proportion of second generation Afro–Caribbeans may be included in the Black–Other category in the census rather than with the Black–Caribbean group. Similar questions arise with regard to the large number of children of the many Black and White unions. In summary, the categories used by the LFS and GHS have a greater coincidence with everyday terms than the census, which includes a higher proportion of synthetic groups, which are not strictly 'ethnic'.

It is clear that the census, LFS and GHS categories of ethnicity fall within 'racially' defined Black boundaries. The ethnic categories do not refer to the Welsh or Scots, Germans or Italians for example. The census tables on ethnicity give a surrogate measure of the Irish population, using either 'Persons born in Ireland' or 'Persons in households with household head born in Ireland'. Neither measure is directly comparable with Irish ethnicity, but the LFS abandoned questions on Irish ethnicity in 1979, because of confusion among respondents, and there is no comparable question on the Irish in the GHS.

The result is that ethnicity, as defined by this volume, is a relatively restricted subset of the available ethnic identities in Great Britain and applies almost exclusively to relatively recently immigrated non-European groups and their children. It is also clear that while the core membership of some groups is unambiguous, the census contains many more residual portmanteau groupings than the LFS or the GHS and that these composite groups have no real ethnic identity; they are the remainders from more definite categories. This presents researchers writing on the portmanteau groups with a much harder task than for those for whom the groups are clear. Children of unions between the ethnic minority population and the White population occupy ambivalent positions and their allocation or non allocation to the major groups is the subject of some dispute. It means that groups such as the Black–Caribbean group, which seem clearly defined, may not, in fact, include all their members. These points need to be taken into account in the development of this introduction and the individual chapters that follow, but at this point it is necessary to outline some of the main facts that emerge from the census questions in the form in which they were collected. The starting point is numbers.

2   Results

From Table 4, it can be seen that the Indian population constitutes the largest numerical group, at 840,255. This is slightly larger than the Irish-born total of 837,464. The Irish figure, however, refers to birthplace rather than ethnicity and understates the Irish ethnic population; the 1,089,428 persons living in households whose head was born in Ireland (OPCS/GRO(S), 1993) may represent a closer approximation. The next largest group, Black–Caribbeans, numbers just under half a million followed by the Pakistani population at 477,000. Overall the non-European ethnic groups amount to 3,015,050 or 5.5 per cent of the total population of Great Britain (see Table 4).

Table 4 *Ethnic population for selected groups, Great Britain, 1991*

Ethnic group	England	Wales	Scotland	Great Britain	Per cent of GB Total
Total persons	47,055,204	2,853,073	4,998,567	54,888,844	100.0
White	44,144,339	2,793,522	4,953,933	51,873,794	94.51
Black–Caribbean	495,682	3,348	934	499,964	0.91
Black–African	206,918	2,671	2,773	212,362	0.39
Black–Other	172,282	3,473	2,646	178,401	0.33
Indian	823.821	6,384	10,050	840,255	1.53
Pakistani	449,646	5,717	21,192	476,555	0.87
Bangladeshi	157,881	3,820	1,134	162,835	0.30
Chinese	141,661	4,801	10,476	156,938	0.29
Other – Asian	189,253	3,677	4,604	197,534	0.36
Other – Other	273,721	7,660	8,825	290,206	0.53
Total minorities	2,910,865	41,551	62,634	3,015,050	5.49
Percentage of regional population	6.2	1.5	1.3	5.5	
Persons born in Ireland	767,439	20,841	49,184	837,464	1.53

Source: OPCS/GRO(S) (1993) Volume 2, Table 6; Irish birthplace from table L06 abstracted from ESRC Census Dissemination Unit, University of Manchester.

Growth of the ethnic minority population, 1951–91

The ethnic minority population of Great Britain has grown rapidly since the end of the second world war and more particularly since the mid-1950s. Before this time, the ethnic minority population was small and largely confined to a small number of dockland areas (Little, 1947; Banton, 1955; Collins, 1957; Halliday, 1992), but thereafter it became an industrial and service industry replacement labour force located in the main urban centres, particularly those which had difficulty in maintaining their White labour force (Peach, 1968). In 1951, the combined Caribbean and South Asian population of Great Britain amounted to less than 80,000; by 1961 it had reached 500,000 or about 1 per cent of the total population; by 1971 it was about 1,500,000 (3 per cent) and by 1981 it was 2,200,000 or 4.1 per cent. The 1991 Census figure puts the ethnic minority population at just over 3,000,000 or 5.5 per cent of the total population. Thus the overall percentage of the population formed by ethnic minority groups is not high, but it is characterised by a high rate of growth. Growth rates differ for the main groups and vary from a steady or possibly declining Black–Caribbean total to a very rapidly expanding Bangladeshi population. Figures given in Table 5 are rather speculative because of the absence of ethnic figures before 1981. However, they indicate the possible size and rates of growth of the main ethnic components of the British population.

Table 5 *Estimated size and growth of the Caribbean, Indian, Pakistani and Bangladeshi ethnic populations in Great Britain, 1951–91*

	West Indian or Caribbean	Indian	Pakistani	Bangladeshi
1951	28,000	31,000	10,000	2,000
1961	210,000	81,000	25,000	6,000
1966	402,000	223,000	64,000	11,000
1971	548,000	375,000	119,000	22,000
1981	545,000	676,000	296,000	65,000
1991	500,000	840,000	477,000	163,000

Sources: Caribbean figures, 1951–81 from Peach (1995) Chapter 1, this volume;
Pakistani figures 1951–66 based on Peach and Winchester (1974) adjusted for separation of Bangladeshi component. Figures for 1971 based on Peach 1990;
Bangladeshi population 1971–81 from Peach (1990). Figures for 1951, 1961, 1966 based on Peach and Winchester (1974) adjusted from Peach (1990);
Indian figures based on Vaughan Robinson's Table 4.1, Chapter 4, this volume.

Timing of arrivals

The main ethnic groups differ somewhat in the timing of the arrival of their primary immigrant groups. The bulk of the immigrants from the Caribbean arrived in the period between 1955 and 1964, while the main time of arrival of the Indians and Pakistanis was between 1965 and 1974. Bangladeshi arrivals peaked in the period 1980–84 (see Figure 1 and Table 6).

Figure 1 *Dates of arrival in Great Britain of the Caribbean, Indian, Pakistani and Bangladeshi population present in 1988*

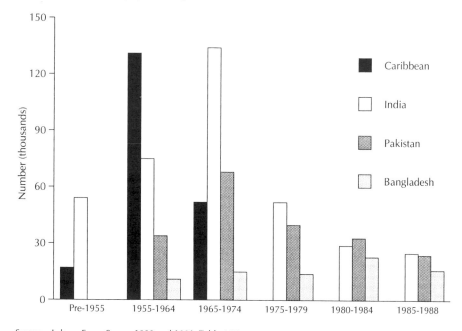

Source: Labour Force Survey 1990 and 1991, Table 6.39

Table 6   *Commonwealth-born population of Great Britain, 1989-91, by year of entry (000s)*

	Year of entry							
	Pre 1955	1955–64	1965–74	1975–79	1980–84	1985–88	No reply	Total entrants
Caribbean	17	131	52	nil	nil	nil	11	231
India	54	75	134	52	29	25	19	388
Bangladesh	nil	11	15	14	23	16	nil	85
Pakistan	nil	34	68	40	33	24	11	216

Source: Labour Force Survey 1990 and 1991 (1992) Table 6.39.

3   Demographic structure

Figure 2 presents the age/sex pyramids for the nine ethnic groups together with the total population and the Irish-born population. The dark shading in the diagram represents the British-born elements in the population and the lighter shading the overseas-born. The first point to emerge is that all of the non-European ethnic minority groups have a much younger age structure than the total, the White or the Irish-born populations. The Black–Caribbean population has an hour glass structure with the bottom half of the structure representing the British-born children of the first generation immigrants. The second point is that in all cases, the British-born element is most marked in the younger age-groups and decreases sharply with increasing age. The Black–Other population is overwhelmingly British-born.

There are some notable asymmetries in the sex structures. Bangladeshi men greatly outnumber women in the older age-groups and the Pakistani pattern is similar, albeit less pronounced. Black–Caribbean women outnumber Black–Caribbean men, although part of this phenomenon may be due to under-recording of young Black–Caribbean men (OPCS/GRO(S), 1993, Table (ii)). Among Other–Asians, there is again a predominance of females.

4   Geographical distribution

There are significant differences in the geographical distribution of the groups in Britain. First, there are differences between the regions. While the overall minority percentage in Great Britain is 5.5 per cent, they are concentrated in England, where they form 6.2 per cent of the population, and relatively absent from Wales, where they form 1.5 per cent, and Scotland, where they form 1.3 per cent (see Table 4). Over 70 per cent of the combined ethnic minorities are found in just two standard regions of Great Britain, the South East and the West Midlands which together contain 40 per cent of the total population. These are the only regions of the country where the region's share of the minority population is higher than its share of the total population (see Table 7).

Table 7 *Ethnic population by standard regions, Great Britain 1991*

Region	Total	Per cent of Great Britain	Minority	Per cent of Minority
North	3,026,732	5.5	38,547	1.3
Yorks and Humberside	4,836,524	8.8	214,021	7.1
East Midlands	3,953,372	7.2	187,983	6.2
East Anglia	2,027,004	3.7	43,395	1.4
South East	17,208,264	31.3	1,695,362	56.2
South West	4,609,424	8.4	62.576	2.1
West Midlands	5,150,187	9.4	424,363	14.1
North West	6,243,697	11.4	244,618	8.1
Wales	2,835,073	5.2	41,551	1.4
Scotland	4,998,567	9.1	62,634	2.1
Great Britain	54,888,844	100.0	3,015,050	100.0

Source: OPCS/GRO(S), (1993) Volume 2, Table 6.

Not only is the minority population unevenly distributed regionally, but it is highly concentrated in the largest urban centres(see Table 8). For example, a quarter of the total population of Great Britain lives in Greater London, Greater Manchester and the metropolitan counties of the West Midlands and West Yorkshire combined. However, 83 per cent of the Black–Africans, 79 per cent of the Black–Caribbeans, 75 per cent of the Bangladeshis and nearly two thirds of the Black–Other, Indians and Pakistanis do so. Only the Chinese, at still nearly double the rate of the total population, are less concentrated than the other ethnic groups.

Table 8 *Relative concentration of ethnic minority population in selected metropolitan counties, Great Britain, 1991*

	Total	White	Black–Carib-bean	Black–African	Black–Other	Indian	Pakist-ani	Bangla-deshi	Chinese
Great Britain	54,888,844	51,873,794	499,964	212,401	178,401	840,255	476,555	162,835	156,938
Greater London	6,679,699	5,333,580	290,968	163,635	80,613	347,091	87,816	85,738	56,579
West Midlands metropolitan county	2,551,671	2,178,149	72,183	4,116	15,716	141,359	88,268	18,074	6,107
Greater Manchester metropolitan county	2,499,441	2,351,239	17,095	5,240	9,202	29,741	49,370	11,445	8,323
West Yorkshire metropolitan county	2,013,693	1,849,562	14,795	2,554	6,552	34,837	80,540	5,978	3,852
Percentage ethnic group in named areas	**25.04**	**22.58**	**79.01**	**82.66**	**62.83**	**65.82**	**64.21**	**74.45**	**47.70**

Source: OPCS/GRO(S) (1993), Volume 2, Table 6.

Figure 2 Age/sex pyramids for the eleven ethnic groups together with the Irish-born population

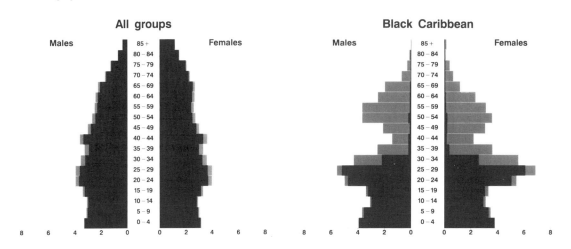

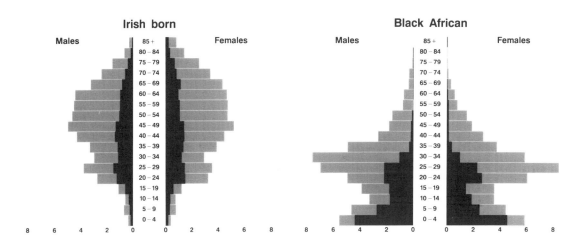

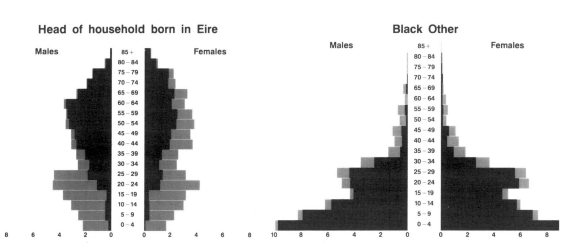

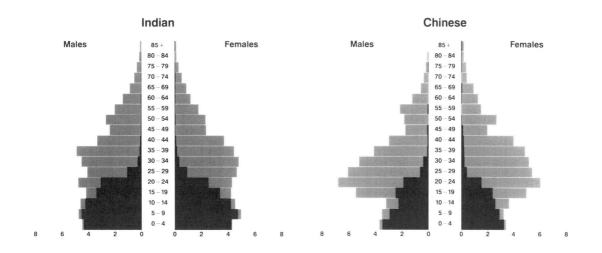

Indian

Males — Females

85 +
80 – 84
75 – 79
70 – 74
65 – 69
60 – 64
55 – 59
50 – 54
45 – 49
40 – 44
35 – 39
30 – 34
25 – 29
20 – 24
15 – 19
10 – 14
5 – 9
0 – 4

8 6 4 2 0   0 2 4 6 8

Chinese

Males — Females

85 +
80 – 84
75 – 79
70 – 74
65 – 69
60 – 64
55 – 59
50 – 54
45 – 49
40 – 44
35 – 39
30 – 34
25 – 29
20 – 24
15 – 19
10 – 14
5 – 9
0 – 4

8 6 4 2 0   0 2 4 6 8

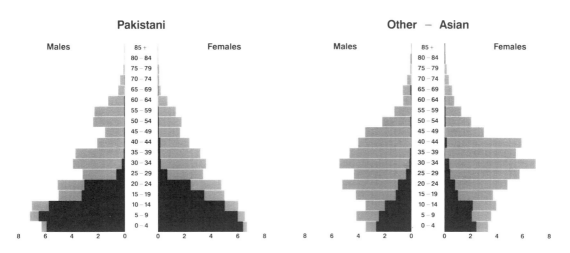

Pakistani

Males — Females

85 +
80 – 84
75 – 79
70 – 74
65 – 69
60 – 64
55 – 59
50 – 54
45 – 49
40 – 44
35 – 39
30 – 34
25 – 29
20 – 24
15 – 19
10 – 14
5 – 9
0 – 4

8 6 4 2 0   0 2 4 6 8

Other – Asian

Males — Females

85 +
80 – 84
75 – 79
70 – 74
65 – 69
60 – 64
55 – 59
50 – 54
45 – 49
40 – 44
35 – 39
30 – 34
25 – 29
20 – 24
15 – 19
10 – 14
5 – 9
0 – 4

8 6 4 2 0   0 2 4 6 8

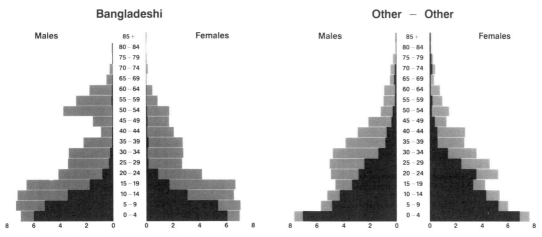

Bangladeshi

Males — Females

85 +
80 – 84
75 – 79
70 – 74
65 – 69
60 – 64
55 – 59
50 – 54
45 – 49
40 – 44
35 – 39
30 – 34
25 – 29
20 – 24
15 – 19
10 – 14
5 – 9
0 – 4

8 6 4 2 0   0 2 4 6 8

Other – Other

Males — Females

85 +
80 – 84
75 – 79
70 – 74
65 – 69
60 – 64
55 – 59
50 – 54
45 – 49
40 – 44
35 – 39
30 – 34
25 – 29
20 – 24
15 – 19
10 – 14
5 – 9
0 – 4

8 6 4 2 0   0 2 4 6 8

Dark shading refers to UK-born; light shading to overseas born

Ward level

A very high proportion of the ethnic minority population is concentrated into a relatively small number of districts, which, in turn contain a small minority of the White population. Figure 3 demonstrates from the Lorenz curve that at least 60 per cent of all of the ethnic minority groups (including the Irish-born) are found in wards that contain only 30 per cent of the total population and that for the Indians, Black–Caribbeans, Black–Africans, Pakistanis and Bangladeshis, about 70 per cent are found in wards which contain less than 10 per cent of the population. However, unlike the USA, there are no towns or cities in which ethnic minorities constitute a majority and this is also true at district level. The London Borough of Brent is the local authority with the highest percentage of its population comprised of ethnic minority groups at 44.8 per cent, followed by Newham (42.3) Tower Hamlets (35.6).

The highest percentage that Black–Caribbeans form of a single ward in Great Britain, is 30.1 per cent in Roundwood in Brent in London. The Black–African population reaches 26.6 per cent in Liddle ward in Southwark. For the Indian population, the highest percentage that they form of a ward is 67.2 per cent in Northcote in Ealing, London (though there are several almost as high in Leicester). The most highly concentrated Bangladeshi ward is Spitalfields in Tower Hamlets, at 60.7 per cent. The highest concentration of Pakistanis is in University ward in Bradford, where they form 52.8 per cent of the total population. By comparison, the highest proportion of a ward's population formed by the Irish-born is 17.7 per cent in Cricklewood ward in Brent. However, if all minorities are taken together, very high levels can be achieved, if not sustained. Northcote ward in Ealing has a non-White ethnic population of 90 per cent. Two other wards in the country have percentages above 80.

Enumeration district level

As the size of area decreases, the degree of ethnic minority dominance of the most concentrated areas increases (Woods, 1976). At ward level, 61 per cent of Spitalfields ward in Tower Hamlets is Bangladeshi. At enumeration district level, 90 per cent of the most densely Bangladeshi-dominated enumeration district in Spitalfields was Bangladeshi. However, this level of concentration is very unusual. The highest level of Black–Caribbean concentration in any London enumeration district was 62 per cent (in Brent). These figures do not achieve the sustained 100 per cent levels common for block and tract data for African Americans in US cities.

Taking these figures together, a number of conclusions can be drawn: (1) The proportions that individual ethnic minorities form of the population of quite small areas like wards, is nowhere near as high as that formed regularly by the African American population in the United States. (2) The number of wards with high concentrations is small and the proportion of a given ethnicity living at such high densities is generally low. (3) There are significant differences between the ethnic groups in the extent to which they form the population of the wards in which they have the highest concentrations. Detailed discussion of the level of segregation can be found in Volume 3 of this series, edited by Peter Ratcliffe.

Figure 3 *Lorenz curve of Great Britain 1991, ward level concentration of population*

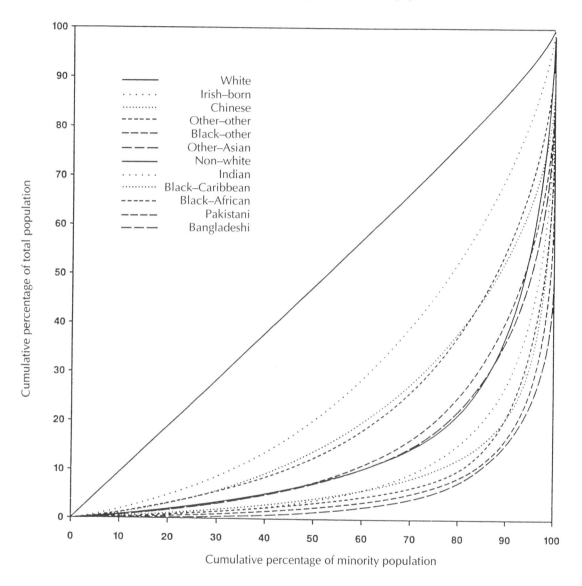

5 Social and economic characteristics

One of the illuminating generalisations about ethnic minority groups in Britain has been to divide them into the Jewish and the Irish models of settlement. Broadly speaking, what I have termed the 'Irish' model is seen as blue collar, manual labour dominated, council house tenured, inner city, while the 'Jewish' model is seen as white collar, self-employed,

Table 9   *Ethnic group for men aged 16 and over, by socio-economic class, Great Britain, 1991*

	Economically active	In employment	I	II	III Non-manual	III Manual	IV	V
Total	73.3	87.4	6.8	27.4	11.5	32.2	16.4	5.7
White	73.2	88.0	6.7	27.6	11.3	32.4	16.3	5.7
Black–Caribbean	80.1	73.8	2.4	14.2	12.2	38.9	23.6	8.7
Black–African	69.0	66.8	14.3	24.5	17.5	17.6	17.3	8.9
Black–Other	81.9	70.5	3.2	24.8	17.2	30.2	17.6	7.1
Indian	78.1	84.9	11.4	27.2	14.4	23.8	18.1	4.0
Pakistani	73.3	68.9	5.9	20.3	13.5	29.9	24.1	6.3
Bangladeshi	72.4	67.3	5.2	8.5	12.9	31.5	35.0	6.8
Chinese	70.1	88.1	17.6	23.3	19.3	29.5	8.0	2.4
Other – Asian	76.2	83.0	15.9	34.3	18.2	16.0	12.3	3.3
Other – Other	75.4	77.7	14.5	30.5	16.1	19.8	14.0	5.1
Irish–born	70.1	84.3	6.9	23.3	7.7	34.3	16.9	10.9

Source: GB Local Base Statistics, Table 9 and Two per cent SARs.

owner-occupied and suburban. As with most broad generalisations, there are many exceptions, but it is instructive to use it as a starting point.

If the ethnic groups were to be divided on the basis of the proportion in the professional classes, then the Chinese, Other–Asian, Other–Other, Black–African and Indian groups would stand out as having more than 10 per cent of their male workers in the top class (see Table 9). The White, the Irish, Pakistanis, Bangladeshis, Black–Other and Black–Caribbean have less than 7 per cent. Some of the groups with high professional representation have bimodal distributions, with high representation in manual categories as well. The White, the Irish, Pakistanis, Bangladeshis, Black–Other and Black–Caribbean all have strong skews towards the manual end of the distribution, albeit with significant representation in the managerial classes. Most of the Asian groups are in the white collar category, while most of the Black groups are in the blue collar category. However, there are significant exceptions. The Black–Africans are in the white collar group because many have migrated to achieve academic qualifications (see Chapter 2). The Pakistanis and, more particularly, the Bangladeshis have a much less favourable profile than the Indians.

Participation rates are generally high, notably so for the Black–Caribbean (80.1 per cent) and the Black–Other (81.9 per cent) groups. The lowest economically active rates are for the Black–African population, which has high student numbers. Employment rates, on the other hand, show large variations (see Figure 4). Only two thirds of the Black–Africans are in employment compared with nearly 90 per cent of Whites and Chinese. Employment rates for the Pakistanis and Bangladeshis are similar to those of Black–Africans

Unemployment

Rates of unemployment among the ethnic minorities are above those of the White population. The Chinese rates are only marginally higher and those for the Irish-born and the Indian populations rather more. However, Black–Caribbean unemployment rates are double the national average, Black–African rates are three times as high, while Pakistani and Bangladeshi rates are highest of all reaching 29 and 32 per cent respectively (see Figure 4). If the groups are disaggregated by age and gender, dramatically high rates are recorded by young Black men.

The socio-economic class of ethnic minorities needs to be interpreted in relation to academic qualifications. There are distinct patterns of educational achievement. Among first generation men, the most highly qualified are the Chinese, Black–African, Other–Asian and Indian groups, all with higher levels than British-born Whites. The Black–Caribbean, Bangladeshi, Pakistani and Black–Other men are much less likely to have higher-level qualifications than White British-born men. Among the first generation women, the patterns are similar to those of the men, with the exception that women tend to have higher qualifications than men. This is particularly the case for the Black–Caribbean, Black–African and Black–Other groups, where the women are more likely to have a post-18 non-degree qualification than the men (Heath and McMahon, 1994). Work by Yuan Cheng (Chapter 7 of this volume) and by Anthony Heath and Dorren McMahon (see Volume 3 of this series) indicate that occupational attainments of many groups are lower than their academic attainments would have produced for equivalent Whites. Their studies are of great interest in that they quantify the degree of 'ethnic penalty' paid by different groups for their ethnicity. They indicate that most ethnic minorities are doubly disadvantaged. They have poorer chances of obtaining employment than do British-born Whites with similar qualifications and they have poorer chances of entering the secure, well remunerated jobs of the service class.

Figure 4 *Percentage unemployment by ethnic group, Great Britain, 1991*

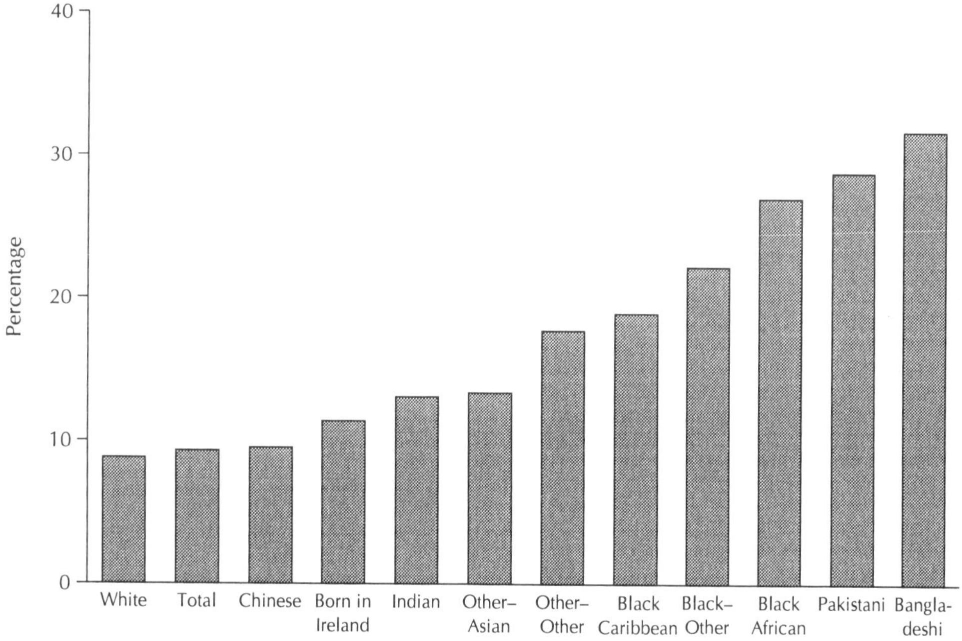

Source: OPCS (1993) Volume 2, Table 10

Female participation rates are much lower than those for men (see Table 10). Whereas nearly three quarters of men are economically active, for women the figure is just under half. For the strongly Muslim groups, the Pakistanis and Bangladeshis, where working outside the home is generally frowned upon for women, the rates drop to just above a quarter and a fifth respectively. While less than half of all men in employment are in the non-manual white collar jobs, the majority of women are in such occupations. Women are notably less represented in socio-economic Class 1 than men. The Chinese and Other–Asians do best with 7.6 per cent and 6.0 per cent respectively.

The South Asian and Chinese groups show a strong concentration in self-employment (see Figure 5). Just under a quarter of the economically active Chinese are self-employed, while the Indian and Pakistani rates are 16 and 17 per cent respectively. Bangladeshi rates are marginally above the national average, while the three Black groups have the lowest rates. High self-employment rates seem to be related to the catering industry for the Chinese and Bangladeshis in particular, while taxi-driving is an important additional element for the Pakistanis (see Chapter 5). The Bangladeshi economic position is exceptionally dependent on the restaurant industry. Two thirds of the Bangladeshi male residents aged 16 or over, both employees and self-employed, were in the distribution or catering trade (OPCS/GRO(S) 1993, Vol 2, Table 14). Only the Chinese with a 60 per cent concentration in this sector come close to this figure. The Indian and Pakistani figures are half that of the Chinese. For the Pakistani male population, the figure is 18 per cent and for the Indian male population 21 per cent. The national average is 15 per cent.

Table 10 *Ethnic group for women aged 16 and over, by socio-economic class, Great Britain, 1991*

	Econom- ically active	In employ- ment	I	II	III Non- manual	III Manual	IV	V
Total	49.9	92.1	1.7	25.9	38.8	7.6	18.0	7.9
White	49.7	92.6	1.7	25.9	39.0	7.6	17.8	8.0
Black–Caribbean	66.9	84.1	1.0	30.3	33.7	6.9	19.5	8.5
Black–African	60.1	71.0	3.0	31.8	30.8	5.6	16.9	12.0
Black–Other	62.9	77.9	1.3	25.2	40.6	9.3	19.1	4.6
Indian	55.4	85.3	4.4	20.9	34.9	6.4	29.2	4.1
Pakistani	27.1	65.5	2.7	22.3	34.2	6.5	31.7	2.6
Bangladeshi	21.8	57.6	1.8	22.9	35.8	6.4	26.6	6.4
Chinese	53.1	90.0	7.6	28.5	31.6	13.0	13.9	5.4
Other – Asian	53.9	84.9	6.0	30.7	33.8	7.0	16.6	6.0
Other – Other	53.9	82.5	4.5	30.8	38.4	6.2	15.1	4.9
Irish–born	49.9	92.4	2.6	33.2	26.8	6.3	18.5	12.6

Source: GB Local Base Statistics, Table 9 and Two per cent SARs.

Figure 5 *Percentage of the economically active who are self-employed, Great Britain, 1991*

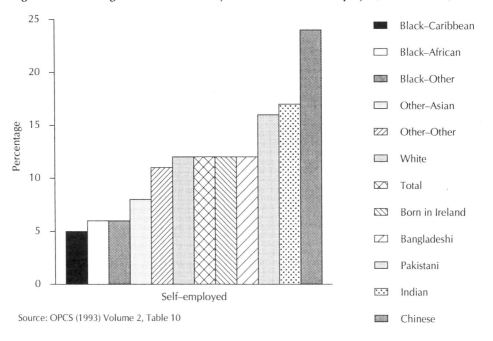

Source: OPCS (1993) Volume 2, Table 10

Housing

In terms of housing tenure, the Irish/Jewish analogy is again instructive. Taking the Irish as representing a working class tradition, in which council housing is a major source of accommodation, then the Black–Caribbean, Black–African, Black–Other and Bangladeshi populations emerge with a high dependence on this sector, while the Indians and Pakistanis have astonishingly high levels of owner occupation. Figure 6 shows that while the Indians have an owner occupation rate of over 80 per cent, closely followed by the Pakistanis, and while the White and Chinese rates of owner occupation are above 60 per cent, the Black groups are below 50 per cent and with a correspondingly higher dependence on local authority and housing association property. The Bangladeshis have a tenure profile closer to the Black–Caribbean group than to the other South Asian groups and again emerge as a particularly distinctive and disadvantaged population. Paradoxically, since this has been called the Irish model, the Irish themselves (as represented by households headed by a person born in Ireland) are not far below the average for ownership, nor much above the White average for private rentals and council housing (see Figure 6).

Tenure does not convey information about housing quality. Much of the Indian and Pakistani owner-occupied property is inner city, 19th century and terraced. Much of the local authority property occupied by the Black–African population, on the other hand, is more modern. However, it tends to be flatted accommodation rather than individual houses. The distribution of house types for the ethnic groups is given in Figure 7.

Figure 6 *Percentage tenure by ethnic group, Great Britain, 1991*

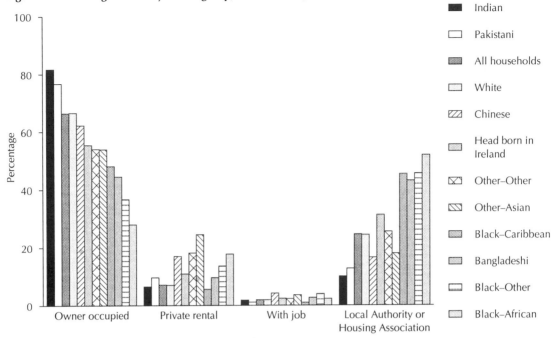

Source: OPCS (1993) Volume 2, Table 11

Figure 7 *Percentage distribution of ethnic groups by house type, Great Britain 1991*

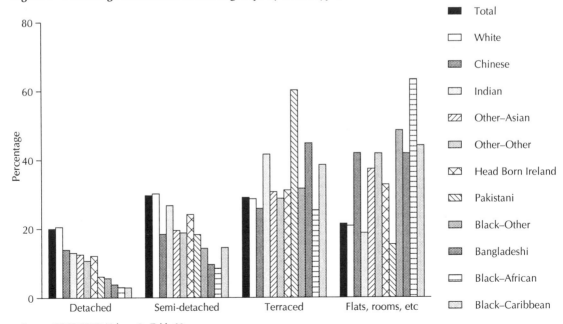

Source: OPCS (1993) Volume 2, Table 12

If the figures for crowding (set at over 1.5 persons per room) are examined, the Black–African population has a relatively high proportion. The most disadvantaged groups, however, are the Pakistanis with 8 per cent and the Bangladeshis with nearly 20 per cent (see Table 11).

Table 11 *Proportion of ethnic groups living at over 1.5 persons per room, Great Britain, 1991*

Ethnic group	Percentage living at over 1.5 per room
White	0.4
All household heads	0.5
Household head born in Ireland	0.9
Black – Caribbean	1.3
Black – Other	1.9
Other – Other	2.5
Indian	2.7
Other – Asian	3.6
Black – African	6.0
Pakistani	7.9
Bangladeshi	19.1

Source: OPCS/GRO(S) (1993) Volume 2, Table 11.

Family structure

There are significant differences between the ethnic minority groups in terms of family structure. South Asians have very few single person households in comparison with most other groups: Indians, Pakistanis and Bangladeshis have less than 10 per cent in such households in comparison to about a quarter for all other groups (with the exception of Other–Asians). On the other hand, the South Asian ethnicities have very much higher proportions in extended families (households with two or more families) than other groups: Indians, Pakistanis and Bangladeshis have just under 10 per cent in such households in comparison to under 3 per cent for other ethnicities. Similarly, cohabitation is rare for the South Asian ethnicities, with less than 2 per cent in such households compared with at least double that proportion for all other non-Asian groups. Lone parent families with dependent children are very much more prominent for Black groups than for others. A fifth of Black–Caribbean and Black–African households are in this category and just under a quarter of Black–Other households. The figure for all other groups is below 10 per cent and for the total, the average is 5.2 per cent (see Table 12). The Samples of Anonymised Records (SARs, see Marsh and Teague, 1992) give interesting insight into the ethnic mixing within households. For the Caribbean households, this is significant (see Peach, Chapter 1) but for Asian households it hardly exists.

Table 12 *Ethnic groups by household structure, Great Britain, 1991*

	Total	White	Black–Carib-bean	Black–African	Black–Other	Indian	Paki-stani	Bang-ladeshi	Chinese	Other – Asian	Other – Other	Born in Ireland
Households with no family												
One person household	26.3	26.6	27.7	25.1	26.5	9.5	7.6	6.2	21.1	17.8	26.4	30.0
Two or more person household	3.3	3.2	4.2	11.7	5.9	2.7	2.9	4.3	9.1	6.8	6.9	4.9
Households with one family												
Married couple family												
With no children	24.3	24.8	10.3	8.2	8.3	12.7	7.3	4.7	13.7	12.9	12.9	21.0
With dependent children	22.4	21.8	13.8	24.6	19.0	49.7	58.3	63.6	38.6	42.7	29.3	17.3
With non-dependent children	8.6	8.7	7.5	1.5	2.8	8.1	4.1	2.4	4.9	4.8	4.3	10.5
Cohabiting couple family												
With no children	3.3	3.4	3.4	2.5	5.1	0.8	0.5	0.3	1.8	1.7	3.8	3.0
With dependent children	1.8	1.8	3.5	2.0	4.3	0.5	0.5	0.4	0.5	0.9	1.9	1.3
With non-dependent children	0.2	0.2	0.4	0.1	0.1	0.0	0.1	0.0	0.1	0.1	0.1	0.3
Lone parent family												
With dependent children	5.2	5.0	20.2	20.6	24.1	4.5	7.2	8.3	5.3	7.3	10.6	5.2
With non-dependent children	3.7	3.7	7.4	2.6	3.1	2.6	1.9	0.8	2.5	2.7	2.8	5.6
Households with two or more families	**0.9**	**0.8**	**1.6**	**1.1**	**0.8**	**8.9**	**9.6**	**9.0**	**2.5**	**2.4**	**1.1**	**1.0**
Total households	100.0	100.0	100.0	100.0	100.0	100.0	100.0	100.0	100.0	100.0	100.0	100.0

Source: OPCS/GRO(S) (1993) Volume 2, Table 11.

6 Conclusion

The ethnic groups covered by the 1991 Census ethnic group question have a number of features in common. The categories are drawn from the non-White population of Great Britain and are, for the most part, post-war immigrants and their children. The groups are generally small, but rapidly growing, including an increasing proportion, and in some cases a majority, of children born in Britain. The largest ethnic group in Britain is probably the Irish, but the census has not categorised this population in the same way as the non-White groups. There were over one million persons living in households headed by a person born in Ireland, compared with 857,000 living in households headed by an ethnic Indian.

The socio-economic position of the nine ethnic categories differs significantly. The Chinese, Other–Asian, Other–Other, Black–African and Indian men are strongly represented in Class I (the professional group). On the other hand, Black–Caribbean, Black–Other, Pakistani and Bangladeshi men are over-represented in semi-skilled and unskilled manual work (Classes IV and V). Advantages and disadvantages are not uniformly distributed across all variables, however. Pakistanis, for example, who are poorly placed in terms of socio-economic class and unemployment, stand out strongly in terms of owner occupation of homes and self-employment. Black–Africans, who stand out well in terms of professional occupations, nevertheless suffer from overcrowding in their homes. However, there are some groups who do consistently well on measures of socio-economic well-being and some who do exceptionally badly. The Indians, Chinese and Other–Asians are among the groups of high performers, well educated, property owning and professional. The Bangladeshis are at the other end of the scale, found in manual labour, with high rates of unemployment and exceptionally high levels of overcrowding.

The Black–Caribbean population's position in Britain stands out in strong contrast to that of African Americans in the USA. Its structure is more working class than the population as a whole, but it does not differ dramatically in terms of housing tenure, jobs or residential segregation from the White population. It has an exceptionally high proportion of mixed Black and White households and in this way appears as one of the most integrated groups.

Depending on whether the criteria for categorisation are social or economic, the grouping of ethnicities differs considerably. The key social differences come between those groups who might be considered encapsulated and those with an open structure. The Indians, Pakistanis, Bangladeshis and Chinese show traditional family patterns. Single person households are rare. There are few ethnically out-married households and few single parents households, while extended families are significant. Self-employment is above average. The Black groups have a more open and assimilated social structure. Single parent households with dependent children are common. Ethnically mixed households are frequent and multi-family households are rare.

However, if the applied criteria are economic rather than social, the Asian social group becomes split into contrasting sections. The Indians and the Chinese occupy a much more advantageous position than the Bangladeshis and the Pakistanis. The Indians and Chinese have above average professional percentages and relatively low unemployment rates. Bangladeshis and Pakistanis have a concentration in manual employment and very high unemployment rates. The Black social group is similarly divided between the more professional Black–Africans and the more manual Black–Caribbeans and Black–Others.

Gender also highlights significant differences between the ethnic groups. Religion and gender intersect to designate Bangladeshi and Pakistani women as the least participant groups in the formal labour market. These two groups also have the highest unemployment rates. At the other end of the scale, all three Black groups have the highest levels of participation. Black–Caribbean women show paradoxical traits of having a higher socio-economic profile than Black–Caribbean men, but also of having a high proportion of single parents.

A significant proportion of the ethnic minority population is derived from mixed unions and new ethnic identities are being forged which will be increasingly difficult to capture within the existing census categories. Therefore, the categories presented by the census have limitations that will need to be addressed before the census of 2001. Indeed, one of the lessons to be derived from the 1991 Census, is that new ethnicities are emerging in Britain.

References

Anwar, M. (1990) Ethnic classifications, ethnic monitoring and the 1991 Census. *New Community,* 16(4) 607–15.

Banton, M. (1955) *The Coloured Quarter.* London: Jonathan Cape.

Collins, S. (1957) *Coloured Minorities in Britain.* London: Lutterworth Press.

Halliday, F. (1992) *Arabs in Exile: Yemeni Migrants in Urban Britain.* London: I. B. Taurus.

Islamic Secretariat (1991) Leaflet headed *Census 1991*

Little, K. S. (1947) *Negroes in Britain.* London: Kegan Paul, Trench, Trubner and Co.

Marsh, C. and Teague, A. (1992) Samples of Anonymised Records from the 1991 Census. *Population Trends,* 69, 17–26.

OPCS/GRO(S) (1993) 1991 Census, *Ethnic Group and Country of Birth, Great Britain.* Two volumes. London: HMSO.

Peach, C. (1991) *The Caribbean in Europe: Contrasting Pattern of Migration and Settlement in Britain, France and the Netherlands.* Research Paper in Ethnic Relations 15. Centre for Research in Ethnic Relations, University of Warwick.

Peach, C. (1990) Estimating the growth of the Bangladeshi population of Great Britain. *New Community,* 16(4), 481–91.

Peach, C. (1968) *West Indian Migration to Britain: A Social Geography.* London: Oxford University Press.

Peach, G.C.K. and Winchester, S.W.C. (1974) Birthplace, ethnicity and the underenumeration of West Indians, Indians and Pakistanis in the Censuses of 1966 and 1971. *New Community,* 3(4), 386-93.

Registrar General (1958) *Census 1951 England and Wales: General Report.* London: HMSO.

Sillitoe, K. (1978) Ethnic origins: the search for a question. *Population Trends,* 25–30.

Sillitoe, K. (1987) Questions on race/ethnicity and related topics for the Census. *Population Trends,* 49, 5–11.

Woods, R. I. (1976) Aspects of the scale problem in the calculation of segregation indices: London and Birmingham, 1961 and 1971. *Tijdschrift voor Economische en Sociale Geografie,* 67(3), 169–74.

Chapter 1
Black–Caribbeans: class, gender and geography

Ceri Peach

1.1 Introduction

The 1991 Census gives an ethnic population of 499,964 Black–Caribbeans living in Great Britain. This is the first time that the census has produced an ethnic figure from a 100 per cent count, but the figure is in line with estimates based on birthplace in earlier censuses and from small percentage sample surveys. Although the 1991 Census was the first census to ask a direct ethnic group question, two official government surveys, the Labour Force Survey (LFS) and the General Household Survey (GHS), had regularly asked such questions during the 1980s. The surveys, however, were small in relation to the 100 per cent coverage of the census and collected relatively small ethnic samples within their broader coverage. They were helpful in giving a snapshot of the country as a whole, but less helpful in pinpointing geographical differences within the country or in measuring change over time. Small numbers meant that the surveys of several years had to be amalgamated to create a sample size large enough to be robust and this militated against measuring change over time. Similar problems of sample size made anything other than coarse regional disaggregation impossible.

Although the LFS and the GHS had asked questions on ethnic identity, the 1991 Census did not follow the categorisations used by those enquiries. In particular, as far as this chapter is concerned, it seems likely that Black British would have identified themselves as 'West Indian (including Guyanese)', the nearest category available to them under the LFS and GHS self-identification labels. Those writing themselves into the census as Black British, amounted to 58,106 (OPCS/GRO(S), 1993, vol 2, Table A). Including this figure would suggest a total of 558,070 Black–Caribbeans.

There are difficulties in measuring the change of the Caribbean population over time, as given in Table 1.1, because of the lack of consistency in definitions between earlier censuses and surveys. Before the 1991 Census, reliance had to be placed on the birthplace figures. However, a growing proportion, and since 1984 a majority, of the Caribbean ethnic population has been British born. Parental birthplace was used as a surrogate measure for ethnicity in the 1971 Census, but even this question was not included in the 1981 Census. The result is that it is not possible to state with certainty whether the Black–Caribbean population in Britain has increased or decreased between 1981 and 1991.

Calculation of the number of children born in the UK to Caribbean ethnic group parents given in Table 1.1 have been calibrated from a variety of sources. The 1991 Census gives figures for Black–Caribbeans born in the UK by age (OPCS/GRO(S), 1993, Volume 2, Table 7). These figures have been

Table 1.1 *Caribbean ethnic population Great Britain, 1951–1991*

Year	Caribbean birthplace	UK–Born children of WI born (est)	Best estimate Caribbean ethnic population
1951	17,218	10,000	28,000
1961	173,659	35,000	209,000
1966	269,300	133,000	402,000
1971	304,070	244,000	548,000
1981a	295,179	250,565	546,000
1981b	268,000	244,000	519,000
1984	242,000	281,000	529,000
1986–8	233,000	262,000	495,000
1991	264,591	268,337–326,443	499,964–558,070

Sources: 1951   Census.

       1961   Census.

       1966   Census (10 per cent count) Sample Census 1966, Great Britain, <u>Commonwealth Immigrant Tables</u> British Caribbean born, Table 2. Total British Caribbean population calculated from Table 15, giving total persons in households headed by person or spouse born in the British Caribbean. Children calculated as the difference between the two numbers.

       1971   Census 1971, Great Britain, <u>Country of Birth Tables</u>, New Commonwealth America-born, Table 3. Table 7 of the same publication gives a total of 163,210 children born in the UK to fathers and mothers born in the New Commonwealth America. The 1991 Census for Black–Caribbean born in UK aged 20+ (OPCS, 1993, vol 1, Table 7) is 137,000. However, <u>Population Trends</u>, Winter 1975, 4, estimates the New Common wealth America figure at 548,000. The latter figure is given in the table.

       1981a   Census 1981, <u>Country of Birth Great Britian</u>. Caribbean–born taken from Table 1, New Commonwealth Caribbean. Caribbean total taken from Table 3, persons usually resident in private households headed by a person born in the New Commonwealth Caribbean.

       1981b   <u>Labour Force Survey</u>, 1981.

       1984   <u>Labour Force Survey</u>, 1988.

       1986–8   Population Trends, 1990, 60, 35–8.

       1991   Census 1991 Great Britain, <u>Ethnic Group and Country of Birth</u> (OPCS, 1993). The official ethnic Black–Caribbean total is 499,964 (OPCS, 1993, Table 5). Note that if those who designated themselves 'Black British' were included (58,106) (OPCS, 1993, vol 2, Table A) the total would be 558,070. The figure for Black–Caribbeans with non–UK birthplace is 231,627. Black–Caribbean–born in the Caribbean number 224,126 (OPCS, 1993, volume 1, Table 5).

used to estimate the number of children who would have been born by the time of the 1951 and 1961 Censuses. The 1981 estimates are based on persons living in private households in which the head of household was born in the New Commonwealth Caribbean. This gives a figure of 250,565 compared with about 200,000 expected on the basis of the UK-born Black–Caribbean population in 1991. This suggests that it is possible that about 50,000 British-born Afro–Caribbeans present in 1981 were no longer present in 1991.

Census estimates based on household headship, parental birthplace and so on, all assume that the Caribbean birthplace equates with Afro-Caribbean ethnicity. It is apparent from the 1991 Census that this is only partly true. Most (85 per cent) of the population originating from the Caribbean in

Britain is of Afro-Caribbean ethnicity, but 15 per cent is not: 7 per cent of the Caribbean-born population is White (OPCS/GRO(S), 1993, Volume 1, Table 5) and 2 per cent is of South Asian origin. In comparing 1991 figures with those based on censuses for earlier dates, no allowance has been made for this fact (see Table 1.1). Thus estimates for the census years before 1991 are based on a more catholic definition of the Caribbean population than that for 1991.

Although the 1991 Census figure given in Table 1.1 is of the expected size, there is some controversy as to whether it is accurate. Ballard and Kalra (1994) have argued that to understand the demographic profile of the Afro-Caribbean population in Great Britain, it is necessary to join together the Black–Caribbean and the Black–Other populations. The Black–Caribbean population has many adults and few children, while the Black–Other population has the reverse. Ballard and Kalra's claim would add 178,401 to the Black–Caribbean numbers and increase the census figure by over one third to 678,365. Since this figure would be substantially out of line with the earlier census and LFS estimates, it seems that one should view the claim with cumspection. It seems probable, that the Black–Other group comprises a varied set of ethnicities, including children of mixed parentage (the LFS gives a total of 309,000 in this category for 1989/90 (LFS,33)). However, the 58,106 who recorded themselves on the census forms within this category as 'Black British' (as a write-in category, rather than ticking a box) should probably have been categorised as Black–Caribbean, rather than Black–Other. This would give a Black–Caribbean total of 558,070 (see footnotes to Table 1.1).

The Caribbean population of Britain has grown from tiny numbers at the end of the second world war (about 28,000 in 1951) to a peak of 550,000 in 1971. Overall numbers seem to have remained fairly steady at around the half million mark since 1971, while those actually born in the Caribbean have been in decline since 1971 (see Table 1.2). The 1971 Census put the Caribbean-born population at 304,070. Ten years later, the 1981 Census showed a decrease of 9,000 and the 1991 Census a further decrease of about 30,000. All in all, there has been a decrease of about 40,000 in the Caribbean-born population between the censuses of 1971 and 1991. Rather little of this decrease is likely to have been caused by death (Peach, 1991; Balarajan and Bulusu, 1990, Table 9.8). Return migration for retirement or onward migration to North America seem probable as causes for the decrease.

Table 1.2 shows that Jamaicans form the majority of the Caribbean-born population (54 per cent in 1991), with Barbadians at just below one tenth of the population and Guyanese and Trinidadians just behind them. The Windwards and Leewards are amalgamated in the 1991 and other censuses into a rather unsatisfactory group or groups. However, as a rough estimate, about one third of the 'Other Caribbean' category in Table 1.2 comes from the Leewards (Antigua, St Kitts, Nevis, Anguilla) and two thirds from the Windwards (Dominica, Grenada, St Lucia and St Vincent) (Peach, 1991). The proportions originating in different territories has remained fairly constant between 1971 and 1991, but within this broadly stable pattern, decreases have been more marked for the Jamaicans than other islanders.

Table 1.2 *Changes in persons born in the Caribbean living in Great Britain, 1971–1991, absolute numbers and percentages*

Caribbean born population in Great Britain	1991	1981	1971	1991	1981	1971
		Numbers			Percentages	
Barbados	22,224	25,247	27,055	8.5	8.6	8.9
Jamaica	142,115	164,119	171,775	54.0	55.6	56.5
Trinidad and Tobago	17,127	16,334	17,135	6.5	5.5	5.6
Belize	1,126	1,043		0.4	0.4	0
Guyana	20,254	21,686	21,070	7.7	7.3	6.9
Other Caribbean	60,115	66,750	67,035	22.9	22.6	22.0
Total	262,961	295,179	304,070	100	100	100

Sources: 1991 figures from OPCS/GRO(s) (1993) Volume 1, Table 5; 1981 (Peach, 1991); 1971 (OPCS, 1974, Country of Birth tables, Table 3).

1.2 History of migration and settlement

Of major significance for the history of Caribbean settlement, was Britain's active recruitment of labour in the Caribbean to help in the war effort: 8,000 men were recruited to serve in the RAF (Glass, 1960). Patterson refers to 7,000 Jamaicans serving overseas in the armed forces while smaller numbers volunteered from other parts of the Caribbean (Patterson, 1963). Foresters were recruited in British Honduras (now Belize) to work in Scottish forests (Richmond, 1954, cited by Patterson, 1963) and workers were also recruited to work in the munitions industry. In all, 345 men arrived in Britain under the latter scheme, which was wound up in 1946 (Patterson, 1963). However, the post war movement in earnest from the former British West Indies to Britain is often dated to the arrival of 417 Jamaicans on the Empire Windrush in 1948 (Glass, 1960) or to the arrival of 100 Jamaicans on the Ormonde a year earlier (Harris, 1987). By the time of the 1951 Census there were about 17,000 persons born in the Caribbean living in Britain.

Large-scale Caribbean migration to Britain effectively started in 1948 (Glass, 1960; Peach, 1968) (although it has much longer antecedents), peaked in the early 1960s and was effectively over by 1973. By this time, the population had reached about 550,000 (see Table 1.1). Caribbean migration to Britain was essentially powered by free market labour forces, but it had its origins in government-sponsored war time recruitment. Post-war direct recruitment by British Rail, London Transport and the National Health Service, although not numerically dominant, was important in shaping the movement. In Barbados, for example, the island most affected by direct recruitment, just under a quarter of the emigrants in 1960, left on sponsorship schemes (Peach, 1968). However, these schemes were introduced after the migration had got under way. Family and island social networks were by far the most important channel of diffusing information and arranging initial footholds in Britain (Davison, 1962; Philpott, 1977: Byron, 1991;1994).

During the 1950s and early 1960s net West Indian immigration tracked the demand for labour in Britain, with perhaps a three month lag (Peach, 1968) (see Figure 1.1). The threat of legislation to curb immigration by British passport holders, who often had no citizenship other than that of the United Kingdom and Colonies, had the paradoxical effect of increasing immigration in a rush to beat the ban (see Figure 1.1). However, it seems to have restricted the movement to Britain without drying up the supply of migrants. After 1962, net immigration to Britain decreased considerably, but liberalisation of the US and Canadian immigration legislation led to renewed migration, particularly of skilled workers (Thomas-Hope, 1986; 1992).

Jamaica was the island earliest affected by emigration. In 1948, 547 Jamaicans emigrated to Britain (Glass, 1960). By 1951 when about 1,000 West Indians migrated, only about 100 of them were not from Jamaica. Migration from Barbados was already well established by 1955 when 2,754 people left (Peach, 1968) but for the smaller islands it was just becoming established. Migration from the Leewards seems to have been going in earnest by 1955 and movement from the Windwards by 1956 (Peach, 1968). Trinidad also seems to have moved to large-scale emigration in 1956, while Guyana did not get into its stride until 1960 (Peach, 1968). Belize was hardly affected by the movement; in 1981 there were only 1,043 persons born in Belize in Britain out of a Caribbean total of 295,179 (OPCS, 1983, Census 1981, Country of Birth, Great Britain, Table 1) and by 1991, there were only 1,122 (OPCS/ GRO(S), 1993, Table 2).

Figure 1.1 *Net West Indian migration to Britain, 1948–1974, against average annual unemployment*

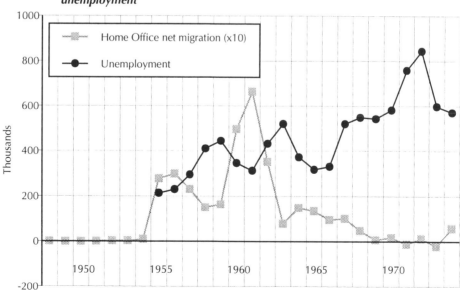

Direct recruitment of labour by British agencies post-dates the beginning of the serious emigration. The Barbadian government set up a sponsorship scheme in 1955 under which the British Transport Commission, the London Transport Executive, the British Hotels and Restaurants Association, and the Regional Hospital Boards received workers. The London Transport Executive sent a direct recruiting team to Barbados in 1956 (Glass, 1960) and by 1958 it had recruited almost 1,000 workers. By the end of 1961 it had recruited over 2,000 Barbadians (Patterson, 1963). Between 1955 and 1960, the Barbadian government scheme had sponsored 3,680 workers of whom 40 per cent went to the London Transport Executive. The main conclusion to draw from this is that directly recruited or sponsored labour was an important but minority element in the migratory flow affecting people only from Barbados. In Jamaica, the government tried, if anything, to restrict the flow (Davison, 1962). It is also important to note that direct recruitment came into play after the migratory streams had been established.

The movement to Britain acted as a 'replacement population', moving to gaps left by the upward mobility of the White population. Migration sustained significant parts of the service industries in Britain, including hospitals and transport, and industrially migrant workers were concentrated in some of the least dynamic industries (Peach, 1967). Since the radical analysts of migration stress the dependence of the capitalist system on the inputs of raw labour, it is worth noting that it was the flagging social services and the weaker parts of the industrial economy which used migration as a prop.

Net immigration from the West Indies to Britain for the period 1955 to 1974 was highly and significantly inversely related to unemployment rates in Britain (Peach, 1978/9). The Home Office ceased keeping embarkation figures after 1974, so that the sharp reduction in net immigration cannot be monitored as clearly as one would hope (see Figure 1.1). However, an alternative, though not entirely satisfactory (Jones, 1981; Peach, 1981) measure of gross immigration, gross emigration and net inflow is available in the International Passenger Survey (IPS). These data confirm the inverse relationship between net immigration and average annual unemployment (Peach, 1991).

The growth of the Caribbean population in Britain since the mid 1960s has come essentially from natural increase. The second generation formed 45 per cent of the total Caribbean population in 1971 and has constituted the majority of the Caribbean population in Britain since 1984. In 1991 it formed 53 per cent of the total. The size of the Caribbean ethnic population seems to have been stable at about the 500,000 mark from 1971 to 1991. However, the Caribbean-born element has shown a significant decrease between 1966 and 1991 and if one takes the 1991 ethnic Black–Caribbean population of 499,964 enumerated by the census at its face value (without including the Black British population classified as Black–Other) it is possible that the Caribbean ethnic population itself is beginning to decrease.

The result is that, of the Commonwealth Caribbean-born population living in Great Britain, covered by the Labour Force Surveys of 1989 to 1991, 57 per cent entered the country between 1955 and 1964; 23 per cent entered between 1965 and 1974 and none entered after 1975.

1.3   Demography

Age

The Black–Caribbean population of Great Britain is young in comparison with the population as a whole, but not as youthful as more recently arrived groups such as the Pakistanis or Bangladeshis. The youthfulness shows up not so much in the younger age-groups as in those of retirement age, where only 6 per cent of the Caribbean population is found, compared with 19 per cent of the total population (see Figure 1.2). The age structure of the Black–Caribbean population is hourglass shaped. The peak of Caribbean migration to Britain was in 1961, 30 years before the 1991 Census and this is reflected in the upper segment of the hourglass of those aged 45 and over. Hardly any Caribbean-born persons aged 20 or under are present. The British-born children born of the first generation dominate the lower segment of the hourglass in the 0 to 30-year-old section.

Gender

Unlike the South Asian ethnic minority groups, the Black–Caribbean population shows a slight preponderance of women: 239,484 men:260,480 women. It is notable that the migration from the Caribbean was always balanced in gender terms and did not show the South Asian pattern of male advance migration with a marked lag before their womenfolk joined them (see Table 1.3). This gender imbalance is true both of those born inside and outside the UK. It partly reflects a degree of under-enumeration of young males. The 1991 Census is known to have a 2.2 per cent overall under-enumeration (OPCS/GRO(S), 1993), which is unevenly distributed across ethnicities,

Figure 1.2 *Population pyramid*

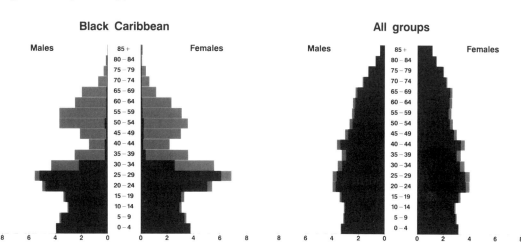

Table 1.3 *Gender balance in selected ethnic minority groups, Great Britain, 1991*

Ethnic group	Men	Women	Male: female
Black–Caribbean	239,484	260,480	100:105
Indian	422,891	417,364	100: 98
Pakistani	245,572	230,983	100: 94
Bangladeshi	84,944	77,891	100: 92
Chinese	77,669	79,269	100:102

Source: OPCS/GRO(s) (1993) Volume 2, Table 7.

gender and location. The Black–Caribbean population is thought to have an overall undercount of 3 per cent, but this rises to 11 per cent for those aged 25 to 29 and to 16 per cent for young men in this age bracket. Undercounting for this group is thought to be higher still in inner London.

Household size

Black–Caribbean household size is rather similar to that of the total population and in turn differs substantially from that of the South Asian groups. Household size tends to be small: while 29 per cent of Indian households, 54 per cent of Pakistani and 61 per cent of Bangladeshi households are five persons or larger, only 11 per cent of the Caribbean and 8 per cent of total households are in this category (see Table 1.4 and Figure 1.3)

Family structure

Although household size is similar to that of the White population, there are significant differences in family structure. In particular, the Caribbean pattern of female-headed households (and allied to this, single female-headed households with dependent children) is much more common than in the White population or in the South Asian ethnic minority groups. The 1991 Census (OPCS/GRO(S), 1993, Volume 2, Table 18) shows that 20 per cent of households headed by a Black–Caribbean was a lone parent family with dependent children. The corresponding figure for the White population was 5 per cent, for Indians 4 per cent, for Pakistanis 7 per cent and for Bangladeshis 8 per cent. If the calculation were to exclude households with no families, the prominence of single parent families for the Black–Caribbean

Table 1.4 *Household size (percent) by birthplace group of household head, Great Britain, 1991*

Household size (persons)	1	2	3	4	5	6	7+	Average size
Total households	27	34	16	16	5	2	1	2.47
Caribbean	27	27	20	15	7	3	1	2.60
India	14	20	15	22	15	8	6	5.36
Pakistan	8	11	11	15	16	17	21	3.58
Bangladesh	5	7	10	15	15	17	29	4.81

Source: OPCS/GRO(s) (1993) Volume 2, Table H.

Figure 1.3 *Percentage distribution of household size for selected groups, by birthplace of head, Great Britain, 1991*

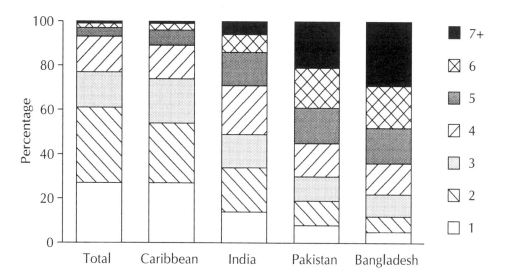

population would appear greater. Figure 1.4 illustrates the contrasts between the White, Black–Caribbean and Indian household types. Single person households are common for both White and Black–Caribbean ethnic groups. However, the high proportion of lone parents with dependent children is prominent for the Black–Caribbean population, but not for the White or Indian populations. Extended, or multi-family household families are significant for the Indian population but not for the other two groups.

Figure 1.4 *Household type (per cent) for total, Black–Caribbean and Indian headed households, Great Britain, 1991*

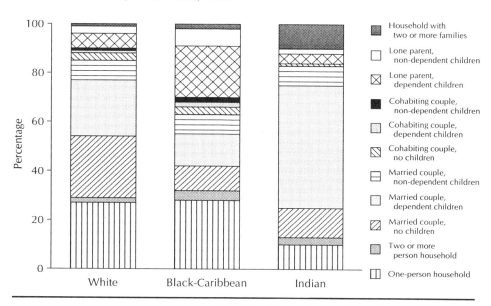

Ethnically mixed households

The SARs (Samples of Anonymised Records, see Marsh and Teague, 1992) allow us to gain a little insight into this matter and indicate a significant proportion of mixed Black and White households. The SARs differ from the traditional output of census tables in that abstracts of individual records are released. There are two samples, the individual SAR, which is a 2 per cent sample of individuals in households and the household SAR which is a 1 per cent sample of the household and the individuals in each of these households. The SARs allow the researcher to make all kinds of cross tabulations not available from the published tables. Of the households in which either the head or partner gave their ethnic group as Black–Caribbean, 37.2 per cent were headed by a female with no male present and 18.1 per cent were headed by a male with no female present. In 26.8 per cent of cases, both the head and partner were Black–Caribbean; in 10.1 per cent of cases there was a Black–Caribbean male with a White female partner while the obverse case obtained only half as frequently (4.8 per cent of cases). There were very few cases of other ethnicities being partners in Black–Caribbean households, although, given the relative sizes of the different ethnic populations, this is to be expected.

Socio-economic status

Table 10 of Volume 2 of the *Ethnic Group and Country of Birth* report (OPCS/GRO(S), 1993) shows a high participation rate of the Black–Caribbean population in the labour force: 285,442 out of the 390,557 aged 16 and over were economically active (73 per cent). This high participation rate was true of both men (147,419 out of 184,147 or 80 per cent) and women (138,023 out of 206,410 or 67 per cent), but the lower female rate probably reflects the high proportion of female-headed households with dependent children.

Female unemployment was 13.5 per cent compared with 6.3 per cent for White women. Black–Caribbean male unemployment was 23.8 per cent compared with 10.7 per cent for White men. For Black–Caribbean men aged 18–19, unemployment stood at an appalling 43.5 per cent and the unemployment rate in each age cohort was generally double that of the White male population. Thus, Black–Caribbeans fared worse than Whites, Black–Caribbean men fared worse than Black–Caribbean women and young Black–Caribbean men were in particularly vulnerable positions.

The occupational structure for Black–Caribbean men is skewed towards the manual categories: two thirds of the men are in such occupations in comparison with only half of the White male working population (see Figure 1.5). Similarly, the proportion in professional occupations is the least of any of the ethnic groups (2.6 per cent compared with 7.1 per cent for White men)

Black–Caribbean female employment is much more similar to White female employment (see Figure 1.6). Unlike the male pattern, it is skewed towards the non-manual side of the distribution. Two thirds of Black–Caribbean females are in non-manual occupations. Thus while Black–Caribbean men

Figure 1.5 *Socio-economic class of men aged 16 and over by ethnicity, Great Britain, 1991*

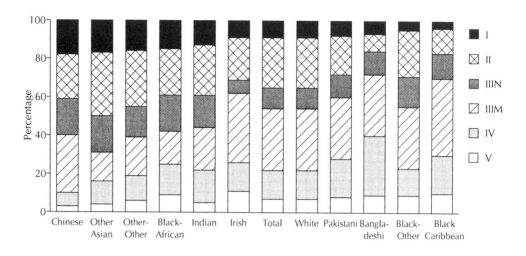

Figure 1.6 *Socio–economic class of women aged 16 and over by ethnicity Great Britain, 1991*

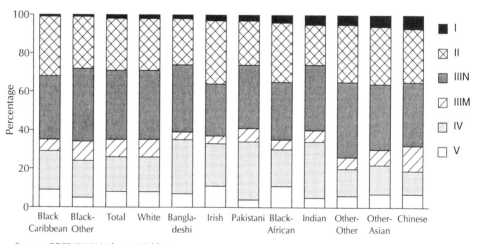

Source: OPCS (1993) Volume 2, Table 16

are blue collar workers, on the whole, Black–Caribbean females are white collar, and while the Black–Caribbean male occupation pattern differs significantly from that of Whites, that of the females is much more similar.

Housing tenure

Black–Caribbean housing tenure is distinguished from that of the White, Indian and Pakistani populations by its higher concentration in the public sector. Local authority housing accommodates 21.4 per cent of White households but 35.7 per cent of Black–Caribbean households. Housing Associations accommodate a further 9.7 per cent of Black–Caribbean households compared with 3 per cent for White households. However, it should be noted that nearly half Black–Caribbean households own their own homes, even though this is less than the two thirds of White households in this position.

The proportion of Caribbean households in council housing is in line with expectations from their socio-economic class position, particularly for men, but less so for women (Peach and Byron, 1993), and there is evidence of decrease in this category with the advent of the 'right to buy' legislation (Peach and Byron, 1994). The 1991 picture represents a major shift in the tenure pattern over the last 30 years. In the 1950s and early 1960s, private rentals dominated, but since that time, there has been a breakthrough into public housing, an increase in owner occupation and the collapse of the private rental sector.

Figure 1.7 *Percentage tenure by ethnicity for selected groups, Great Britain, 1991*

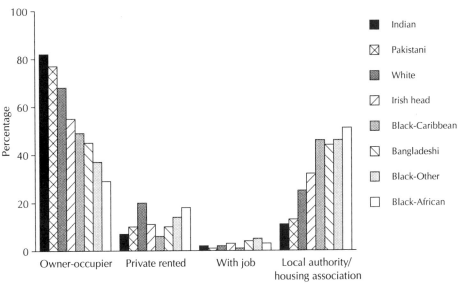

1.4 Geographical distribution

The Black–Caribbean population of Great Britain is heavily concentrated into the English conurbations. Nearly 80 per cent of the total is found in four main metropolitan clusters: Greater London and the metropolitan counties of the West Midlands (Birmingham), Greater Manchester and West Yorkshire. This compares with less than a quarter of the White population. Greater London alone accounts for 58 per cent of the Black–Caribbean population (see Table 1.5). Within these metropolitan areas, the Caribbean population has an inner city concentration, although it does not exhibit the ghetto scale of concentration of the North American cities.

Segregation levels

Black–Caribbean levels of segregation show some variability between the south east and Midlands, on one hand and northern towns on the other. Greater London and Birmingham, which contain over two thirds of the Caribbean population have Indices of Dissimilarity (ID) of 47 and 46, respectively, at enumeration district level (see Table 1.6). The ID represents the percentage of the population which would have to shift from its area of residence in order to replicate the distribution of the total population in the city. It has a range from 0 (no segregation) to 100 (total segregation). To put these values into perspective, the average ID for African–Americans in cities in the United States is about 80.

The level of segregation is not only moderate, but is decreasing (see Table 1.7). The London value of 49 seems to represent a significant decrease in levels of concentration compared with earlier studies. We do not have measures of segregation for ethnicity in the past, but only birthplace. Taking the birthplace group, for which direct comparisons can be made, the ID at enumeration district level was 50 for Greater London. Comparison for Greater London, at a variety of scales from 1961 to 1991, shows a progressive decrease in the levels of segregation at all available scales (borough, ward

Table 1.5 *Relative concentration of ethnic minority population in selected metropolitan counties, Great Britain, 1991*

	Total	White	Black–Carib-bean	Black–African	Black–Other	Indian	Paki-stani	Bang-ladeshi	Chinese
Great Britain	54,888,844	51,873,794	499,964	212,362	178,401	840,255	476,555	162,835	156,938
Greater London	6,679,699	5,333,580	290,968	163,635	80,613	347,091	87,816	85,738	56,579
West Midlands Metropolitan County	2,551,671	2,178,149	72,183	4,116	15,716	141,359	88,268	18,074	6,107
Greater Manchester Metropolitan County	2,499,441	2,351,239	17,095	5,240	9,202	29,741	49,370	11,445	8,323
West Yorkshire Metropolitan County	2,013,693	1,849,562	14,795	2,554	6,552	34,837	80,540	5,978	3,852
Percentage ethnic group in named areas	**25.04**	**22.58**	**79.01**	**82.66**	**62.83**	**65.82**	**64.21**	**74.45**	**47.70**

Source: OPCS/GRO(s) (1993) Volume 2, Table 6.

Table 1.6 *Indices of segregation of the Caribbean ethnic population at enumeration district (ED) level in selected cities, Census 1991*

City	Caribbean index of segregation at ED level	Caribbean total population
Leicester	43	4,070
Oxford	46	1,732
Birmingham	48	42,431
Greater London	49	289,712
Bradford	56	3,223
Greater Manchester	56	10,390
Liverpool	68	1,479
Leeds	72	4,102

Table 1.7 *Comparison of Caribbean-born IDs in Greater London, 1961–1991*

Year	Borough level ID	Ward level ID	Enumeration district ID
1961		56.2	
1971	37.7	49.1	64.5
1981	36.5	46.0	53.0
1991	34.0	41.0	50.0

Source: 1961 data Lee (1973); 1971 data Woods (1976); 1981 data, author's calculations.

and enumeration district). Given that the initial levels of segregation were not high by US standards and that the trend in segregation is downwards, this suggests significant differences in terms of ethnic tolerance between Great Britain and the USA.

Coupled with this decrease in the IDs of the Caribbean-born population, there is evidence of progressive outward diffusion. Map 1.1 shows the absolute change in the Caribbean-born population of Greater London between 1981 and 1991. It is clear that substantial decreases have taken place in areas of inner concentration while the major areas of increase are further away from the centre. Running a regression of absolute change in the Caribbean-born population against absolute numbers of that population, shows a very high inverse relationship: the higher the numbers in 1981, the greater the decrease in 1991

The highest proportion that the Black–Caribbean population forms of any ward in Great Britain is 30.1 per cent in Roundwood in Brent, London (see Table 1.8). Nine out of the top 10 such wards are in London (Moss Side in Manchester is ranked 9). Even if the Black–Other and Black–African populations are added, the highest proportion is still less than 50 per cent (see Table 1.9)

Even when all ethnic minority groups are taken together there is only one ward in England and Wales where the proportion of ethnic minority groups exceeds 90 per cent and only two between 80 and 90 per cent. These very high proportion wards are mainly associated with South Asian settlement.

Map 1.1 *Change in Caribbean–born population, Greater London, 1981–1991. Absolute change by ward*

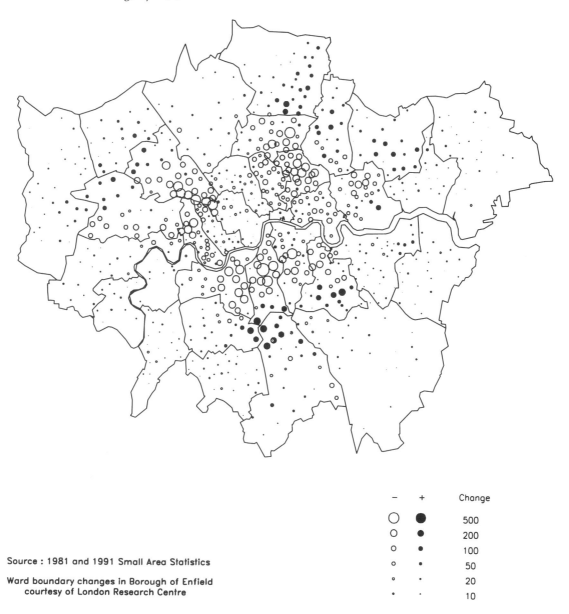

	−	+	Change
	○	●	500
	○	●	200
	○	●	100
	○	●	50
	○	·	20
	·	·	10

Source : 1981 and 1991 Small Area Statistics

Ward boundary changes in Borough of Enfield
   courtesy of London Research Centre

Table 1.8 *Top ranking wards in terms of Caribbean percentage of total population, Great Britain, 1991*

Local authority		Ward	Black–Caribbean Total	Ward Total	Black–Caribbean per cent
1	Brent	Roundwood	2,043	6,783	30.12
2	Brent	St. Raphael's	2,768	10,667	25,95
3	Brent	Stonebridge	1,387	5,746	24.14
4	Lambeth	Tulse Hill	2,643	11,367	23.25
5	Brent	Carlton	1,370	6,156	22.25
6	Lambeth	Ferndale	2,706	12,479	21.68
7	Brent	Kensal Rise	1,273	6,042	21.07
8	Brent	Harlesden	1,216	5,927	20.52
9	Manchester	Moss Side	2,659	13,106	20.29
10	Haringey	Bruce Grove	2,124	10,488	20.25

Source: 1991 Census SAS.

Table 1.9 *Top highest ranking wards by percentage of combined Black populations of the total ward population, Great Britain, 1991*

Local authority		Ward	Black–Caribbean Total	Ward Total	Black–Caribbean per cent
1	Southwark	Liddle	5,115	10,984	46.57
2	Brent	Roundwood	2,902	6,783	42.78
3	Brent	St Raphael's	4,358	10,667	40.85
4	Brent	Stonebridge	2,044	5,746	35.57
5	Hackney	Kings Park	2,383	6,700	35.57
6	Lambeth	Angell	3,807	10,739	35.45
7	Lambeth	Ferndale	4,395	12,479	35.22
8	Lambeth	Tulse Hill	3,965	11,367	34.88
9	Haringey	Bruce Grove	3,601	10,488	34.33
10	Brent	Carlton	2,096	6,156	34.05

Source: 1991 Census SAS.

Micro scale segregation

Chain migration has meant that groups from different islands and territories had somewhat different centres of settlement both between and within cities. People from St Vincent, for example, had a notable concentration in High Wycombe and those from Nevis in Leicester. Within London, Jamaicans were particularly dominant south of the river, while Leeward and Windward islanders reproduced a kind of archipelago of concentrations north of the river — Dominicans around Paddington, Montserratians around Finsbury Park and so on. The census does not give us a high degree of resolution on the distribution of small islanders, but indices of dissimilarity calculated from the birthplace tables indicate that a degree of segregation of islanders from one another still exists in 1991 (see Table 1.10). The high levels of segregation of the Belizeans is probably a function of the small numbers rather than any sociological phenomenon.

Table 1.10 *Indices of Dissimilarity for selected Caribbean birthplaces, ward level, Greater London ,1991*

Birthplace	Barb–ados	Jam–aica	Trini–dad	Other independent states	Caribbean dependent territories	West Indies	Belize	Guy–ana	ID	IS	N
Barbados	0								15	16	13,451
Jamaica	22	0							13	26	76,529
Trinidad	27	33	0						25	27	10,204
Other independent states	26	34	32	0					23	29	27,675
Caribbean dependent territories	46	50	44	39	0				43	44	2,847
West Indies	30	36	35	24	42	0			28	29	5,136
Belize	80	81	79	82	84	81	0		80	80	228
Guyana	26	26	25	35	50	39	79	0	21	24	14,752

Source: 1991 Census, Local Base Statistics, Table 7.

1.5   Conclusion

The picture which emerges from this analysis is of a population which has matured from a first generation immigrant population, which arrived between 1948 and 1974 and which now has a larger number of second than first generation. It is a group with a high concentration in London and Birmingham, within which traces of the original chain migration from different islands can still be seen. Levels of segregation are much lower than for African–Americans in the United States and for Pakistanis and Bangladeshis in Britain. Surburbanisation of the population is clearly evident in their London distribution.

There are also high levels of mixed Black–Caribbean and White households and evidence of the emergence of a Black British identity. It is both a hardworking and a disadvantaged population. Participation rates in the workforce are among the highest of all groups for both men and women. On the other hand, unemployment rates are unacceptably high, more than double the White average, and double this figure again for young men.

Housing tenure has shown a remarkable degree of change from the patterns of the 1960s. At that stage, the Caribbean population was largely concentrated in private rentals and almost entirely absent from public housing. Since then, there has been a substantial advance into both the private sector and into local authority and housing association property. Even in council housing, there has been significant evidence of purchase. The Caribbean population is much more concentrated into flats than houses. Even after controlling for the position of lone mothers with dependent children, who are exceptionally highly concentrated in the Caribbean population, the degree of flatted accommodation is high.

One of the most telling summaries of the differences between the Caribbean and Asian settlements in Britain was that the Caribbeans faced what I term an 'Irish future' while the Asians faced a 'Jewish future'. Apart from the ironic drawback that we have little firm information on the Jewish and Irish populations in Britain, the implication of the statement is that the Black–Caribbean popu-lation is working class, waged labour, state educated and council housed, while the Asian population will become self-employed, owner-occupiers and white collar workers, with professional qualifications. There is some truth as well as counter evidence for such an assertion for both groups. The Jewish future seems to be coming about for the Indian popula-tion and to an extent the Pakistani population, although not for the Bangla-deshis. However, in the case of the Black–Caribbean population, there seems to be a gender divide between the white collar, female, socio-economic structure and the manual, male structure. Certainly, the other model for Caribbean settlement that has haunted the literature, that of the African–American ghetto, has not come about.

References

Balarajan, R. and Bulusu, L. (1990) Mortality among immigrants in England and Wales, 1973–1983. In: Britton, M (ed.), *Mortality and Geography*. OPCS Series DS no 9. London: HMSO, pp. 135–50.

Ballard, R. and Kalra, V. S. (1994) *The Ethnic Dimensions of the 1991 Census*. Manches-ter: The University of Manchester, Manchester Census Group.

Byron, M. (1991) Social networks and housing: West Indians in a British city. Unpublished paper delivered at the Association of American Geographers 1991 Annual Meeting, Miami, Florida, April 13–17.

Byron, M. (1994) *Post-war Caribbean Migration to Britain: The Unfinished Cycle*. Aldershot: Avebury.

Davison, R. B. (1962) *West Indian Migrants. London:* Oxford University Press.

Glass, R. (1960) *Newcomers: The West Indians in London* (assisted by Harold Pollins). London: George Allen and Unwin.

Harris, C. (1987) British capitalism, migration and relative surplus population: a synopsis. *Migration*, 1 (1), 47–90.

Lee, T.R. (1977) *Race and Residence: The concentration and dispersal of immigrants in London*, Oxford: Clarendon Press.

Jones, P. (1981) British unemployment and immigration: two case studies. *New Community*, 9(1), 112–16.

Marsh, Cathy and Teague, A (1992) Samples of Anonymised Records from the 1991 Census, *Population Trends*, 69, 17–26.

OPCS (1974) Census 1971, Great Britain, *Country of Birth Tables*. London: HMSO.

OPCS/GRO(S) (1993) 1991 Census, *Ethnic Group and Country of Birth, Great Britain*. Two volumes. London: HMSO.

OPCS (1983) 1981 Census, *Country of Birth, Great Britiain*, London: HMSO

Patterson, S. (1963) *Dark Strangers*. London: Tavistock Publications.

Peach, G. C. K. (1967) West Indians as a replacement population in England and Wales. *Social and Economic Studies*, 16(3), 259–94.

Peach, C. (1968) *West Indian Migration to Britain: A Social Geography*. London: Oxford University Press.

Peach, C. (1981) Ins and outs of Home Office and IPS migration data. *New Community*, 1, 117-19.

Peach, C. and Byron, M. (1993) Caribbean tenants in council housing: race, class and gender. *New Community*, 19(3), 407–23.

Peach, C. and Byron, M. (1994) Council house sales, residualisation and Afro Caribbean tenants. *Journal of Social Policy*, 23(3), 363–83.

Philpott, S. B. (1977) The Montserratians: migration dependency and the maintenance of island ties in England.In Watson, J. L. (ed.), *Between Two Cultures: Migrants and Minorities in Britain*. Oxford: Basil Blackwell.

Thomas-Hope, E. (1986) Transients and settlers: varieties of Caribbean migrants and the socio-economic implication of their return. *International Migration*, 24(3), 559–71.

Thomas-Hope, E. (1992) *Explanation in Caribbean Migration*. London: Macmillan.

Woods R. I. (1976) Aspects of the scale problems in the calculation of segregation indices: London and Birmingham 1961 and 1971. *Tijdschrift voor Economische en Sociale Geografie* 67, 169–174.

Chapter 2
Black–Africans: students who stayed

Patricia Daley

2.1 Introduction

The 1991 Census of Great Britain recorded 213,362 persons who classified themselves as Black–African. Africa has a very heterogeneous population; during the period of colonial occupation and after, some parts of the continent witnessed substantial in- and out-migration of Europeans, Asians and other ethnic groups. Consequently it would be deceptive to categorise the African-born population as Black, and in recognition of the importance of Black as a political category, a significant proportion of the 213,362 may conform to a political, as opposed to racial, definitions of Black. There were, for example, over 2,000 persons born in the Caribbean who classified themselves Black–African (OPCS/GRO(S), 1993, Volume 1, Table 5). With 53 potential countries of origin and varied social backgrounds the Black–African population is characterised by diversity, both internally and in comparison with other ethnic groups.

The United Kingdom's African population is a relatively understudied social group in British race relations. Black–Africans have a long history of residence in the UK well before the more recent period of large-scale immigration in the 1960s. The history of their migration differs significantly from those immigrants who were recruited directly for the purposes of employment. Well established African communities existed in the seaports of Liverpool, London and Cardiff, peopled by seamen and stowaways, many of whom settled in Britain in the late 1940s.

Since the immediate post-independence period of the 1960s there has been a marked increase in the number of Africans travelling to the UK for higher education and technical training. It is understood that a significant proportion of this group settled in the UK where their newly acquired skills were in demand. Marriages, family reunions, the births of offspring and ensuing economic crises in their countries of origin have all assisted in creating a settled population. Political instability in the 1970s and 1980s generated refugee in-migration.

Historical background

Africans have resided in Great Britain since antiquity. They were, however, few in number and it was not until the twentieth century that their numbers showed a substantial increase. Colonisation fuelled a desire to investigate the source of the colonisers' power and offered the prospects of employment as seamen to many Africans from coastal communities. West Africans, particularly from Sierra Leone, Nigeria and the Gold Coast, and east Africans from British Somaliland, settled in the docklands of Cardiff, Liverpool,

London and other ports (Banton, 1955; Killingray, 1994). Nevertheless, before the 1950s the African population of Britain was less than 10,000.Students from Africa have been a feature of Britain's educational institutions since the eighteenth century (Carey, 1956). Many were sons of chiefs or were sponsored by missionaries or traders of African companies. Data for the early twentieth century show that until 1940 there were less than 100 African students in British universities in any year. The figure rose rapidly in the post-war years and West Africans rose from being 14 per cent of the total colonial student population in 1939 to 2,009 or 43 per cent in 1950. By this time the West African Students' Union, which was formed in 1925, was already the focus of students campaigning against colonial rule and discrimination in Britain (Adi, 1994).

This migration for education took on a greater momentum in the run up to independence in the 1950s and in the immediate post-independence period of the 1960s. After the second world war the Colonial Office, under pressure from aspiring Africans for social and economic development and self-government, recognised that 'it was essential that the people of these territories be given the opportunity to train for posts in the professional and technical fields' (Little, 1948:52). New universities were created and British universities were able to establish links with colleges in Africa: Fourah Bay College in Sierra Leone, Legon in the Gold Coast, Ibadan in Nigeria and Makerere in East Africa. Other forms of educational links were formed with specific countries in Africa. The Colonial Office, independent governments and the British Council also sponsored a number of training programmes for civil servants.

Goody and Groothues (1977) attributed the 'quest for education' among West Africans to the wealth and prestige gained by studying abroad. English education was held in great esteem by Africans. Little (1948:52) comments that the 'most common assumptions are that, in England, education is available to everyone, almost without exception, to a university level' (Little,1948, quoted in Banton, 1955). He goes on to say 'the graduate returning from England may possibly bring with him a European wife; in any event his stay in the imperial country will of itself serve to heighten his prestige, he will be introduced to strangers as someone who 'has been to England' [which was abbreviated in Nigeria to 'been-to ']' (Little, quoted in Banton, 1955). A similar function was served by the seamen who spread amongst the 'illiterate population exaggerated tales of luxurious standards of living in Britain.' They helped spread the idea that 'England holds the secret of success and that by going there a man can improve his status or make his fortune' (Banton, 1955:45).

In West Africa the absence of a settled white population during the colonial era meant that western-educated Africans were assured high status positions in the civil service and in the professions. As independent governments attempted to improve local educational institutions, the importance of foreign qualifications declined. On returning to some African countries, doctors and lawyers had to take local examinations before they could practise (Goody and Groothues, 1977). By the 1980s the situation had radically changed; political instability meant that universities were more often closed than opened, while economic crisis resulted in the reduction of state expenditure on education. Equipment in some of the best universities became outmoded and many could no longer guarantee a high quality of education. Consequently in the 1990s education abroad is more sought after than ever. However, the increasing cost of overseas students' fees in the UK ensures that only the African elite can now fund overseas education.The earliest cohort of students sought professional qualifications, but later, once African universities were established and travel was easier, many students came to acquire a variety of higher degrees or technical qualifications. A survey carried out in London in the 1950s show law, engineering, medicine, education and nursing to be the most popular subjects among Africans (Carey, 1956). Due to the gendered nature of early western education in Africa the majority of the student population were men.

Country of birth

Country of birth is a particularly unhelpful guide to ethnicity of the African-born population living in Great Britain in 1991. The East African-born population is largely Indian, the Southern African-born population is largely White and only the West African-born population is largely Black–African. Most of the African-born population of Britain comes from Commonwealth countries, but there is, in addition, African-born population from non-Commonwealth countries, largely from the Maghreb (Mediterranean North Africa) and the Republic of South Africa. The Republic was not a member of the Commonwealth at the time of the 1991 Census and most South Africans (61,000 out of 68,000) were White. The North African population was also largely White, presumably children born to British forces stationed in Egypt and Libya.

Thus, although previous censuses contained data on birthplace, it was not always possible to distinguish between Whites, Asians or Africans, especially for countries such as Kenya, Uganda, Zimbabwe (formerly Rhodesia) and South Africa. The 1971 Census recorded a population of 176,060 whose birthplace was on the continent of Africa (see Table 2.1). This figure increased to 267,252 in the 1981 Census. One can assume that a significant proportion of these were White. Of the 331,313 persons born in New Commonwealth Africa living in Britain in 1991, one fifth were White (OPCS/GRO(S), 1993, Table 5). Of the 146,869 persons born in the rest of Africa, 94,973 were White. Thus, 210,740 of the 478,182, or nearly half (44 per cent), of the population born in Africa were White.

Over 84 per cent of the African-born population in the 1971 Census were born between the years 1935 and 1965, during the period of effective colonial rule and White settlement. In the 1960s many African countries with settler colonies saw a mass exodus following independence, mainly by Whites who retained their British citizenship and educated their children in the United Kingdom. Nevertheless, in the 1991 Census nearly 90 per cent of the African-born population whose birthplace was Nigeria, Ghana, Gambia and Sierra Leone was Black–African (OPCS/GRO(S), 1993, Volume 1, Table 5).

Table 2.1 *Country of birth of the African–born population 1971–1991*

Country of birth	1971 Total	Males	Females	1981 Total	Males	Females	1991 Total	Females	Males
Kenya	59,500	32,170	27,330	102,144	53,299	48,845	112,422	57,762	54,660
Malawi	2,545	1,380	1,165	9,407	4,935	4,472	10,697	5,541	5,156
Tanzania	14,375	8,035	6,340	27,151	14,483	12,668	29,825	15,575	15,240
Uganda	12,590	6,925	5,655	45,937	24,356	21,581	50,903	26,639	24,264
Zambia	5,740	2,990	2,750	12,558	6,450	6,108	16,758	8,313	8,445
Zimbabwe (Rhodesia)	7,905	3,795	4,110	16,330	8,189	8,141	21,252	10,071	11,181
Botswana, Lesotho & Swaziland				1,069	527	542	2,001	1,099	902
Gambia				619	396	223	1,388	773	615
Ghana	11,215	6,385	4,835	16,887	8,918	7,969	32,672	15,867	16,805
Nigeria	28,565	16,415	12,155	31,310	17,946	13,364	47,085	23,483	23,602
Sierra Leone	3,175	3,715	750	3,840	1,961	1,879	6,310	2,961	3,349
Algeria				2,417			3,672	2,460	1,272
Egypt				23,463			22,849	12,103	10,746
Libya				6,004			6,604	3,791	2,813
Morocco				5,818			9,073	5,244	3,829
Tunisia				2,037			2,417	1,468	949
South Africa	45,825	20,430	25,400	54,207			68,059	31,450	36,609
Other Africa	18,590			17,040	8,867	8,173	34,194	18,290	15,899
Africa	164,205	90,245	73,960	378,238	150,327	133,965	331,134	168,084	163,229

Source: OPCS: 1971, 1981 and 1991 Census. Crown Copyright.

The West African population is the core of the Black–African population of Great Britain. Of the total population of 212,362, just under half were African-born (96,653) and just over a third were born in the UK. Three quarters of the African born Black–Africans were from New Commonwealth West Africa. If it is assumed that the UK-born children were distributed proportionately to the non-UK birthplaces, then 43,000 could be thought of as West African children. This suggests that nearly 60 per cent (56 per cent) of the Black–African population of Great Britain is West African in origin. Table 2.1 shows a 50 per cent increase in the Nigerian-born population in the intercensal period 1981 to 1991 and a 100 per cent increase in the Ghanaian population from 16,887 in 1981 to 32,672 in 1991. This cannot be attributed purely to natural increase.

The growth in the number of Nigerians may be the indirect consequence of the availability of surplus capital derived from the post-1973 oil boom. This caused a proliferation of higher education institutions in Nigeria and a growth in higher qualification scholarships from central and state governments. The increase in Ghanaians has to be related to political upheavals in that country following the two 'revolutionary' coups of 4 June 1979 and 31 December 1980 and the subsequent outflow of students, refugees and exiles. The latter coup was marked by the flight of progressive elements after 1983 (Yeebo, 1991; Atampugre, 1992). This pattern of flight is reflected in the data showing applicants for asylum in the UK (Table 2.2).

Table 2.2 *Application for asylum status by country of origin, 1980–1991*

Africa	1980	1981	1982	1983	1984	1985	1986	1987	1988	1989	1990	1991	Total
Angola						7	8	22	47	235	1,160	5,780	7,259
Congo							1	1	5	20	70	370	467
Ethiopia	97	90	90	126	135	209	212	266	230	560	1,975	1,685	5,675
Ghana	29	13	407	689	337	175	220	153	155	330	1,020	2,405	5,933
Libya	41	41	48	26	78	60	125	72	60	15			566
Nigeria						17	8	10	10	20	115	335	515
Seychelles	15	19	20	25	31	90	90	201	65	35			591
Somalia	14	11	14	50	83	244	214	356	390	1,850	1,920	1,995	7,141
South Africa	27	62	54	61	54	53	73	73	35	40	15		547
Sudan	3	14	11	19	57	27	42	42	35	110	255	1,150	1,765
Togo/Ivory Coast										20	110	1,910	2,040
Uganda	28	99	66	199	165	203	189	440	565	1,235	1,905	1,450	6,544
Zaire	2	0	2	4	11	8	18	63	100	525	1,730	7,010	9,473
Other	32	43	49	80	130	120	102	85	110	205	560	3,405	4,921
	288	392	761	1,279	1,081	1,165	1,270	1,751	1,745	5,200	10,835	27,495	53,262
Granted asylum or refugee status	94	117	168	380	156	297	235	243	720	1,675	450		4,535
Granted exceptional leave to remain	87	92	80	229	95	233	201	581	820	1,050	480		3,948

Source: Home Office, Statistical Bulletin, Issue 25/89(1), 20 July 1989 & Issue 12/92(2), June 1992; British Refugee Council, Statistics on Refugees and Asylum Seekers in the UK, 1989; British Refugee Council, Asylum Seekers in the UK - Essential Statistics, 1989.

Refugees

In-migration of refugees occurred before the last intercensal period. At various times since the last century members of the African elite, such as Seretse Khama of Botswana, sought refuge in Britain (Parsons, 1994). Mass refugee movements from Africa began with the Ugandan Asians in 1968. Since the 1970s, political instability and human rights abuses have led to an increase in the number of Africans seeking refuge in the UK from countries such as Eritrea, Ghana, Uganda, Somalia and Ethiopia and more recently from Angola, Congo and Nigeria (Table 2.2). According to Oguibe (1994) This group of Africans consisted of: 'fallen politicians and their families, opposition and pressure group leaders, political misfits, disgruntled and dissappointed idealists, deviants for whom the new dispensations had no place, and in a great number of cases, dispossessed populations fleeing from war and deprivation'.

Although the number of people seeking asylum rose dramatically in the 1980s, the actual number granted refugee status or exceptional leave to remain has been too small to be significant. Between 1980 and 1991 there were some 53,262 applications for asylum but only 8,500 were granted refugee status or exceptional leave to remain. Of these the Somalis, Ethiopians and Ugandans were the major beneficaries, with Somalis forming 25 per cent of successful applicants. Despite their small number, these refugees may have undue influence on certain features of the Black–African population.

2.2 Demographic characteristics

The introduction of the ethnic category Black–African in the 1991 Census should enable, for the first time, more accurate documentation of the Black population with roots in Africa. Neither earlier country of birth statistics or the use of the ethnic category Black–African in the 1991 Census can provide reliable measures of the number of Africans in Britain. There are, however, caveats about the reliability of the census data. Post-enumeration checks on the 1991 Census suggest that 1.2 million or 2.2 per cent of the total population of Great Britain was missed (OPCS/GRO(S), 1993, Volume 1). Undercounting was particularly marked for young men, and Black–African men between the ages of 20 and 29 have the highest rates of under-enumeration of any of the recorded ethnic groups. It amounted to 15 per cent of the age-group 20 to 24 and 17 per cent of the 25-to 29-year-olds. Under-enumeration of Black–African women was small and close to the national average. Difficulties with immigration officials are among the reasons suggested for this under-enumeration.

In the 1991 Census the number of people in Great Britain who identified their ethnic group as Black–African numbered 212,362 or 0.4 per cent of the total population. This group also comprised 7 per cent of the ethnic minority population. About 7 per cent of this group had a former residence outside the UK in the year preceding the census. This figure is much lower than that for the White (18 per cent) and Asian (22 per cent) populations. One assumes that foreign students, refugees and visitors form a significant proportion of Black–African recent migrants. The age structure of the migrants with 20 per cent under the age of 15 and 64 per cent between the ages of 20 and 44 may be a reflection of this origin. There is a tendency for members of the African elite to favour British private education for their children, and for African university students to be slightly older than the British norm as many pupils do not finish their secondary education until they are in their early twenties.

Over a third (36 per cent) of the Black–African population in the 1991 Census was British-born. This reflects the more recent history of migration and the increasingly settled nature of the population. Using the two per cent individual Sample of Anonymised Record (SAR), it was possible to examine the country of birth of the Black–African population. The two per cent SAR contained 4,171 Black–Africans. Almost a third (32 per cent) of those belonging to this ethnic group were born in England. The other major countries of birth were Nigeria (19 per cent), Uganda (4 per cent), Kenya (2 per cent) and South Africa (1 per cent). Only these African countries could be identified in the two per cent SAR. There are no major differences between the number of men and women in terms of country of birth for Commonwealth Africa, but non-Commonwealth Africa had a higher percentage of men: 60 per cent.

The ambiguity of the term Black–African has been shown through the examination of the country of birth statistics. Since it can be assumed that children born in Britain of Black–African parents or of mixed race unions may not always be assigned to that ethnic category, it is possible that the Black–African category does not reflect some of the internal diversity in the population of African origin. A cursory glance at the Black—Other category in the SAR shows about 2 per cent of the sample being born on the continent of Africa.

Using the one per cent household SAR, it was possible to look at the ethnic categories in households headed by Black–Africans. Here it was found that the children of mixed marriages (African–non-African), which came to 2.5 per cent of all marriages, may place themselves in five other ethnic group categories: 8 per cent identified themselves as Black–Other; 3 per cent as Other–Other; 2 per cent as White; 1 per cent as Black–Caribbean and less than 1 per cent as Indian and Pakistani. Although, it is possible that some sons and daughters, especially those claiming to be White, may be stepchildren of previously all White unions, it is not unknown for children of mixed parents to claim the White ethnic status of one parent.

Age and sex structure

The age structure of the Black–African population is what would be expected from a recent immigrant community. The Black–African group is very youthful, with 29 per cent of the population below the age of 16 (62,290) and a sharp reduction after 40 years (Figure 2.1), resulting in fewer people of retirement age than among the Black–Caribbean and Indian ethnic groups. This may be the consequence of return migration.

It can be assumed that up until the economic crisis of the 1980s a significant proportion of Black–African students would return to their country of origin on the completion of their studies. The standard of living for professionals

Figure 2.1 *Population pyramid*

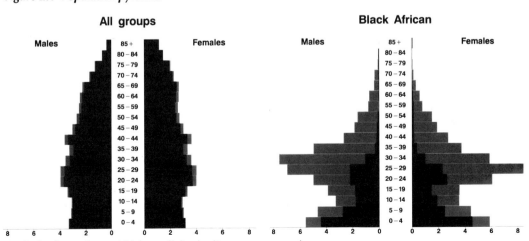

Dark shading refers to UK–born; light shading to overseas– born

would have been much higher in African countries than in Europe and many professionals moved into business and became entrepreneurs in their field. This may be one case where the propensity to return was high and was achieved, although this did not necessarily result in total decamping from Britain. The birth of offspring in the UK and their acquisition of British passports, until quite recently, provided some households with an insurance system which could be drawn upon in times of crisis, as in the 1980s

The age structure of the group shows marked differences if the sample is subdivided according to country of birth. The bulk (89 per cent) of the British born population is below the age of 30, with 26 per cent below four years. These figures reflect the increase in immigration during the 1960s and the very young children of second or third generation settlers. Looking at the age structure of the non-UK-born population, the chart is highly skewed in the 25 to 34 age-group. This reflects the earlier pattern of migration for education (some of this group being students) and also the children of students who were brought to this country in the 1960s. West Africans had specific cultural strategies to maximise the gains they and their offspring could obtain from residence in the UK.

One such strategy was the fostering out of their children to White families with the hope that they would assimilate into British society and improve their chances of success. The novelist, Buchi Emecheta in her novel *Second Class Citizen*, which portrayed African immigrant life in the Britain of the 1960s, wrote: 'No sane couple would dream of keeping their children with them. So rampant was the idea of foster-parents that African housewives in England came to regard the foster-mother as the mother of their children... No one cared whether a woman was suitable or not, no one wanted to know whether the house was clean or not; all they wanted to be sure of was that the foster-mother was white. The concept of 'whiteness' could cover a multitude of sins' (Emecheta, 1974:50).

The loss of the extended family meant that the burden of child care was borne in isolation. Many women became the only breadwinners in their family as they supported 'student' husbands or partners. Fostering was an economic strategy in situations where paid child care was unaffordable. A 1970s survey by Goody and Groothues (1979) of 300 African families in the UK showed that 50 per cent either had children in care at the time of the survey or had previously fostered out one or more of their children. They attributed this to 'crowded and sub-standard housing, the husband's determination to study as well as support his family, and the wife's need to work and her attempts to train as well; [also the] opportunity for the children to learn English language and customs'. Goody and Groothues also recognised 'the role of the cultural paradigm which defines the rearing of children outside the parental family as a valued form of education' (p78).

Putting children into local authority care was not a permanent solution and parents often planned to return for them once the more difficult years of child rearing had passed. Alienated from their customs and often losing their first language altogether, these children can often experience difficulty fitting back into West African communities. Fostering as a survival strategy was essentially a phenomenon of the 1960s and 1970s; by the 1980s it had started to decline, as community workers highlighted some of the racial and psychological problems such children might experience in care.

African women

Like the character of Adhana in Emecheta's novel, most women attempted to join their husbands or partners in the UK. Many migrated on their own for training, but it was infinitely easier if they were joining a spouse. Historically, studies of African student population often failed to distinguish between men and women. Because of the gendered nature of colonial education in Africa the early student population would have exhibited huge sexual imbalances. The main activists in the student movements were men, even though Adi (1994) notes the formation of a West African Women's Association founded in Britain in the 1940s, and in the early 1950s the Nigerian Women's League. Many of these women migrated for professional training as in the field of nursing. However, recognition of the value of female education among the growing African bourgeoisie meant that later female migrants were, like their male counterparts, encouraged to follow professional careers as lawyers, doctors and teachers.

Female migration from Africa whether on their own account or to join spouses has in recent years kept pace with male migration. By the 1991 Census the historical difference in the sex ratios had disappeared with the Black–African population now split 51 per cent males to 49 per cent females. This numerical balancing of the sexes furthered the establishment of marital unions and the consequent emergence of a settled community among migrants from the same ethnic group.

Marital status

Over 33 per cent of the Black–African population is married. This compares with 47 per cent of the White and 30 per cent of the Black–Caribbean populations. The youthfulness of the African population may account for this low figure, since there is no evidence to suggest that marital rates among Africans are similar to that of the Caribbean group. In African societies generally, there are considerable social pressures on couples to marry rather than cohabit. In the one per cent household SAR, there were 694 households headed by Black–Africans, but only 12 per cent contained a spouse; less than half of those who were reported to be married. The pattern of migration may be responsible for this anomaly. It is not peculiar for a spouse (either husband or wife) to permanently reside in Great Britain with the children, leaving the other in their country of origin. There is also a high degree of inter-continental commuting among Africans with permanent residence in the UK; the more successful of whom may retain a second home and possibly a business venture in their country of origin.

Research on gender relations in Africa has shown that the western concept of joint family responsibilities for husbands and wives does not hold true in a number of African societies. Instead men and women have different spheres of activities and different sources of income and duties. Modernisation and the introduction of western household structures and property rights have generated considerable conflict and mobility in African households. Some researchers have argued that this is more evident in households from matrilineal societies such as the Ashanti (Goody and Groothues, 1979; Atampugre 1992). Migration can lead to stress in marriage as documented by Goody and Groothues (1979), but can also facilitate the generation of independent sources of income for women. In the UK, husbands and wives seek to improve their income and status through work and further education. The satisfaction of these two goals is in some way influential in determining the geographical location of the population.

2.3 Geographical distribution

Black–Africans are perhaps more highly concentrated than others in the metropolitan areas of Greater London, Liverpool, Cardiff and Leeds; the historical centres of early African communities. Seventy-nine per cent of the total Black–African population live in Greater London and of this group 66 per cent live in Inner London (see Figure 2.2 showing their distribution in London). The highest concentrations are in Lambeth where almost 10 per cent of the population live and where they constitute 7 per cent of the borough's population. A survey of the top 20 Black–African wards shows those wards in the London Borough of Southwark as having some of the highest concentrations of Black–Africans in Britain (Table 2.3). A similar survey of the top 10 enumeration districts (EDs) show high concentrations in Southwark, and Barking and Dagenham, with almost 50 per cent in one ED (Table 2.4).

This high level of residential concentration can be explained to some degree by the cultural strategies that are utilised during the process of migration. Access to housing, national foodstuffs and social networks are part and parcel of migrants' survival strategies. And among Africans these occur along ethnic, national or regional lines. For instance, Yorubas may congregate in the same areas, but may also depend on links with other Nigerian and West African ethnic groups. Within London it is possible to identify residential areas associated with specific national groups: Ugandans, Ghanaians and Nigerians in south London, and Somalis in east London. Regional and national associations are closely linked with the settlement process (Atampugre, 1992). Many perform social welfare functions providing mutual and financial support in times of bereavement or other crises, and fund raising for activities in their home areas. Among Ghanaians, Atampugre (1992) identifies some 19 village and town, eight ethnic and clan, 24 district and regional, and seven old boys' associations with representation in the major urban centres of the UK.

Figure 2.2 *Black–African ethnic group, Greater London, 1991*

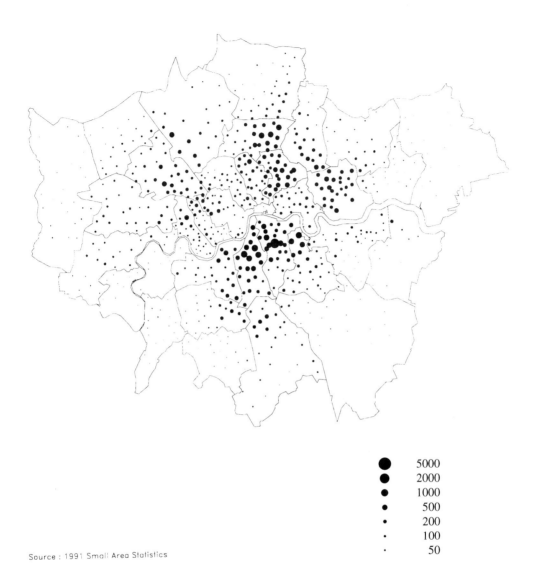

5000
2000
1000
500
200
100
50

Source : 1991 Small Area Statistics

Table 2.3   Black–Africans: top 20 wards, 1991

Area	Ward	Africans	Total in ward	Per cent Black–Africans
Southwark	ALFR	2,920	10,984	26
Lewisham	AJFJ	1,299	9,765	13
Hackney	ACFJ	830	6,700	12
Southwark	ALFQ	1,034	8,470	12
Lambeth	AHFA	1,272	10,739	12
Lambeth	AHFJ	1,533	13,227	11
Lewisham	AJFS	1,071	9,948	11
Haringey	AEFD	1,093	10,488	10
Hackney	ACFG	644	6,241	10
Cardiff	TNPB	372	3,663	10
Lambeth	AHFE	1,254	12,479	10
Haringey	AEFE	1,093	10,882	10
Haringey	AEFX	1,130	11,334	10
Lambeth	AHFY	1,409	14,169	10
Lewisham	AJFL	960	9,776	10
Southwark	ALFK	899	9,287	10
Southwark	ALFG	954	9,881	10
Southwark	ALFP	1,153	11,966	10
Brent	ATGA	637	6,676	9
Haringey	AEFK	668	7,174	9

Source: 1991 Census SAS (ESRC/JISC purchase). © Crown Copyright.

Table 2.4   Black–Africans: top 10 enumeration districts

Enumeration district	Ward	Africans	Total in ward	Per cent
Southwark	ALFR	190	418	45
Barking and Dagenham	AQFD	49	114	43
Haringey	AEFX	140	331	42
Lewisham	AJFL	88	213	41
Hackney	ACFW	159	409	39
Southwark	ALFR	227	588	39
Barnet	ARFE	159	431	37
Southwark	ALFR	149	439	34
Southwark	ALFR	121	365	33
Southwark	ALFR	233	715	32
Southwark	ALFR	167	523	32

Source: 1991 Census SAS (ESRC/JISC purchase). © Crown Copyright.

2.4 Social and economic characteristics

Education

From the highly selective nature of early African migration to Great Britain, it is not surprising that in 1991 Black–Africans were the most qualified ethnic minority group in Britain with 26 per cent of the population over 18 years possessing higher qualifications (Table 2.5). Students comprised some 18 per cent of the population compared to 3 per cent for Whites, while 27 per cent of Nigerians in the two per cent SAR have student status. If one considers levels of qualifications the majority of qualified Africans have qualifications of above A–level or equivalent.

The most qualified age-groups are the 30 to 44 years and 45 to 59 years. This is not surprising judging from the student origins of the first generation of Black–African migrants. Evidence suggests that the younger generation may yet achieve equivalent levels of qualifications. Among Africans there continues to be a strong emphasis on professional qualifications as the main route to higher social status. For many, education is pursued for far longer into adulthood than for most other ethnic groups.

When the country of birth by level of qualification is considered, Black–Africans who were born on the continent of Africa tend to be better qualified than those born in the UK. Of those qualified, 31 per cent were born in Nigeria; 16 per cent in England; 33 per cent in Other Commonwealth Africa; and only 8 per cent in Other Africa (Table 2.6).

Again, this is not unusual for a population in which a substantial proportion migrated for educational purposes. Considering level of qualifications among recent migrants, 29 per cent of those who moved to the UK in the year preceding the 1991 Census had post A–level or equivalent qualifications; 29 per cent first degree and 37 per cent higher degrees. The poor showing of non-Commonwealth Africans can be partially attributed to the presence of the refugee populations from Somalia and Ethiopia; yet the prevalence of higher degrees among recent migrants indicates the more recent influx of qualified professional refugees.

Table 2.5 *Black–Africans: qualified and level of qualifications*

	Black–Africans		Whites	
	No.	Per cent	No.	Per cent
Total persons age 18 and over	13,233		3,991,91	
Proportion qualified	3,512	26	561,488	14
Higher degrees	457	3	35,915	9
First degree and equivalent qualifications	1,425	11	244,958	6
A–level or equivalent	1,630	12	252,146	6

Source: OPCS/GRO(S) (1993) 1991 Census Ethnic Group and Country of Birth.

Table 2.6 *Level of highest qualification by country of birth (percentage) of Black–Africans*

Country	Higher degree	First degree or equivalent	A–level or equivalent
England	12	21	12
Nigeria	34	31	31
Other Africa	31	31	37

Source: 1991 Census, two per cent SAR (ESRC/JISC purchase). © Crown Copyright.

The principal fields of qualifications for Black–Africans are: management studies, nursing, sociology, education, clinical medicine, engineering, accountancy and law. When looked at according to gender, men dominate the traditionally 'masculine' fields of management studies, accountancy and law, while women outnumber men two to one in education, nursing, vocational studies, and in art and design.Major generational differences are apparent between the subjects studied by the 30–44 age-group and younger cohorts. For example, among the over–50 age–group nursing and education are the most popular qualifications, while 30–year–olds prefer management studies and clinical medicine. Forty per cent of qualified 30–year–olds had their highest qualification in management studies. Among those in their twenties, nursing and education lose their popularity and a more diversifed curricula is followed. This represents a shift away from education purely for vocational qualifications to its merit as an intellectual pursuit, and it symbolises the wider range of career choices open to UK–based Africans.

Social class

Another distinctive feature of the Black–African group is its distribution across the social classes. This is a facet of Black–African life that is rarely considered in the literature on immigrants in the UK. The tendency to merge Black–African with Black–Caribbean has meant that in the area of social class the more distinct characteristics of Black–Africans are often submerged in the broader category.

If the occupational definition of social class is accepted, then 8 per cent of the Black–African group are in Social Class I compared to 5 per cent of the White population and 2 per cent of Black–Caribbean group. Nigerians are over-represented with 14 per cent. The 1970s' expansion of institutions of higher education in Nigeria can explain partially this difference between Nigerians and other Black groups. Furthermore, Nigerians tended to account for a higher proportion of the African student population in Britain from the 1960s onwards.

Table 2.7 shows that the labour force participation of Black–Africans is more varied than has been assumed. Africans have higher than expected representation in the top three socio-economic groups. Their pattern of distribution is comparable, if not better than that of the White population. This has to be attributed to the higher level of qualifications within the Black–African group.

Table 2.7 Black–Africans: social class based on occupation (percentage)

		White	Black–Africans		Nigerians
		10 per cent sample	10 per cent sample	2 per cent SAR	1 per cent SAR
I	Professional	5	8	8	14
II	Managerial and technical	28	27	26	26
III	Skilled non-manual	23	22	22	18
III	Skilled manual	21	12	11	8
IV	Partly skilled	15	16	16	18
V	Unskilled	6	9	10	11
	Armed forces	1	1	1	
	Inadequately described			10	1
	Not stated	1	4	4	4
	Total	100	100	100	100

Source: OPCS/GRO(S) (1993) 1991 Census Ethnic Group and Country of Birth and two and one per cent SARs (ESRC/JISC purchase). © Crown Copyright.

Employment

Historically, there has been no direct recruitment of Africans. Unlike other ethnic groups there are few traditional industrial sectors of Black–African employment, with the exception of the National Health Service, where many occupied low status positions as ancillary staff: domestics (auxiliary) and caterers. Institutionalised discrimination made the acquisition of state-enrolled nurse status difficult and confined most Blacks within low status positions (Lewis, 1994).

As with the population statistics from the 1991 Census, it is difficult to get an accurate picture of the pattern of employment among Africans. Many of those who were not enumerated may be working illegally. It is well known among Black Londoners that the first tube train of the morning carries an army of African cleaners to the office blocks of the City, the department stores of the West End and various educational institutions. Many such workers run the gamut of immigration officers who often operate in dawn swoops on suspected premises.

In deconstructing the employment data account must be taken of the student worker: full-time students who work part time and full-time workers who study part time or at evening classes. Africans with student permits may work illegally to substitute grants that ended prematurely after 1980s collapse of African economies. Only 2.5 per cent of the economically active claim to be studying. Qualitative assessment suggests that the figure should be higher. Which socio-economic category the student worker assigns him or herself is important because a significant number of Africans straddle the boundary between work and study. With all these potential anomalies, the employment data in the 1991 Census has to be treated with a certain degree of scepticism. What it provides is an insight into the myriad occupational choices of Africans particularly of those permanently settled in the UK.

Hypothetically, with their higher levels of qualification Africans could be more selective of their occupational choices than Caribbean migrants. However, apart from the professional minority they seem to have similar occupational trajectories as other immigrant groups. The employment profile of the Black–African group shows 65 per cent of over 16-year-olds to be economically active (Table 2.8). As is expected the proportion economically active is lower among the 16 to 24 age-groups, but only 66 per cent of the 30 to 34 age-group are economically active compared to 81 per cent of the 50 to 54 age-group.

Africans proliferate in manual and non-manual service sector occupations as clerical assistants, cleaners, sales assistants, cashiers, kitchen porters and security guards. In the two per cent SAR, 32 per cent of those employed are working in professional occupations as managers and administrators; local government is a particular favourite, as are science and engineering, teaching and health (Table 2.9). Expected gender differences are apparent, and, as is common to all ethnic groups, more women (17 per cent) work part time than men (7 per cent). The 1991 Census is unable to illuminate clearly the complexity of the known work patterns among Africans, especially the presence of multiple occupations, for example, the combination of part-time early morning and evening cleaning, and daytime job.

Table 2.8   *Economic position of Black–Africans - age 16 and over, Great Britain*

	Total		Males		Females	
	Number	Percentage	Number	Percentage	Number	Percentage
Age 16 and over	150,072		75,405		74,667	
Economically active	96,919	65	52,026	69	44,893	60
Economically active – age under 25			36,991	71	33,802	75
Employees – full time	49,952	51	27,017	52	22,935	51
Employees – part time	11,289	12	3,611	7	7,678	17
Self-employed						
– with employees	1,521	2	1,143	2	378	0.8
– no employees	3,891	4	3,003	6	888	2
On a government scheme	4,140	4	2,217	4	1,923	4
Unemployed	26,126	27	15,035	20	11,091	15
Unemployed under age 25						
Economically active student	1,775	2	989	2	786	2
Economically inactive	53,153		23,379	31	29,774	66
Students	27,014	18	15,992	29	11,022	25
Permanently sick	3,337	35	1,741	2	1,596	2
Retired	3,579	2	2,033	3	1,546	2
Other inactive	19,233	13	3,613	5	15,610	21

Source: OPCS/GRO(S) (1993) 1991 Census Ethnic Group and Country of Birth, Volume 2.

Table 2.9 *Principal occupations of Black–Africans*

Occupation	Number	Percentage of total sample
Occupation in sales and service	212	12.0
Sales assistants and check-out operators	92	7.0
Numerical clerks and cashiers	86	5.2
Secretaries, typists, word processors operators and personal assistants	62	3.5
Managers and proprietors in service industries	59	3.3
Teaching professionals	57	3.2
Catering occupations	50	2.8
Administration, clerical officers in civil service and local goods	49	2.8
Health professionals	42	2.4
Clerks (n.o.s.)	42	2.4
Security and protective services	34	1.9
Road transport operators	33	1.9
Health and related occupation auxilaries	32	1.8
Textiles, garments and related trades	29	1.6
Specialist managers	29	1.6
Business and financial professionals	28	1.6
Librarians and related professionals	25	1.4
Scientific technicians	23	1.3
Stores and despatch clerks and book keepers	23	1.3

Source: OPCS, 1991 Census, two per cent SAR (ESRC/JISC purchase). © Crown Copyright.

Africans employed in many of these occupational categories often do shift work or work unsociable hours. Even senior medical doctors find employment within an agency system as peripatetic doctors, working long hours in a variety of locations. Africans work in industries that were more vulnerable to subtle changes in the economy and fared worse than other groups in the 1980s decline in inner city service sector employment.

Unemployment

Black–Africans have the third highest rate of unemployment, 27 per cent behind that of the Bangladeshi and Pakistani ethnic minority groups. This compares to a national unemployment rate of 9 per cent and a Greater London regional rate of 7 per cent for men and 6 per cent for women. Fifty-eight per cent of the unemployed are men. Unemployment among men is higher than for women in absolute numbers and for almost all age-groups (Figure 2.3) and alarmingly high among men in the 16–19 age-group. In the two per cent SAR, over a third of all households had no residents in employment.

Among the Black–African group, qualifications do not necessarily guarantee access to the labour market. Fourteen per cent of those with qualifications are unemployed (48 per cent of those unemployed have A-levels, 39 per cent with first degree or equivalent, and 13 per cent have higher

Figure 2.3 *Percentage of economically active Black-African population unemployed, by sex, age-group, Great Britain, 1991*

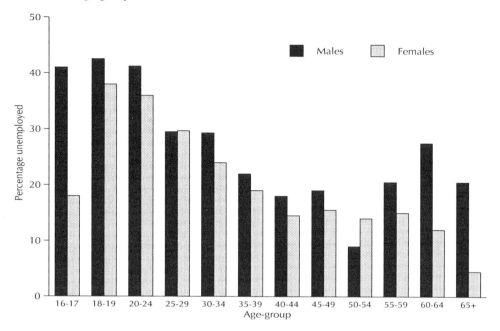

degrees). Of the total qualified persons (682) 15 per cent of those with A-levels, 14 per cent of graduates and 13 per cent of higher degree holders are unemployed. Black–African men have high qualifications, but 20 per cent of those with higher qualifications are unemployed. The limited potential for Africans to fulfil their career choices is not reflected in the earlier social class data. Even among those employed it is possible to find a high degree of under-employment, with professionals working as taxi drivers, cleaners or security guards. Job status often becomes irrelevant so long as the wages surpass that earned as a professional in the home country. This is increasingly the case since currency devaluation and wage freeze under structural adjustment programmes have had deleterious effects on the purchasing power of the professional salary. In the UK low status occupations restrict severely people's housing choice.

Housing tenure

The price seemed reasonable, location
Indifferent. The landlady swore she lived
Off premises. Nothing remained
But self–confession. 'Madam, ' I warned,
I hate a wasted journey — I am an African.
Silence. Silence transmission of
Pressurized good-breeding. Voice, when it came
Lipstick coated, long gold-rolled
Cigarette-holder pipped. Caught I was, foully.
'HOW DARK?'.....I had not misheard....'ARE YOU LIGHT OR VERY DARK?'
(Extract from Wole Soyinka's, *Telephone Conversation*, 1984)

For most Africans, living in close proximity to one's countrymen was a necessity if accommodation was to be found. Racism was a major factor affecting the residential choices and housing tenure adopted by early migrants. Africans congregated in areas where landlords were known to rent houses to people from ethnic minority groups and where countrymen who purchased homes let rooms in order to meet mortgage repayments. Such houses were often in slum areas with overcrowded and poor facilities.

Even though the upsurge in Black–African migration was coterminous with the expansion in slum clearance and housing development, studies have shown that local authorities were reluctant to initiate redevelopment programmes in areas with a high concentration of immigrants (Carter, Harris and Joshi, 1994). Often immigrants and refugees have access only to the poorest quality local authority housing as in areas of Southwark and Lambeth where Black–Africans are concentrated in sink estates such as the North Peckham. Henderson and Karn (1987) document the discriminatory practice in contemporary local authority housing allocation schemes. They write: 'it emerges that no matter what the allocation schemes or the type of housing stock, West indians and Asians in all the local authorities studied have been found to receive the oldest housing with the poorest amenities, and the smallest proportion of houses as compared to flats' . This quote refers equally to Africans. They experience high levels of overcrowding behind the Bangladeshis and Pakistanis and have limited access to amenities such as private cars (Table 2.10).

In the 1991 Census the most distinctive feature in the tenure patterns of Black–Africans was the high number of Africans in rented housing; 42 per cent rented from local authorities, 11 per cent from housing associations and 18 per cent privately; with only 28 per cent owner-occupied (see Table 2.11). The latter is strikingly lower than that of the general population and the lowest for all ethnic minority groups.

Nevertheless, the hetereogeneity of the Black–African population makes it difficult to make generalisations. For example, there is a far greater degree

Table 2.10 *Black–Africans: proportion of households with access to selected amenities (percentage)*

	Black–Africans	Whites	Black–Caribbeans	Bangladeshi
Living at over 1.5 persons per room	6.0	0.4	1.3	19.1
Lacking or sharing use of bath/shower and/or inside WC	5	12	1.4	2
No central heating	15.8	18.9	17.4	23.6
No car	61.9	33	54.8	60.9

Source: OPCS/GRO(S) (1993) 1991 Census Ethnic Group and Country of Birth, Volume 2.

Table 2.11 Tenure of Black–African households in the 1991 Census

	Great Britain	Greater London	Black– African 1 per cent SAR	Nigerian– born 2 per cent SAR	Whites 1 per cent SAR
Tenure					
Owner occupied – own outright	3	2.9	22.6	28.5	24.4
Owner occupied – buying	25	21.3	45.1	38.8	42.2
Rented privately	18	16.5	9.7	9.8	8.9
Rented from housing association	11	11.7	2	3.3	3.0
Rented from a local authority or new town	42	46	20.6	19.6	21.4
Total	100	100	100	100	100

Source: OPCS 1991 Census, one and two per cent SARs (ESRC/JISC purchase). © Crown Copyright.

of house ownership among the Nigerian-born population (67 per cent). Geographical variations can also be found. The two per cent individual SAR shows a decline in the proportion renting from local authorities and a marked increase in private ownership. This may reflect the greater geographical spread in the selected sample.

Local housing market constraints can be influential. The increasing cost of housing in Greater London may account for the higher proportion of Africans renting their accommodation in the city. Concentrations of Africans in the boroughs of Lambeth, Southwark and Hackney are a reflection of the availability of local authority housing rather than lower cost of private housing stock. Escalating house prices in the 1980s have put most inner city houses beyond the reach of most residents. In the London boroughs of Southwark and Lambeth respectively, 71 and 62 per cent of all households live in rented accommodation.

The high representation in rented housing may also be attributed to the migrants' perception of the temporary nature of their settlement in Britain and related economic objectives. Rented accommodation becomes a cultural strategy allowing resources to be transferred to home countries to assist relatives or for the construction of a future home. Unauthorised transfer of tenancy is another cultural strategy adopted by Black–Africans. As households move between Africa and Great Britain, local authority tenancies can pass between kin relations, people from the same region, or close friends. This does mean that the expected pattern of social class and tenure does not hold true for Black–Africans. There are representatives from all social classes living in housing rented from local authority (Table 2.12). These include high status refugees who on arrival are first housed by the local authority and who choose to remain tenants in order to take advantage of lower rents. Among Africans, local authority housing does not hold the same social stigma as for the indigeneous population. As with employment, Africans may opt to adopt underclass positions in Britain to secure a higher status lifestyle on their return home.

Table 2.12 *Black–Africans: tenure by social class (percentage)*

Tenure	I Profes- sional	II Manag- erial	III N Skilled	III M Skilled	IV Part Skilled	V Unskilled	Armed forces	Inade- quately described	Not stated	% of sample
Owner occupied – outright	1.8	7.2	5.4	2.4	3.1	1.3	0	0.37	0.5	22
Owner occupied – buying	3.5	9	14	4.2	8.7	2.4	0.4	0.2	2.2	45
Rented private furnished	1	0.9	2.4	0.7	1.1	0.2	0	0	0.2	5.7
Rented private unfurnished	0	0.4	0.4	0.4	0.4	0.2	0	0.2	0.5	2.4
Rented job/business	0	0.4	0.7	0	0.7	0	0.2	0	0.2	2.2
Rented housing association	0	0	0.7	0	0.5	0.2	0	0	0.5	2
Rented local authority	2	5.4	4.8	3.1	2.6	0.9	0.2	0	1.5	21
% in each social class	7.6	23.3	28.5	10.9	17.2	5.4	0.7	0.7	5.7	100

Source: OPCS, 1991 Census, one per cent SAR (ESRC/JISC purchase). © Crown Copyright.

2.5   Conclusion

An analysis of census data alone cannot illuminate a population which has hitherto remain understudied. This problem is worsened by the fact that the population is so fragmented and diverse making it difficult to generalise with any degree of confidence. Consequently this chapter focuses on those unifying and distinguishing characteristics of the Black–African ethnic category: education, employment and housing. Even under these broad topics, considerable differences exist between nationalities, ethnic groups, and across class.

Black–African is a census remnant category that defines geographic origins without conferring internal ethnic identity. It is a category of imposition rather than one of self-proclamation. Yet it does, in some ways, produce an identity of political aspiration. While Bangladeshis, for example, as clearly an ethnic group, originating in a single country, having the same language and overwhelmingly the same religion, Black–Africans originate from potentially 53 different countries. Most, however, originate from countries with a British colonial past and West Africa is the source area of nearly 60 per cent of the total living in Britain.

Academic qualification has been a strong motivation for many of the settlers and the contrast between the social and the economic conditions of the group as a whole is a reflection of this student origin. The Black–African population is young, highly qualified, concentrated in London and living in poor student conditions. In social status terms it has done well, in economic terms less so.

References

Adi, H. (1994) West African students in Britain, 1900–60: the politics of exile. In: Killingray D., *Africans in Britain*. London: Frank Cass & Co., pp.107–28.

Atampugre, N. (1992) Migrants and Development: A Study of Ghanaian Migrant Associations in London. Mimeo produced for the Panos Institute, London.

Banton, M. (1955) *The Coloured Quarter: Negro Immigrants in an English City*. London: Jonathan Cape.

Carey, A. T. (1956) *Colonial Students: A Study of Social Adaptation of Colonial Students in London*. London: Secker Warburg.

Carter, B., Harris, C. and Joshi, S. (1994) The 1951–55 Conservative Government and the racialisation of Black immigration. In James, W. and Harris, C. (eds.), *Inside Babylon: The Caribbean Diaspora in Britain*. London: Verso.

Emecheta, B. (1974) *Second Class Citizen*. London: Fontana.

Goody, E. N. and Groothues, C. M. (1973) *Factors Relating to the Delegation of Parental Roles among West Africans in London*, London: SSRC.

Goody, E. and Groothues, C. M. (1977) The quest for education: West Africans in London. In: Watson J. L. (ed.) *Between Two Cultures: Migrants and Minorities in Britain*. Oxford: Blackwells.

Goody, E. and Groothues, C. M. (1979) Stress in marriage: West African couples in London. In: Saifullah Khan, V. (ed.), *Minority Families in Britain: Support and Stress*. London: Macmillan.

Henderson, J. and Karn, V. (1987) *Race, Class and State Housing: Inequality and the Allocation of Public housing in Britain*, CURS: Studies in Urban and Regional Policy, 4. Aldershot: Gower.

Killingray, D. (ed.) (1994) *Africans in Britain*. London: Frank Cass & Co.

Lewis, G. (1994) Black women's employment and the British economy. In: James, W. and Harris, C. (eds), *Inside Babylon: The Caribbean Diaspora in Britain*. London: Verso.

Little, K. (1948) *Negroes In Britain: A Study of Race Relations In English Society*. London: Routledge, revised 1972.

Oguibe, O. (1994) *Sojourners: New Writings by Africans in Britain*. London: African Refugee Publishing Collective.

OPCS/GRO (S) (1993) *Ethnic Group and Country of Birth, Great Britain*, Volume 1 and 2. Ref: CEN91 EGCB. London: HMSO.

Parsons, N. (1994) The impact of Seretse Khama on British public opinion, 1948—56 and 1978. In: Killingray, D. (ed.), *Africans in Britain*. London: Frank Cass & Co., pp.195–219.

Soyinka, W. (1984) Telephone conversation. In: Moore G. and U. Beier (eds), *The Penguin Book of Modern African Poetry*, New Edition.

Yeebo, Z. (1991) *Ghana: The Struggle for Popular Power*. New Beacon Books.

Chapter 3
Black–Other: the melting pot

David Owen

3.1 Introduction

This chapter is concerned with an ethnic minority group which is not as readily identifiable as most of those appearing in the ethnic group tables from the 1991 Census. For example, the White, Indian and Chinese categories appear to be clear and unambiguous descriptions of particular types of people that correspond with the box in the ethnic group question on the census form ticked by the respondent (though there are ambiguities even in these categories). In contrast, there is no clear perception of what types of people fall into the Black–Other category. Hence, since OPCS has released little information about how this question was answered, many analysts may be drawn into making sweeping assumptions about the members of this ethnic group, such as regarding them all as the British-born children of Black–Caribbean people or all as people of mixed Black and White parentage. In reality, the category contains a fairly diverse range of people, and none of its components are dominant.

The Black–Other category derives from the option in the ethnic group question for the form-filler (usually the household head) to provide further details of the ethnic origin of household members who were Black, but for whom neither Black–Caribbean nor Black–African adequately described their ethnicity. As will be discussed below, this option was incorporated into the ethnic group question in an attempt to improve the quality of responses, especially from African Caribbean people. However, in the majority of the output from the census, the composition of the category is not specified, which thus means that it is not possible to determine the extent to which it represents the same types of person in different areas. These issues will become more important over time, since this is a very youthful ethnic group, and it is likely that an increasing part of the Black population born in the UK will fall into this category.

This chapter reviews the way in which the Black–Other category came to be included in the ethnic group question and examines the composition of the category in greater detail. It goes on to consider the demographic composition, geographical distribution and socio-economic characteristics of people from this ethnic category.

The OPCS ethnic group classification and the composition of the Black–Other ethnic group

The nature of the census ethnic group question and the debate over the inclusion of such a question in the census have been reviewed in detail by Bulmer (1996) in Volume 1 of this series. Here, the way in which the Black–Other category originated and how people come to be classified as such will be briefly described.

The origins of the Black–Other ethnic group

During the 1970s, a series of tests of a possible question on ethnic group to be included in the 1981 Census were carried out. A number of alternative designs for the question were considered. During this process it became apparent that many members of ethnic minority groups would like to have the option of describing themselves as British. This reflected both the increasing numbers of people from these ethnic groups born in the UK and the resistance of many West Indian parents to describing their children born in the UK as West Indian. One solution considered was to add a category of Black British (using the term Black to describe persons of African descent) to the ethnic group question, but this was rejected because 'it placed too much emphasis on racial or colour distinctions' (Sillitoe and White, 1992). In the event, the final census tests undertaken in 1979 met with considerable resistance, with nearly a third of West Indian and Asian households object-ing on principle to the inclusion of an ethnic group question. Resistance to the question was heightened by the inclusion of a question on the countries of birth of parents, which aroused fears that the census would be used in conjunction with new legislation to check on the immigration status of persons from ethnic minority groups. Moreover, a high percentage of people from Black and Asian backgrounds who cooperated with the test did not answer the ethnic group question in accordance with the intentions of the Census Offices. Both the ethnic group and parent's birthplace questions were omitted from the 1981 Census.

In the 1980s, a second series of field trials was carried out, following the recommendation of the House of Commons Home Affairs Sub-Committee on Race Relations and Immigration that a question on ethnic group should be included in the 1991 Census. This report recommended that the design of the question should not compel persons to define themselves solely in terms of their own or their ancestors' immigrant origin, and hence the terms White and Black were adopted. The Committee suggested a possible design for the question which included the categories 'Black British', 'Black Other', 'Asian British' and 'Asian Other'. Instead, the Census Offices tested a question which simply included the categories 'Black British' and 'British Asian' for persons born in the UK. This form of the question proved unsuccessful (with regard to the type of information the Census Offices were trying to obtain) because many Asian people born elsewhere in the Commonwealth wanted to describe themselves as British.

The Census Offices argued against the inclusion of an alternative option for all ethnic groups to describe themselves simply as British on the grounds that a large proportion of ethnic minority groups would prefer to describe themselves in this way, thus diminishing the usefulness of the data on individual ethnic groups (especially as many UK-born people would continue to choose the ethnic group option while many born overseas would describe themselves as British).While the Census Offices felt 'Black British' and 'British Asian' would be more successful than a category of simply 'British', their view was that the inclusion of a British option would, in practice, simply reduce the ethnic group question to one of colour, as reliable information could only be produced for Black or Asian people as a whole. Field trials conducted in January 1986 found that three quarters of UK-born persons of immigrant descent were categorised as 'White British', 'Black British' or 'Asian British'. A question that omitted the 'British' categories was tested in October 1986, which again aroused objections from African Caribbean people on the grounds that they were identified in terms of their immigrant origins. The term Black was therefore adopted, and following the desire of African Caribbean groups for greater details of ethnic origin, the category was subdivided into Black–Caribbean, Black–African and Black–Other. A test conducted in April 1989 yielded acceptable results, with a much smaller level of resistance to the inclusion of a question on ethnic group than had been the case in 1979, while responses to the ethnic group question were judged by the Census Offices to be 90 per cent accurate (in terms of their assessment of the ethnic group of respondents).

The final version of the question adopted for the 1991 Census did not include a British category for any ethnic group. Instead, the census question included a Black–Other option in which respondents were invited to write in full details of the ethnic origin of the individual(s) concerned if Black–Caribbean or Black–African did not adequately describe their ethnic background. The answers written in for the Black–Other and 'any other ethnic group' categories in the responses to the 1989 Census Test were used to devise a flow diagram for processing written answers into 35 possible ethnic groups (which is used to present the detailed local breakdown of ethnic origin in Table A of the *Ethnic Group and Country of Birth* report (OPCS/GRO(S), 1993), upon which this chapter draws). A coding framework was also devised to allocate these 35 groups into the 10-fold classification of ethnic group to be used in the bulk of the census output (Bulmer, 1996).

The composition of the Black–Other ethnic group

In 1991, the Black–Other category was large compared to other ethnic minority groups, accounting for more than a fifth of all Black people. It comprised four categories of answer: British, Black/White parentage, Other Mixed and Other answers (Figure 3.1). The largest single component of this category was people for whom the description British was written into the Black–Other box, but the categories for mixed parentage and other answers together accounted for more than two thirds of all Black–Other people. Persons falling into the category 'mixed, with Black and White parents' should probably be added to the first category as representing the British-born children of African Caribbean fathers or mothers.

Modood, Beishon and Virdee (1994) showed that around half the African Caribbean people they interviewed were willing to accept relationships

Figure 3.1 *Composition of the Black–Other ethnic group, 1991*

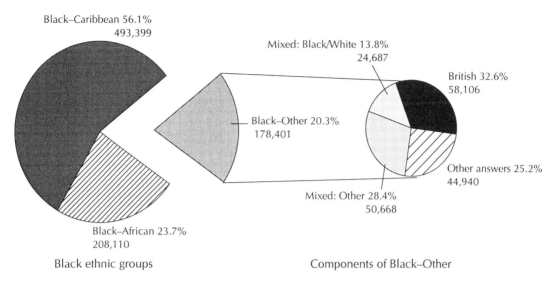

Black–Caribbean 56.1%
493,399

Mixed: Black/White 13.8%
24,687

British 32.6%
58,106

Black–Other 20.3%
178,401

Other answers 25.2%
44,940

Mixed: Other 28.4%
50,668

Black–African 23.7%
208,110

Black ethnic groups   Components of Black–Other

between Black people and people from other ethnic groups (while people from South Asian ethnic groups wished to maintain marriages within the ethnic group). The relatively large number of people of mixed parentage in the Black–Other ethnic group reflects the high incidence of inter-ethnic partnerships among people of Caribbean descent. Coleman (1985) found that a quarter of the partners of West Indian men were White in 1981, though Berrington (1994) shows that inter-ethnic partnerships are less common for West Indian women (during 1989–91, 16.7 per cent of West Indian women with partners had White partners, compared to 26.8 per cent of West Indian men with partners). Partnerships between second-generation Black–Other people and White people were even more common in 1991, especially among people who were cohabiting (Berrington, 1996). More than a quarter of all Black–Other people fell into the Mixed–Other category (which includes the children of mixed partnerships involving a Black person and another person from a minority ethnic group) in 1991. Many of these would have been born in areas with long-standing ethnic minority group populations (such as Liverpool or Cardiff), where a large number of children from ethnic minority groups have parents from different ethnic groups, or who themselves are the offspring of a mixed partnership.

Further details of people with mixed Black and White parents or other types of mixed parentage may be obtained by comparing the ethnic groups of the parents of children who were recorded as Black–Other on the census form. Table 3.1 presents the results of this cross-tabulation, using the one per cent Household Sample of Anonymised Records (SAR) (Marsh and Teague, 1992). Households containing Black and White partners contained 43.9 per cent of all Black–Other children, with Black–Caribbeans the most likely of the Black ethnic groups to have children in a partnership with a White person. A further 20.5 per cent of Black–Other children resided in households with two Black partners, mainly either both Black–Caribbean or both

Table 3.1 *Ethnic origin of household head and partner for children from the Black–Other ethnic group in 1991*

Ethnic group of household head	Ethnic group of partner						
	White	Black–Caribbean	Black–African	Black–Other	South Asian	Chinese and Other	Total
	% of Black–Other children in each partnership type						
White	27.2	4.2	2.0	2.0	1.2	0.5	37.1
Black–Caribbean	18.2	8.8	0.2	1.2	1.4	0.4	30.1
Black–African	3.9	0.7	0.4	0.3	0.3	0.1	5.7
Black–Other	13.6	1.3	0.1	7.5	0.5	0.1	23.0
South Asian	0.7	0.0	0.0	0.0	0.3	0.1	1.1
Chinese and Other	1.7	0.0	0.0	0.3	0.0	1.1	3.1
Total	65.2	15.0	2.7	11.3	3.6	2.2	100.0

Source: One per cent household SAR.
Note: There were a total of 1,090 Black–Other children in the one per cent household SAR.

Black–Others. Only 3.1 per cent of Black–Other children lived in households in which the partners were from the Black and South Asian or Chinese and other ethnic groups (and all but 0.3 per cent were in households with Black heads). Of the remainder, 27.2 per cent resided in households with only White partners. This could include children from ethnic minority groups who had been adopted by a White person and were recorded as Black by the person filling in the census form, but may also reflect high rates of partnership break-up. A White mother may have had a child in a partnership with a Black man, and then gone on to another relationship with a White man once the first partnership had ended. It should also be noted that this analysis does not include the children of parents who were not in a partnership at the time of the census. It is possible that if the ethnic group of the single parents of Black–Other children were analysed, a high percentage would also be White.

It is clear that children in the Black–Other ethnic group are much more likely to have a White parent than to be the child of two Black parents (and this parent is more commonly the partner rather than the household head). Thus for children, this ethnic group is more a reflection of mixed ethnic origin than identification as 'Black British'. A total of 35.7 per cent of such children lived in households with a Black head and White partner, and a further 8.2 per cent in households where the head was White and the partner Black.
In addition to the Black British, a relatively high percentage of this ethnic group was represented by those who supplied other answers. Although none of the census output permits further disaggregation of this category, some clues to what sort of person might be included within it can be obtained by analysing the countries of birth of persons classified as Black–Other. Table 3.2 presents the 10 countries that individually accounted for 2 per cent or more of persons in the Black–Other ethnic group born outside the UK. Overall, the Black–Other ethnic group was the most 'British' of all the minority ethnic groups, with 84.4 per cent of its members having been born within the UK. Of the non-UK-born, the most common origins were the

United States, Guyana and Jamaica, which together accounted for more than a third of those born outside the UK. It seems likely that most Black US servicemen and women would have chosen the Black–Other box, since neither of the other categories adequately described their ethnic group. On the other hand, for those born in Guyana, the percentage of all those designated as Black–Other was strikingly high, reflecting a relatively high percentage of the population of mixed descent and possibly a greater likelihood of describing themselves as British. Other countries appearing in the list are less easily interpretable. Persons born in countries such as Cyprus and Germany might be the children of Black members of the British armed forces who had been based there. The appearance of Mauritius in the top 10 countries again probably reflects a high percentage of people of mixed ethnic origin, reflecting its colonial history and location on the trade routes between Africa and Asia. In contrast, the appearance of persons born in South Asian countries was probably a consequence either of confusion over how to answer the ethnic group question or a deliberate decision to describe themselves as Black.

The composition of this ethnic group is also influenced by the degree of reliability with which the ethnic group question was answered. The Census Validation Survey (CVS) which was carried out after the census was taken in order to check the accuracy of the census data was too small to yield reliable information on the performance of the individual ethnic groups, but has shown the degree of overlap which occurred between the White, Black, South Asian and Chinese and other categories (OPCS, 1994). In the CVS, an OPCS or GRO(Scotland) interviewer checked the answers that had been provided on the census form with the form-filler. This revealed that 21 per cent of persons covered by these interviews coded on the census form in the Chinese and other group were described in the CVS interview as being either White or from one of the Black ethnic groups. Moreover, 9 per cent of

Table 3.2 *Geographical distribution of the non-British born Black–Others: countries with more than 2 per cent of the total in 1991*

Country of birth	Black–Others	% of all Black–Others	% born outside UK	All born in country	% of all Black–Others
Outside United Kingdom	27,763	15.6	100.0	3,774,796	0.7
United States	6,361	3.6	22.9	143,484	4.4
Guyana	1,830	1.0	6.6	20,478	8.9
Jamaica	1,732	1.0	6.2	142,483	1.2
Cyprus	1,030	0.6	3.7	78,031	1.3
India	955	0.5	3.4	409,022	0.2
Mauritius	921	0.5	3.3	23,450	3.9
Irish Republic	908	0.5	3.3	592,020	0.2
Pakistan	657	0.4	2.4	234,107	0.3
Germany	568	0.3	2.0	215,534	0.3
Nigeria	555	0.3	2.0	47,085	1.2
Total	15,517	8.7	55.9	1,905,694	0.8

Source: OPCS/GRO (S) (1993) 1991 Census Ethnic Group and Country of Birth Report, Volume 2.

those coded as Black from the responses on the census form were described as being in the Chinese and other category in the CVS interview. This is consistent with some of the evidence presented above about the geographical origins of the members of the Black–Other ethnic group, and implies that there was also uncertainty amongst the British-born of mixed parentage or from a less numerous ethnic group about how to describe themselves on the census form.

The demographic composition of the Black–Other ethnic group

Though the Black–Other ethnic group is clearly diverse, no data has been produced on the demographic and socio-economic features of its constituent parts, and hence analysis of these topics is limited to considering Black–Others in their entirety. The most salient feature of this ethnic group is its extreme youth, with a male median age of 15 years and a female median age of 16.5 years in 1991, compared to 35.8 years for White males, 38.9 years for White females, 30.2 years for Black–Caribbean males and 30.3 years for Black–Caribbean females (Owen, 1993). Females were in the majority, with only 963 Black–Other males per 1000 females. The age distribution is summarised in the population pyramid presented in Figure 3.2, which has a very exaggerated pyramidical shape, with a narrow apex and a wide base. In contrast with other youthful ethnic groups such as the Pakistanis and Bangladeshis (see Owen, 1996; Ballard, 1996), it has a concave shape, with the numbers of pre-school age children greater than the numbers aged 5–9 and 10–14, suggesting that the rate of growth in the numbers of Black–Other people is accelerating. The pyramid also has a notable 'bulge' in the 20–29 age range, for both men and women, with people in their twenties much more common than those in their later teens or early thirties.

Figure 3.2 *Population pyramid for Black–Other people, 1991*

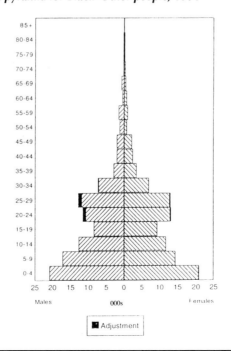

The 1991 Census yielded a significant undercount of people in certain age-groups, notably of men in the 20–34 age range. This was largely due to the difficulties all major social surveys are encountering in contacting this section of the population, exacerbated by failure to cooperate with the census, probably because of a wish to avoid the poll tax. These problems were exaggerated in the inner areas of London and other large cities, where a high percentage of census returns also had to be imputed because absent households did not return a completed form. The Labour Force Survey has also encountered difficulty in surveying young Black men for a number of years, and there is thus a suspicion that ethnic group data from the census significantly underestimates the number of young Black people in some areas.

OPCS and GRO(Scotland) have derived a set of age- and gender-specific adjustment factors from a comparison of census with mid-1991 population estimates, which can be used to modify the ethnic group data to take account of the under-enumeration. These factors are larger for males than females and for ethnic minority group populations than White people. They reflect the tendencies for ethnic minority groups to be more youthful than the White population and to live in areas where the undercount was most severe. These adjustment factors have been applied to the population data for Black–Others, and the effect of the adjustment is illustrated by the dark shading at the end of the individual bars in the pyramid in Figure 3.2. As might be expected, the main effect of the adjustment is to increase the number of people aged 20–34, with the effect strongest for men. For females, the adjustment also increases the number of 0–4 year olds.

As mentioned above, the percentage of people in this ethnic group who were born in the UK is the highest of any of the census ethnic minority groups. Figure 3.3 also contrasts the age structure of persons born within and outside the UK, using information derived from the two per cent Individual SAR (this population pyramid has been adjusted to take account of the undercount). Clearly, the UK-born were dominant for all age-groups up to 35, though the number born outside the UK increased from the age of 20 onwards. Among people aged 35 and over, the majority of both men and women were born outside the UK.

Table 3.3 summarises the age and marital status of people from the Black–Other ethnic group, contrasting it with that of White people and ethnic minority groups as a whole. The percentage of Black–Other people who were married increased steadily with age, with more than a third of those aged over 65 married. The percentage married was similar for males and females throughout the age range in 1991, though there was a tendency for it to be higher for women than men in the younger age-groups and higher for men than women in the older age-groups. However, the percentage married was much smaller than that for White people for all age-groups, with the differential most marked for women (since the percentage married is far higher for White women than White men). The differential with ethnic minority groups as a whole is even greater.

The second section of Table 3.3 presents the percentage of each age-group

Figure 3.3 *Age and sex structure of Black–Other people born within and outside the UK*

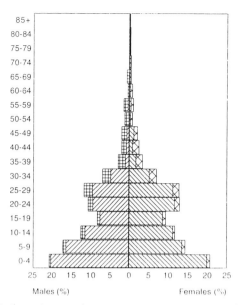

The shading at the ends of each bar represents people born outside the UK

Table 3.3 *Marital status of Black–Other and White people by age and gender in 1991*

Age group	Males			Females		
	Black–Other	White	Ethnic minority groups	Black–Other	White	Ethnic minority groups
	Percentage married					
16–24	4.9	6.6	9.6	7.3	13.9	21.6
25–44	14.5	23.3	25.2	16.1	34.0	38.4
45–64	24.0	39.4	42.9	23.7	49.7	51.7
65+	38.5	59.6	64.4	35.0	67.4	66.1
	Percentage widowed or divorced					
16–24	0.4	0.3	0.4	0.7	1.0	0.7
25–44	1.3	1.8	1.0	2.1	3.5	1.8
45-64	2.8	3.7	1.8	4.0	6.2	3.2
65+	5.2	6.5	3.1	7.2	9.9	5.4
	Percentage single					
16–24	94.7	93.1	90.1	92.1	85.1	77.7
25–44	84.2	74.9	73.9	81.8	62.4	59.8
45–64	73.2	56.8	55.3	72.3	44.1	45.1
65+	56.2	33.8	32.6	57.7	22.7	28.5

Source: OPCS/GRO(S) (1993) 1991 Census Ethnic Group and Country of Birth Report.

that was widowed and divorced in 1991. These percentages were very low for both genders and ethnic groups in the younger age-groups, and there is little variation among them until the 25–44 year age-group is reached. The percentage widowed and divorced was higher for women than men, and higher for Black–Other women than White men. For both women and men, this percentage was higher for White people than for Black–Other people. As a result, the percentage of Black–Other people who were single was higher than that for White people throughout the age range. The percentage single was very similar for both men and women in the Black–Other ethnic group, and declined more slowly with age than for either the White ethnic group or ethnic minority groups as a whole. The differential between Black–Other and White people widened with increasing age and was greater for women than for men.

3.2 Geographical distribution

The broad regional distribution of the Black–Other ethnic group and its four component categories in 1991 is presented in Table 3.4. As is the case for the other Black ethnic groups, the majority of people in this ethnic group lived in the largest urban centres, but their concentration in the London and Birmingham areas was less marked than for Black–Caribbean and Black–African people. Overall, three quarters lived in the South East, West Midlands and North West standard regions. Nearly half lived in Greater London, mostly in Inner London. People in the Black–Other ethnic group represented 0.3 per cent of the population of Great Britain, but their major concentration was in Inner London, where they formed 2 per cent of the resident population. Elsewhere, this percentage exceeded the national average only in Outer London, the West Midlands metropolitan county, Greater Manchester and East Anglia. Only one in a thousand persons living in Wales, Scotland and the more peripheral regions of England (with the exception of East Anglia) was a member of this ethnic group.

There were notable inter-regional contrasts in the composition of the Black–Other ethnic group, as revealed by the written-in answers. For example, in Greater London and Merseyside more than 40 per cent of Black–Others had been identified as British, compared to between 20 and 30 per cent in the other major population centres and only 7.8 per cent in East Anglia. East Anglia and Scotland stood out for the very high percentage who wrote in other answers; around 45 per cent compared to a quarter of all Black–Other people in Greater London and around a fifth in other major cities. People with mixed Black and White parents were most common in East Anglia and other peripheral regions such as the South West, and Scotland. Black–Other people with other mixed origins were most common in Wales, Greater Manchester, the East Midlands, South Yorkshire, Tyne and Wear, and the West Midlands, in all of which they form two fifths or more of all Black–Other people — twice the figure for Greater London.

Table 3.4 *Regional distribution of the Black–Other ethnic group in 1991*

Region or metropolitan county	Black–Other	% of population	% of Great Britain	Composition of Black–Others (%)			
				British	Other answers	Mixed Black/White	Mixed other
South East	100,923	0.6	56.6	39.9	26.5	10.5	23.2
Greater London	*80,613*	*1.2*	*45.2*	*44.9*	*25.4*	*8.1*	*21.6*
Inner London	49,428	2.0	27.7	46.9	23.7	6.8	22.6
Outer London	31,175	0.7	17.5	41.8	28.1	10.2	19.9
East Anglia	7,150	0.4	4.0	7.8	45.2	29.8	17.1
South West	6,572	0.1	3.7	20.8	25.2	21.5	32.4
West Midlands	18,819	0.4	10.5	27.4	16.2	17.4	39.1
West Midlands	*15,716*	*0.6*	*8.8*	*29.6*	*15.9*	*16.5*	*37.9*
East Midlands	10,668	0.3	6.0	19.6	21.9	17.7	40.7
Yorkshire & Humberside	10,236	0.2	5.7	27.8	20.7	18.2	33.4
South Yorkshire	*2,560*	*0.2*	*1.4*	*21.4*	*16.6*	*21.4*	*40.6*
West Yorkshire	*6,552*	*0.3*	*3.7*	*33.0*	*20.7*	*16.2*	*30.1*
North West	16,038	0.3	9.0	29.4	18.8	13.4	38.4
Greater Manchester	*9,202*	*0.4*	*5.2*	*27.7*	*18.7*	*11.9*	*41.7*
Merseyside	*4,283*	*0.3*	*2.4*	*42.4*	*15.3*	*13.1*	*29.2*
North	1,876	0.1	1.1	15.1	31.7	18.1	35.1
Tyne and Wear	*832*	*0.1*	*0.5*	*15.1*	*26.2*	*18.5*	*40.1*
Wales	3,473	0.1	1.9	11.5	30.6	16.0	42.0
Scotland	2,646	0.1	1.5	14.7	44.8	19.5	21.0
Great Britain	**178,401**	**0.3**	**100.0**	**32.6**	**25.2**	**13.8**	**28.4**

Source: OPCS/GRO (S) (1993) 1991 Census Country of Birth and Ethnic Group Report, Volume 2, Table A.

The spatial distribution of the Black–Other ethnic group within Great Britain is mapped in Figure 3.4. The greatest local concentrations occurred in the London area and the belt of greatest urbanisation stretching north-westwards from London to Leeds. However, this ethnic minority group was also more widely distributed within the South East than in other standard regions, with the percentage at or above the British average in the area north of London and in the southern East Midlands. The percentage of Black–Others was low outside the urban centres and particularly low in the peripheral rural areas of Britain, with the exception of Suffolk (notably the Forest Heath district) and Argyll in western Scotland, both of which contained large US military bases at the time of the census.

Figure 3.4 *Geographical distribution of Black–Other people, 1991*

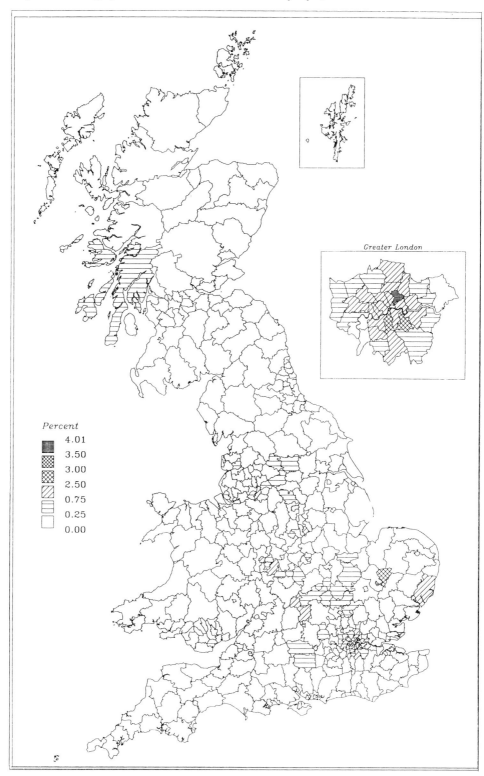

Figures 3.5 (a) to (d) present the geographical pattern of under- and over-representation of the four components of the Black–Other ethnic group. This is the ratio of the difference between the actual number of people in each category and the number that would have been in each if the proportion of the Black–Other ethnic group in each of its component categories was the same as for Great Britain as a whole. Areas of over-representation have values greater than zero, while values of less than zero indicate under-representation. Figure 3.5 (a) shows that the Black British were under-represented in most areas outside London, except in Skye and Lochalsh district in north west Scotland. Those writing in other answers were over-represented in more peripheral rural districts in east Wales, Cornwall, the Northern region of England, western and southern Scotland and East Anglia (including the areas with US military bases in Argyll and Suffolk). The pattern of under-representation is less clear, but includes Wolverhampton, Dudley and a number of districts in north west England. People of mixed parentage with Black and White parents were over-represented outside the main population centres, in the more rural parts of eastern England, in northern and central Scotland, the central Midlands, the South West, and in commuter towns south west of London. Those of mixed parentage with other origins tended to be under-represented in the same areas in which those giving other answers are over-represented, but were also over-represented in a number of districts in the North West, North Yorkshire and the South Wales Valleys.

Table 3.5 lists the 10 local authority districts in which the percentage of the resident population from the Black–Other ethnic group was greatest. This emphasises the concentration of this ethnic group within Greater London. Hackney clearly stands out as having the largest local concentration of Black–Other people, and nine of the top 10 are also boroughs in central and south London. However, Forest Heath in rural Suffolk was the district with the second largest percentage of its population from the Black–Other ethnic minority group. The composition of the ethnic group was clearly quite different in the two types of environment. In the London boroughs, the bulk of Black–Others were those who were described as British on the census form, and the percentage of mixed origin with Black and White parents was extremely low. In contrast, the latter category accounted for a third of Black–Other people in Forest Heath, with nearly all the remainder giving other answers (920 out of 1,516 in the Black–Other ethnic group). This strongly suggests that the Black–Other group in Forest Heath largely consisted of American servicemen and their families.

The final column of Table 3.5 presents the percentage share of Black–Others among children of compulsory school age (approximated to by the 5 to 15 year age-range) in the local education authority (LEA) within which each district falls. This underlines the youth of this ethnic group, and shows that while its share of the entire population was relatively small even where its concentrations are greatest, Black–Other children formed a significant part of the school population in central and south London in particular. Given the shape of the population pyramids presented earlier in this chapter, this share is likely to increase during the 1990s. However, the heterogeneity of the ethnic group means that the needs of Black–Other schoolchildren will probably vary between LEAs, and will be quite different in rural areas and central London.

Figure 3.5 *Patterns of over-and under-representation of the four components of the Black–Other ethnic group 1991*

(a) British

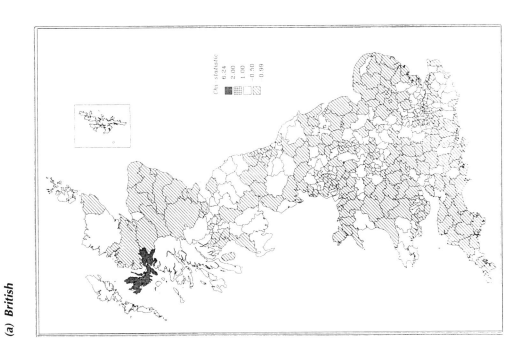

(b) Other answers

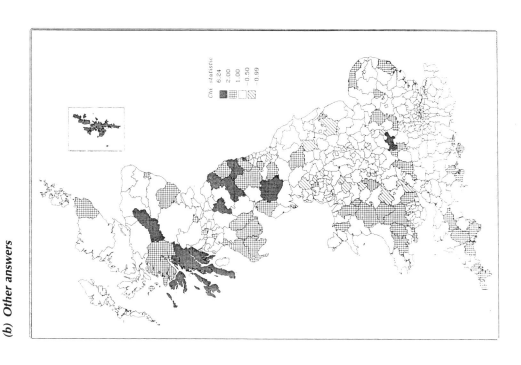

(d Mixed other

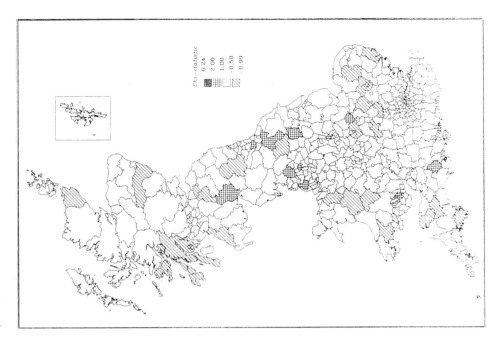

(c) Mixed Black/White

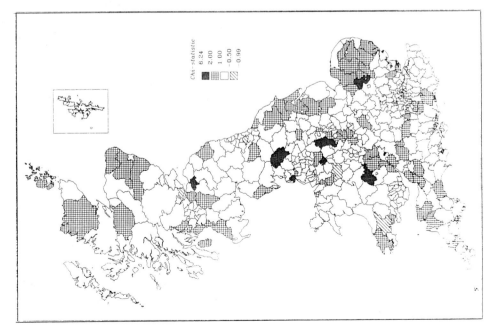

Table 3.5 *Local concentrations of the Black–Other ethnic group in 1991*

Local authority district	Black–Other	% of population	Per cent of Black–Others				% all aged 5-15 in LEA
			British	Other answers	Mixed Black/ White	Mixed other	
Hackney	7,266	4.0	58.7	21.0	4.5	15.8	8.2
Forest Heath	1,516	2.8	0.7	60.7	34.8	3.8	1.2*
Lambeth	6,622	2.7	43.4	22.4	7.6	26.5	6.7
Lewisham	5,741	2.5	51.6	19.6	5.8	23.0	6.0
Haringey	4,613	2.3	44.2	30.3	6.3	19.1	4.8
Southwark	4,870	2.2	52.2	20.6	5.1	22.2	5.3
Brent	5,323	2.2	56.3	24.0	5.4	14.2	4.7
Islington	3,117	1.9	41.4	27.9	5.7	25.0	4.6
Hammersmith & Fulham	2,601	1.8	45.6	22.5	5.7	26.1	5.0
Wandsworth	4,207	1.7	51.8	18.4	7.9	21.8	5.1

* Average for the whole of Suffolk (a single local education authority (LEA)).
Source: OPCS/GRO (S) (1993) 1991 Census Country of Birth and Ethnic Group Report, Table A.

Table 3.6 illustrates how the composition of the Black–Other ethnic group varied according to different local environments, using Craig's (1985) classification of local authority districts into 10 broad types. This again emphasises that more than 30 per cent of Black–Other people lived in central parts of London, and demonstrates a marked urban–rural contrast in their distribution. Few lived in 'rural', 'higher status growth' or 'resort and retirement' areas, while 'traditional manufacturing areas' and 'service centres and cities' accounted for a third of Black–Other people. The relatively high percentage living in 'established high status' areas represents the higher percentages of Black–Other people in the commuter belt of the London metropolitan region. Marked spatial contrasts in the composition of the Black–Other ethnic group are again highlighted. In London, the ethnic group was mainly made up of people identified as British, while in 'rural', 'higher status growth' and 'resort and retirement' areas, people for whom other answers were written in were the largest component of the Black–Others. People of mixed origin with Black and White parents were more common outside than within London, particularly in more rural and peripheral areas, while those of mixed origin with other parents were most common in the more urbanised areas outside London.

3.3   Social and economic characteristics

Having described the demography and geographical distribution of the Black–Other ethnic group in some detail, the economic and social living conditions of its members in 1991 will now be examined. Unfortunately, though the analyses presented thus far have clearly demonstrated that this ethnic group contains quite distinct subgroups living in different parts of Britain, the limitations of the ethnic group classification mean that this analysis must be concerned with the ethnic group as a whole.

Table 3.6 *Distribution of the Black–Other ethnic group across different types of environment, 1991*

Type of district	Black–Other	% of population	% share of GB total	Composition of Black–Others (%)			
				British	Other answers	Mixed Black/ White	Mixed other
Established high status	23,495	0.3	13.2	31.5	29.0	14.5	25.0
Higher status growth	8,672	0.2	4.9	13.1	37.7	21.3	27.9
More rural	7,250	0.1	4.0	6.8	48.1	26.0	19.1
Resort and retirement	2,407	0.1	1.4	12.2	36.4	21.0	30.4
Mixed town and country, some industry	16,209	0.1	9.1	17.7	22.4	25.6	38.4
Traditional manufacturing	31,003	0.6	17.4	32.2	20.4	14.4	33.0
Service centres and cities	29,330	0.4	16.5	30.3	20.3	14.7	34.6
Areas of much local authority housing	5,853	0.1	3.3	24.1	24.7	17.8	33.4
Parts of Inner London	46,342	2.0	26.0	49.2	23.2	6.6	21.0
Central London	7,840	1.2	4.4	36.1	30.2	8.7	25.1

Source: OPCS/GRO(S), 1993 1991 Census Ethnic Group and Country of Birth Report, Volume 2, Table A.

Households and family structure

It has already been shown that this is a youthful ethnic group within which rates of marriage are comparatively low. Table 3.7 disaggregates household and family types and households for Black–Others compared with the White population and ethnic minority groups as a whole. The high percentage of single people was reflected in relatively high values for the percentages of households not containing many multiple families and of single person households. The latter was well above the corresponding figure for ethnic minority groups as a whole, but similar to that for the White population (which includes many pensioners living alone). As is the case for the White population, households tended to be smaller than for ethnic minority groups as a whole and did not contain multiple families. The share of married couples among all families was only just over half the corresponding figure for White people, which was somewhat higher than the ethnic minority group average. For Black–Others, as for ethnic minority groups as a whole, married couples were more likely than White married couples to have dependent children. The most distinctive feature of the family structure was that cohabiting couples and lone parent families were more than twice as common in the Black–Other group than in the White population or all ethnic minority groups. In contrast to White people, cohabiting couples were almost as likely to have dependent children as not to have. Nearly two fifths of Black–Other families were lone parent families with children; the children of Black–Other parents were therefore more likely to live with a single parent than with any kind of couple.

Table 3.7 *Comparison of household and family types for the Black–Other ethnic group, White people and all people from ethnic minority groups, 1991*

Type of household or family	Black–Others	White	Ethnic minority groups
Total households	**3,559**	**2,061,033**	**83,095**
Households with no families (%)	32.4	29.8	23.4
One person (%)	26.5	26.6	18.4
Two or more persons (%)	6.0	3.2	5.0
Households with one family (%)	66.8	69.4	71.9
Households with 2+ families (%)	0.8	0.8	4.7
Total families	**2,543**	**1,462,155**	**67,996**
Married couple family (%)	42.9	79.2	74.2
Married couple, 0 dependent children (%)	11.9	35.6	17.1
Married couple, 1+ dependent children (%)	27.0	31.1	49.0
Married couple, non-dependent children (%)	4.0	12.5	8.1
Cohabiting couple family (%)	13.7	7.7	4.9
Cohabiting couple, 0 dependent children (%)	7.3	4.9	2.6
Cohabiting couple, 1+ dependent children (%)	6.3	2.5	2.1
Cohabiting couple, non-dependent children (%)	0.1	0.3	0.2
Lone parent family (%)	43.4	13.1	20.9
Lone parent dependent children (%)	38.9	7.8	15.8
Lone parent non-dependent children (%)	4.5	5.4	5.1

Source: OPCS/GRO(S) (1993) 1991 Census Ethnic Group and Country of Birth Report.

Housing characteristics

Black–Other households tended to be of similar size to White households, much smaller than the average for ethnic minority groups and containing fewer dependent children. However, pensioner households were much less common than for the White population, reflecting the youthful age structure of this ethnic group. Only just over a third of Black–Other households owned their dwelling, compared to two thirds of White households and three quarters of all households from ethnic minority groups. A further third rented from the local authority (or other public sector body) and of the remainder, most rented from private sector landlords. Three quarters of Black–Other households lived in terraced houses or flats, a much higher percentage than for ethnic minority groups as a whole and quite different to White households, more than half of whom lived in detached or semi-detachd houses. The youthful nature of this ethnic group and the high percentage of unmarried people within it was also reflected in the relatively large percentage living in rooms or bed-sits. Consequently, a relatively high percentage of households lived in overcrowded conditions (despite the relatively small size of Black–Other households) and lacked the exclusive use of amenities such as a WC or bathroom. This and the high percentage of households without a car indicates the poverty of this ethnic group relative both to the White population, and to ethnic minority groups as a whole (rates of car ownership for the population as a whole also tend to be lower in the larger cities where many Black–Other people live, and are lower for young people).

Table 3.8 *Household size, housing tenure and amenities for the Black–Other ethnic group, white people and all people from ethnic minority groups, 1991*

Household characteristics or family type	Black–Other	White people	Ethnic minority groups
All households (100%)	**38,281**	**21,026,565**	**820,757**
Mean household size	2.5	2.4	3.3
Mean number of dependent children	1.8	1.8	2.2
Per cent pensioner households	1.8	25.7	4.2
% households owner-occupied	36.7	66.6	59.5
% renting from private sector	13.6	7.0	10.8
% renting from Housing Associations	11.2	3.0	5.9
% renting from public sector	34.5	21.4	21.8
% living in detached houses	6.8	23.2	9.0
% living in semi-detached houses	17.8	32.7	20.8
% living in terraced houses	40.0	29.7	44.7
% living in flats	34.1	13.7	24.5
% living in rooms	0.4	0.1	0.2
% living in bed-sits	0.8	0.2	0.7
% with 1+ person per room	5.6	1.8	13.1
% lacking/sharing bathroom/WC	2.4	1.2	2.1
% without a car	52.0	33.0	40.8

Sources: 1991 Census Local Base Statistics and 1991 Census one per cent household SAR.

Health and long-term limiting illness

Table 3.9 presents the incidence of limiting long-term illness among Black–Other people, in comparison with White people and people from ethnic minority groups as a whole. The percentage of people suffering such illnesses was considerably lower than that for White people, for both males and females. However, this does not mean that Black–Other people had better levels of health than White people. Rates of long-term limiting illness are strongly influenced by the age structure of a population subgroup: older people have much higher rates of illness than young people. Thus, the percentage of people with long-term illness is smaller for Black–Others mainly because of their youthful age structure.

This is demonstrated by calculating a hypothetical illness rate for ethnic groups, by applying age-specific illness rates for the population as a whole to the age structure of each ethnic group. Using the two per cent individual SAR, it is possible to calculate the percentage of each 5-year age-group in each ethnic group suffering from a limiting long-term illness. Applying the overall average illness rate for each age-group to the population of each

Table 3.9 *Limiting long-term illness for Black–Other people compared with White people and all ethnic minority groups, 1991*

Long-term ill persons and illness rates	Black–Other	White people	Ethnic minority groups
Persons suffering limiting long-term illness (000s)	10.9	6,949.7	251.8
Percent of all persons	6.1	13.4	8.4
Households containing a long-term ill person (000s)	6.0	5,227.4	182.3
Percent of all households	15.6	24.9	20.9
Mean number ill per household	1.8	1.3	1.4
Male age standardised long-term illness rate	4.4	12.0	8.1
Female age standardised long-term illness rate	3.9	13.1	6.1
Male relative illness rate	1.49	0.99	1.15
Female relative illness rate	1.25	0.99	1.32

Sources: 1991 Census Local Base Statistics (ESRC purchase) and two per cent individual SAR; both Crown Copyright.

ethnic group in each age-group and summing across age-groups provides an estimate of the number of persons in each age-group who would be ill if the ethnic group experienced the same illness rate as the population as a whole across the age range. Since the actual illness rate for Black–Others exceeded this hypothetical rate, it is clear that Black–Other illness rates are above average for each age-group. The relative health of Black–Other males was poorer than that of females, their illness rate being nearly 50 per cent higher than the hypothetical rate, while that for females was a quarter higher than the hypothetical rate. This can be seen more clearly in Figures 3.6 (a) and (b), which plot age-specific illness rates for Black–Other and White people, demonstrating that the percentage with long-term illnesses was higher for the Black–Others than for the White population across the age range for both genders. The differential in illness rates widened after the age of 40, and was greater for women than for men. However, illness rates for Black–Other males tended to be higher than those for both White males and ethnic minority groups as a whole, particularly for young men (aged 15–30) and middle-aged men. Rates for Black–Other females tended to follow the average more closely.

Economic activity and unemployment

Table 3.10 summarises the pattern of economic activity of Black–Other people in 1991 and compares their economic activity with that of white people and minority ethnic groups as a whole. For Black–Other people and people from minority ethnic groups as a whole, the economic activity rate was very similar whether calculated over the economically active age range (16–59 for women and 64 for men) or calculated for all persons aged over 16. However, since the white ethnic group is older on average and contains a relatively large percentage of pensioners, the economic activity rate calculated for all persons aged over 16 is much lower than that for white people of economically active age. For the working age population, the activity rate of Black–Other people was substantially lower than that of white people, but was still above the average for minority ethnic groups as a whole.

Figure 3.6   *Incidence of limiting long-term illness by age, 1991*

(a) Males

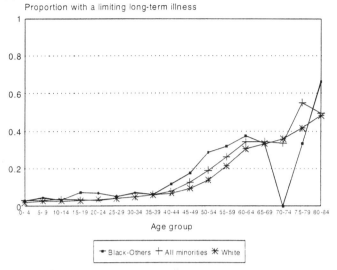

(b) Females

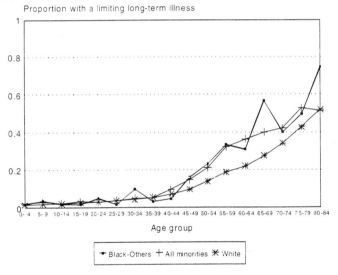

The unemployment rate for Black–Other men was nearly twice that for White men, and that for women was nearly three times the rate for White women. Both rates were well above the overall averages for ethnic minority groups. Of those in work, a much higher percentage of Black–Other people were employees than either White people or other ethnic minority groups, with the percentage working for themselves much smaller than in the other two ethnic categories, for both men and women. For women, the percentage self-employed was less than half the average for ethnic minority groups as a whole. Moreover, self employment was more likely to be an involuntary state for Black–Other people, since the percentage of self-employed people employing others was much smaller than for ethnic minority groups as a whole, and the percentage these entrepreneurs form of the economically active group was similarly much smaller.

Table 3.10 *Economic activity of Black–Other people by gender, 1991*

Type of economic activity	Males			Females		
	Black–Other	White	Ethnic minority groups	Black–Other	White	Ethnic minority groups
All aged 16 and over (000s)	**48.7**	**21,296.7**	**1,102.5**	**53.5**	**23,236.2**	**1,116.7**
Economically active (000s)	38.1	15,445.0	801.9	32.4	11,641.7	574.3
Economic activity rate	78.2	72.5	72.7	60.5	50.1	51.4
Economically active aged 16–59/64 (000s)	47.6	14,423.0	769.6	32.1	11,167.1	564.8
16–59/64 economic activity rate	79.7	87.4	76.4	62.1	67.4	54.5
In employment (000s)	27.8	13,724.2	633.3	26.1	10,844.4	480.0
Employees (000s)	23.0	11,157.8	491.6	23.7	9,990.1	423.2
Full-time employees (000s)	21.2	10,615.5	459.8	18.4	6,093.2	321.4
Part-time employees (000s)	1.7	542.3	31.7	5.3	3,896.9	101.9
% employed part-time	7.5	4.9	6.5	22.3	39.0	24.1
Self-employed (000s)	3.0	2,274.6	119.1	0.9	671.1	37.7
Self-employed with employees (000s)	0.8	738.4	51.0	0.2	241.9	14.6
Self-employed without employees (000s)	2.2	1,536.2	68.0	0.7	429.1	23.1
% self-employed with employees	25.5	32.5	42.9	24.8	36.1	38.8
% of those in work self-employed	10.7	16.6	18.8	3.6	6.2	7.9
self-employed with employees as % of economically active	2.0	4.8	6.4	0.7	2.1	2.5
On government scheme (000s)	1.9	291.8	22.7	1.4	183.2	19.1
Unemployed (000s)	10.2	1,720.8	168.6	6.3	797.2	94.2
Unemployment rate	26.9	11.1	21.0	19.6	6.8	16.4
Economically active students (000s)	0.5	168.8	8.9	0.9	221.0	9.6
Economically inactive (000s)	10.6	5,851.8	300.6	21.1	11,594.6	542.5
Students as a per cent of inactive	68.7	20.7	59.7	41.2	10.7	28.7
Permanently sick as a per cent of inactive	13.5	17.1	16.0	6.4	6.3	6.8
Retired as a per cent of inactive	10.5	59.6	17.4	6.0	40.7	9.6
'Other inactive' as a per cent of inactive	7.3	2.6	6.9	46.4	42.3	66.0

Source: OPCS/GRO(S) (1993) 1991 Census Ethnic Group and Country of Birth Report.

Amongst employees, Black–Other men were more likely to work part time than either white men or men from ethnic minority groups as a whole, while Black–Other women were much less likely to work part time than White women or women from all ethnic minority groups. The high incidence of part-time working by men might be a consequence of the very youthful age structure of this ethnic group, but may also indicate that workers from this ethnic group have to look for employment in the secondary labour market (the structure of employment is examined in greater detail in the next section). The high rate of full-time working for women might result from the concentration of this ethnic group in central London, where more full-time employment opportunities are available.

The composition of the economically inactive Black–Other population was rather different to that of the White population or ethnic minority groups as a whole. More than two thirds of inactive men and two fifths of inactive women were full-time students, well above the average for ethnic minority groups (reflecting the youthful age structure of this ethnic group). A far smaller percentage of Black–Other than of White people were retired, but the percentage of Black–Others permanently sick was similar to that for White people for both men and women, despite the disparity in age. The percentage of women who were 'other inactive' (mainly looking after a home or family full time) was much lower than the average for ethnic minority groups, and only slightly higher than for White women. The corresponding percentage for men was very much lower, but considerably higher than that for White men, perhaps indicating that Black–Other men experience the 'discouraged worker effect' at a younger age than White men, as a result of the high probability of unemployment that they face.

Clearly then, the overall figures for economic activity were powerfully influenced by the youthful age structure of the Black–Other ethnic group. Figures 3.7a and b present the pattern of economic activity by age for men and women (aged 16 and over) from the Black–Other ethnic group. It shows how the bulk of the ethnic group was aged under 35 in 1991 (most being in their twenties) with their numbers declining with increasing age. However, the number aged 16–19 (containing recent labour market entrants) was also markedly smaller than the number of 20–24-year-olds, who had reached economically active age in the mid-1980s. These diagrams show how labour force participation increased as the percentage of full-time students declined in the early part of the economically active age range, and then declined as the percentage in retirement and suffering from permanent sickness increased.

For men, the percentage of the age group in work increased for each successive age-group up to the age of 35, but then became successively smaller with increasing age The numbers on government schemes declined rapidly with age, but unemployment rose in age-groups up to the age of 30, which together contained the majority of unemployed Black–Other men. An interesting feature of the diagram was the number of 'other inactive' men in their twenties (this category includes those looking after home or family full time), suggesting that a small percentage of young men had never joined the formal labour market or had become disillusioned after a very short time. Full-time education accounted for a larger share of young women than young men, but the number of students declined rapidly for women in their twenties. Those in employment increased as a share of the age-group for each age-group up to the age of 55, declining thereafter. A much higher percentage of women than men were economically inactive, most being 'other inactive', the majority of whom will have had full-time family responsibilities.

Figures 3.8a and 8b present the trend of economic activity and unemployment rates for Black–Other men and women, compared to White people and people from ethnic minority groups as a whole. For men, the economic activity rate followed a similar path to that of White men (at a slightly lower

Figure 3.7 *Pattern of economic activity by age, 1991*

(a) Male

(b) Female

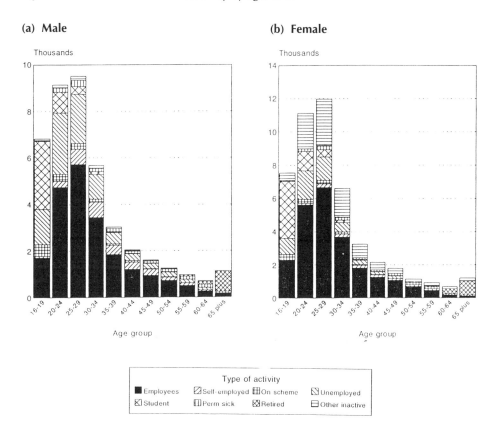

Age group

Age group

Type of activity
■ Employees	▨ Self-employed	⊞ On scheme	◩ Unemployed
⊠ Student	▥ Perm sick	⊠ Retired	⊟ Other inactive

level) and was higher than or close to the average for all ethnic minority groups throughout the economically active age range. Economic activity rates rose steadily through the late teens and early twenties to reach a peak of over 90 per cent in the 25–29 year age-group, remaining fairly constant until the 45–49 year age-group, after which it declined at an accelerating rate. However, this decline was slower than for White men, and thus the economic activity rate for men above retirement age was slightly higher for Black–Other than White men.

The trend for Black–Other women was also very similar in shape and level to that for White women (but well above the average for all women from ethnic minority groups throughout the age range), reaching a peak in the 25–29 year age-group, then declining in the next two 5-year age-groups. reflecting the tendency for many women to withdraw from the labour force in order to raise children. Economic activity rates were higher for 40–44 year olds than for women in their thirties, resulting from the return of mothers to work after childbirth. The rate continued to rise for longer and started to decline later for Black–Other than for White women. For both men and women, Black–Other people experienced unemployment rates about twice as high as those for White people (and also above the average for ethnic minority groups as a whole) throughout the economically active age range.

Figure 3.8 *Economic activity and unemployment rates by age, 1991*

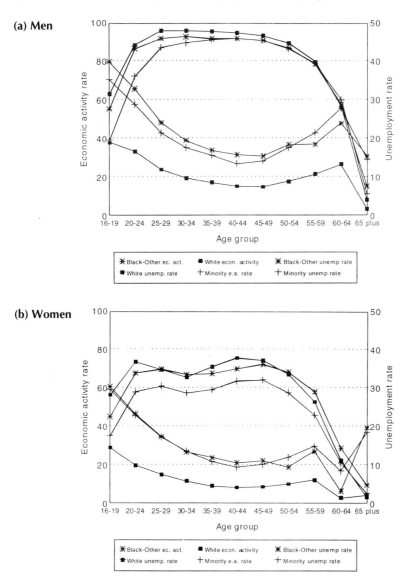

(a) Men

(b) Women

Unemployment rates for both men and women declined with increasing age to reach a minimum in the 45–49 year age group for men and the 50–54 year age group for women. Unemployment rates increased in successively older age groups for men, declining for retired men. For women, unemployment rates were higher for 55–59 year olds than for younger women, but were much lower for 60–64 year olds.

The pattern of employment

Here, the types of work which Black–Other people were engaged in are compared with the employment patterns of the population as a whole in 1991. The two per cent individual SAR was used to estimate the distribution of employment by industry and occupation for men and women. The industrial distribution was simplified into three categories. These were the production sector (primary, energy, manufacturing and construction); distribution, transport and communications, and business services; and other services (which contains public administration and the health and education services as well as miscellaneous private sector services). For each industry, the percentage employed in each of the nine categories of the Standard Occupational Classification was calculated. Table 3.11 highlights the occupational specialisation of Black–Other people by underlining those categories in which the percentage was greater for Black–Other people than for the population as a whole.

Black–Other people had a greater tendency than all people to work in the service sector, with the concentration of Black–Other women in other services particularly marked. The largest occupation for men was craft and related occupations, while that for women was clerical and secretarial occupations. Overall, men were over-represented relative to all working men in lower level white collar jobs, in sales occupations and in less skilled manual occupations. Black–Other women were over-represented in associate professional and technical occupations (which includes occupations such as nursing), craft and related occupations and personal and protective service occupations.

The majority of Black–Other men working in the production industries (primary, manufacturing and construction sectors) were in manual jobs, about equally split between skilled and less skilled occupations. In the distribution, transport, communications and business services sectors, Black–Other men worked in lower-level non-manual jobs, sales occupations and

Table 3.11 *Industrial and occupational specialisation of Black–Other people, 1991*

Standard Occupational Classification major group	Males				Females			
	Primary, manufacturing construction	Distribution, tranpport business services	Other services	All	Primary, manufacturing construction	Distribution, transport business services	Other services	All
Managers/administrators	11.2	14.7	11.9	12.6	10.5	12.0	*6.6*	8.3
Professional occupations	2.1	3.3	14.4	5.5	0.0	1.4	8.0	4.1
Associate professional/ technical	2.7	*7.8*	*28.8*	*10.6*	7.0	6.2	*21.5*	*12.7*
Clerical/secretarial	4.8	15.5	*9.3*	*10.6*	23.3	34.1	32.8	32.2
Craft and related	36.9	15.5	7.6	21.3	*30.2*	1.4	0.0	4.6
Personal/protective service	*2.7*	5.3	16.9	6.7	*2.3*	9.4	24.1	*14.9*
Sales occupations	2.7	13.1	0.0	6.9	1.2	21.4	0.4	9.6
Plant/machine operators	24.6	12.2	2.5	14.0	*30.2*	4.0	0.0	5.8
Other occupations	*11.8*	13.5	7.6	*11.8*	4.7	9.8	6.6	7.9
Employment share (%)	34.1	44.6	*21.5*	100	13.5	43.4	*43.1*	100

Source: 1991 Census two per cent individual SAR.

a range of manual occupations, but a higher percentage than in the other sectors were managers and administrators. In other services, Black–Other men were over-represented in associate professional and technical occupations, in clerical jobs and in personal and protective service occupations.

In contrast, Black–Other women in the production industries were over represented in skilled and semi-skilled manual jobs, with clerical and secretarial occupations also an important source of employment. In the distribution, transport, communications and business services industries, more than half of Black–Other women worked in clerical, secretarial and sales occupations. On the other hand, it was these industries (as was the case for men) in which the percentage in managerial and administrative jobs was highest. In the other services sector, Black–Other women were over-represented in associate professional and technical occupations (reflecting their substantial role as nurses in the health service), but nearly a third worked in clerical and secretarial jobs and 24.1 per cent in personal and protective service occupations. The percentage of both men and women working in professional occupations was highest in other services.

Qualifications

The distribution of highest educational qualifications by gender and age-group in 1991 is presented for the Black–Other population, the White population and the ethnic minority group population as a whole in Table 3.12. For the White population and ethnic minority group population as a whole, a higher percentage of men than women had higher educational qualifications. However, this pattern was reversed for Black–Other people, across all age-groups. Overall, a lower percentage of Black–Other men than White men had educational qualifications better than A-level (or equivalent) standard, with the White figure below the average for ethnic minority groups as a whole. Among women, the differentials were much narrower and Black–Other women displayed the highest percentage with higher education qualifications. However, as is the case for the other ethnic minority groups presented in Table 3.12, a higher percentage of Black–Other men than women held the equivalent of a first or higher degree, and more Black–Other women than men held nursing or teaching qualifications as their highest qualifications.

In common with other ethnic groups, Black–Other people with higher education qualifications displayed a much higher degree of participation in the labour market than the ethnic group as a whole, with their economic activity rate nearly as high as that of the White population. The economic activity rate of qualified Black–Other people was probably depressed by their relative youth, since many with less advanced post-school qualifications would not have finished their education at the time of the census; this factor probably operates more strongly for the Black–African and Asian ethnic groups, resulting in a much lower average economic activity rate for ethnic minority groups as a whole. The percentage of highly qualified Black–Other people in work was much lower than for White people, while the unemployment rate they experience was more than twice as high as that

Table 3.12 *Higher education qualifications for Black–Other people, compared with White people and the average for all people from minority ethnic groups, 1991*

	Black Other		White		Ethnic minority groups	
	Male	Female	Male	Female	Male	Female
All persons aged 18+	**3,505**	**4,132**	**1,893,853**	**2,097,438**	**91,212**	**93,324**
All qualified	417	551	292,137	240,882	16,262	12,207
Percent qualified	11.9	13.3	15.4	11.5	17.8	13.1
Percent with highest qualification:						
A-level or equivalent	4.5	7.6	5.9	6.7	5.5	6.7
First degree	6.2	4.8	8.1	4.4	9.6	5.3
Higher degree	1.3	0.9	1.4	0.5	2.7	0.9
Percentage of age group qualified:						
18–24	4.3	4.9	7.7	7.4	11.3	7.1
25–29	13.0	15.1	19.5	18.4	30.5	17.6
30–44	18.8	19.9	21.5	17.9	30.4	16.7
45–59	15.1	22.9	16.5	11.8	21.5	12.4
60–64	10.0	10.9	12.8	8.1	13.4	6.3
65+	7.4	8.5	8.9	4.7	15.8	3.4
Qualified age 18 to						
pensionable age		*944*		*466,985*		*27,839*
Economically active		828		414,121		23,305
Economic activity rate		87.7		88.7		83.7
Percent in work		79.4		85.2		75.1
Unemployed		66		14,710		1,913
Unemployment rate		7.3		3.6		8.2

Note: This table is based on a 10 per cent sample of Census returns.
Source: OPCS/GRO(S) (1993) 1991 Census Ethnic Group and Country of Birth Report.

for highly qualified White people, though substantially lower than for Black–Other people as a whole. This suggests that while the possession of higher educational qualifications improves the likelihood of success Black–Other in the labour market, substantial barriers to achievement still remain, relative to White people.

3.4 Conclusion

This chapter has demonstrated that the Black–Other ethnic group is quite distinctive in comparison with the other nine categories of the OPCS ethnic group classification. It is a category constructed from the answers provided for people whose ethnicity cannot adequately be described by the categories presented in the ethnic group question, rather than describing a recognisable group of people. Clearly, it includes people of mixed ethnic origin, people who regard themselves as British and possibly object to being classified on the basis of the immigrant origins of their ancestors and those for whom the British-centric classification is not appropriate; for example Black people from the United States.

It has been shown that there were clear geographical patterns in the composition of the ethnic group; people identified as Black British were most likely to live in London, while those with other answers and mixed Black and White parentage were found in more rural areas, and those of mixed ethnicity with other origins tended to live in larger urban areas outside London.

The Black–Other population stands out from other ethnic groups for its extreme youth, the high percentage of its members born in the UK and the high percentage of families represented by cohabiting couples and lone parents. On a range of social and economic measures, it emerges as being relatively disadvantaged. Both men and women experienced relatively high unemployment rates, poorer health than the population as a whole, had poorer standards of housing, tended to work in middle ranking and lower-level jobs and had lower levels of higher education qualifications. Some of these patterns are a reflection of the relative youth of this ethnic group, but high relative unemployment rates apply across the age range. Given the population structure, this ethnic group will grow strongly in the medium term, and will account for a growing percentage of school-age children in the 1990s and labour market entrants in the first decades of the 21st century. Planning to meet the needs of this ethnic group will be complex, because of its diversity and because it tends to represent different types of people in different areas of Britain.

References

Berrington, A. (1994) Marriage and family formation among the white and ethnic minority populations in Britain. *Ethnic and Racial Studies*, 17, 517–546.

Berrington, A. (1996) Marriage patterns and inter-ethnic marriage. In: Coleman, D. and Salt, J. (eds), *Demographic Characteristics of the Ethnic Minority Populations.* Ethnicity in the 1991 Census Series, volume 1 London: OPCS.

Bulmer, M. (1996) The ethnic question in the 1991 Census of Population. In: Coleman, D. and Salt, J. (eds), *Demographic Characteristics of the Ethnic Minority Populations.* Ethnicity in the 1991 Census Series, Volume 1 London: OPCS.

Coleman, D. (1985) Ethnic intermarriage in Great Britain. *Population Trends*, 40, 4–10.

Marsh, C. and Teague, A. (1992) Samples of anonymised records from the 1991 Census. *Population Trends*, 69, 17–26.

Modood, T., Beishon, S. and Virdee, S. (1994) *Changing Ethnic Identities.* London: Policy Studies Institute.

OPCS (1994) First results from the Quality Check element of the 1991 Census Validation Survey. *OPCS Monitor* SS 94/2.

OPCS/GRO(S) (1993) *1991 Census, Ethnic Group and Country of Birth , Great Britain.* London: HMSO.

Owen, D.W. (1993) Ethnic minorities in Great Britain: Age and gender structure. NEMDA 1991 Census Statistical Paper no. 2. Centre for Research in Ethnic Relations, University of Warwick.

Owen, D.W. (1996) Size structure and growth of the ethnic minority populations. In: Coleman, D. and Salt, J. (eds), *Demographic Characteristics of the Ethnic Minority Populations.* Ethnicity in the 1991 Census Series, Volume 1 London: OPCS.

Sillitoe, K. and White, P.H. (1992) Ethnic group and the British census: the search for a question. *Journal of the Royal Statistical Society A*, 155, part 1, 141–63.

Chapter 4
The Indians: onward and upward

Vaughan Robinson

4.1 Introduction

Indians were the largest individual ethnic category listed by the 1991 Census of Great Britain. They numbered 840,255, with the largest proportion being born in the United Kingdom, followed by the subcontinent and East Africa.

Although popular perceptions would suggest otherwise, there has been an Indian presence in the United Kingdom since at least the 18th century. Visram (1986) describes how these early arrivals were highly diverse in nature because they were either wealthy princes, domestic servants to the English gentry, students, artistic performers or seamen with the East India Company. Maan (1992) describes the parallel history of Indians in Scotland, noting that the first arrivals were recorded as early as 1505, and that there was already a 'considerable' number there by 1540.

The significance of this early 'pioneer phase' of the migration was that it established foundations upon which the subsequent mass labour migration of the 1950s and 60s could be built. The pioneers were important as sources of information on Britain and the opportunities which existed there, and were also often instigators of the chain migration which was such a characteristic feature of the 'target migrant phase'. This began to develop from 1955 onwards as the attraction of higher wage levels and job vacancies in British manufacturing industry became synchronised with the availability of cheaper travel from India, population pressure within the subcontinent, and the development of a powerful localised social momentum in certain villages, which saw peasants leaving simply because they felt everyone else was. The intentions of many of these labour migrants was to achieve specific financial or family targets and then return to India. These targets included the acquisition of land, the building of a permanent house or the accumulation of a larger dowry to ensure a more prestigious marriage for their daughters. Because of their target orientation, the labour migrants were demographically unbalanced, with a preponderance of young men who were often unmarried.

Unlike migration from the West Indies, which had perhaps already peaked by 1962, Indian labour migration was really only hitting its stride when it was curtailed by the 1962 Commonwealth Immigrants Act. This was responsible for instigating the third major phase to Indian migration to the UK. 'Family reunion' involved the migration of female and child dependants and the recreation of households in the UK. The migration of fiancées also led to the creation of new households. Migration targets were either abandoned as unrealisable or inflated, and temporary sojourning gradually gave way to permanent settlement within an Anglo-Indian arena.

Progressive tightening of immigration and citizenship laws, and the recessions which have punctuated British economic progress since 1973 have together transformed the migration for a third time. Indian movement to the UK has been gradually professionalised as the pool of eligible dependants has dwindled and greater reliance has been put on labour market skills as entry requirements. Even for professional workers, entry has become more difficult as the number of work vouchers has been reduced and limits have been placed on their duration.

Although Indian migration to Great Britain has a long tradition, post war mass migration was only one of a series of 'waves' of Black and Asian labour migration which began in the mid-1950s and continued until the mid-1970s. The peak of Indian mass migration certainly post-dated that from the Caribbean but pre-dated that from Pakistan and Bangladesh (see Figure 4.1). The demographic and geographical consequences of the different timing of these is still to be seen today (see Robinson, 1993a) and also in the results of the 1991 Census.

Figure 4.1 *Cumulative proportions of the overseas-born ethnic minority populations of Great Britain by year of entry, 1956- to 1987*

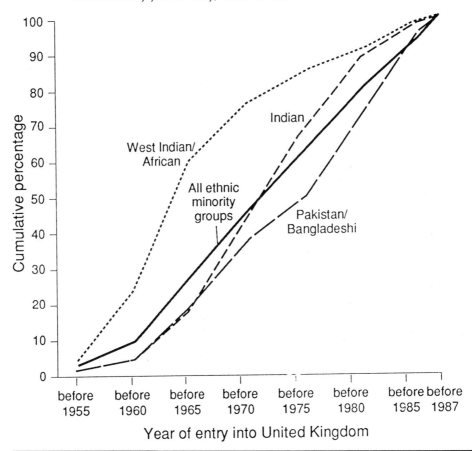

While Indian labour migration thus needs to be viewed alongside other migrations from the New Commonwealth to Britain, it does stand alone in one respect. A sizeable minority of Indians in Great Britain arrived as refugees, either 'acute' or 'anticipatory'. The story of the expulsion of Indians from East Africa has been told elsewhere (most recently in Robinson, 1986 and 1995, and Marret, 1989), but the important elements are that the East African Asians had earned their living either as administrators or businessmen, that many had already embarked on a strategy of inter-generational social mobility centering on education, and that few were able to realise their full financial assets before having to leave. Equally as important, many had been educated through the medium of English and were skilled at negotiating complex bureaucratic systems.

Some contextual constants

Understanding the contemporary social and economic position of Indians in Great Britain requires a knowledge both of the core values which many Indians hold and those of their White counterparts. It also requires a knowledge of the human capital resources which Indians had on their arrival in the UK.

Studies in the early phases of mass migration (Rose, 1969; Smith, 1974) demonstrated that by British standards many Indian immigrants were not highly educated, that they had few transferable skills valued by employers in an advanced industrial economy, and that communication skills in English varied enormously. Anthropological studies demonstrate the emphasis placed by Indians upon the (extended) family and the way in which each member has an allotted role within this, which constrains their actions and aspirations. Furthermore, when other Indians are making assessments of status they do so about the family as a whole, not about individuals within it. Individuals thus see their destinies as intertwined with that of the extended family, and strive to contribute to family, not individual, goals. On a different level, the achievement of economic success, and the status that goes with this, is an integral shared goal within the Indian population, although it is still not clear whether this results from colonialism (Robinson, 1986) or from value systems which pre-date this (e.g. the 'merchant ideo-logy' which Tambs-Lyche (1980) argues all Patidars possess). Nevertheless this drive to achievement has been manifested in a variety of ways (a predilection for landowning, the renunciation of renting of property, business ownership, the acquisition of formal qualifications) and in different geographical contexts (e.g. East Africa (Gregory, 1993) or the United States (Helweg and Helweg, 1990).

Set against these factors, which are internal to the Indian population, are those which are imposed. An extensive literature has demonstrated that Indians in the UK face both overt racism and subtler racial exclusion in contexts ranging from the school, the workplace, the housing market, and even in their leisure time. Moreover the prejudices which drive these actions have been shown to be common to all social classes and to all parts of the United Kingdom. In addition, Indians were recruited by metropolitan society to fulfil a particular role, namely to provide cheap unskilled labour.

4.2 Demographic characteristics

For the first time, the 1991 Census allows the number of people of Indian ethnicity in Great Britain (henceforward known as Indians for brevity) to be quantified accurately. With a total of 840,255, they are the largest of the ethnic categories listed by the 1991 Census of Great Britain, outnumbering the next largest group (Black–Caribbeans) by over 340,000 residents. They form 27.7 per cent of the ethnic minority population and some 1.5 per cent of the total population of Great Britain. The Irish are not treated identically by the census and there is only Irish birthplace rather than Irish ethnicity data. On this basis, the Irish are slightly less numerous than the Indians. However, on a directly comparable basis they would probably constitute a larger group than the Indians (see Introduction and Chapter 10).

The Indian group has diverse places of birth, with 41.2 per cent being born in the UK, 36.8 per cent in India, 16.9 per cent in the East African Commonwealth countries, 0.7 per cent in South East Asia, 0.5 per cent in Pakistan, and 3.9 per cent elsewhere.

Although there are no directly comparable sources of data which would allow an accurate assessment of changes in the size of the Indian population, Table 4.1 brings together best estimates of the size of the Indian minority of the UK at various points in time. What is immediately apparent is how the group increased in size through immigration in the 1960s and early 1970s but how more recently, fertility has taken over as the main engine of demographic growth.

Figure 4.2 demonstrates the impact of this upon the age structure of the group. In comparison with the White population, Indians are over-represented in all of the five-year bands up to 40 years of age, particularly the 5–14 grouping and the 30–39 grouping: in these cases they are over-represented by between a third and a half. Figure 4.2 also shows how the numerical dominance of males in the 'mass labour migration' period has left its mark upon the group, which now records a male:female sex imbalance of 1.01:1 (cf the White ratio of 0.93:1). Family reunion and fertility has, however, modified the very sharp sex imbalance that existed earlier in the migrations (see Robinson, 1986).

Table 4.1 *Changing numbers of Indians in Britain*

	Indians	East African Asians
1951	30,800	
1961	81,400	
1966	223,600	
1971	375,000	(68,000)
1976	550,000	(160,000)
1981	676,000	(252,000)
1983–5	763,000	
1986–8	786,500	
1991	840,255	(142,000)

Note: the data are collected from a variety of sources and should not be taken as strictly comparable.
Source: 1951–66, Rose (1969); 1971–6, ISU (1977); 1981, Population Statistics Division (1986); 1983–5 and 1986–8 Labour Force Survey; 1991, National Census.

Figure 4.2 *Age-sex pyramids for the Indian and White populations*

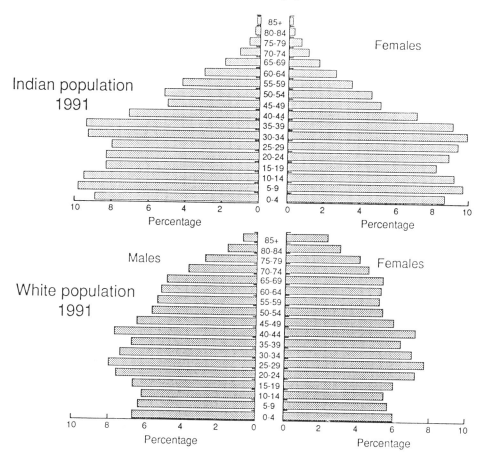

Indian population 1991

Females

White population 1991

Males

Females

4.3 Geographical distribution

The geographical distribution and concentration of the Indian population needs to be considered at a variety of spatial scales. Table 4.2 contains data at two scales, national and economic regions. It shows how the Indian population is overwhelmingly resident in England, and how three regions within England (the South East, West Midlands and East Midlands) contain almost 84 per cent of all Indians within Great Britain. It also indicates the importance of the south east of England for the group, with more than half of all Indians being found in that part of the country. However, comparison of the Lorenz curves shown in Figure 4.3 for the different ethnic minority groups reveals that the Indian population is less geographically concentrated than either the Caribbean or Bangladeshi populations, although it is more concentrated than the Pakistani population. Robinson (1993a) has argued that these differences arise predominantly from the fact that each 'wave' arrived at different times, such that economic conditions and the geography of opportunity had changed. Column 3 of Table 4.2 shows how the regional distribution of the Indian population has changed since the last census, with significant proportional growth in the South East and East Midlands and commensurate decline in the West Midlands, the South West, Yorkshire and Humberside, and the North West.

Table 4.2 *Regional distribution of the ethnic Indian population, 1981 and 1991*

| | Ethnic Indians 1991 | | Indians 1981 | East African 1991 | |
	Number	Per cent	Per cent	Number	Per cent
Great Britain	840,255	100	100	211,535	100
England	823,821	98.0	96.6	209,437	99.0
Scotland	10,050	1.2	2.4	789	0.4
Wales	6,384	0.8	1.0	1,309	0.6
North	7,739	0.9	1.3	437	0.2
Yorkshire and Humberside	40,752	4.8	6.3	4,707	2.2
East Midlands	98,859	11.8	9.2	33,206	15.7
East Anglia	6,492	0.8	1.1	1,954	0.9
South East	444,779	52.9	47.3	139,764	66.0
South West	10,915	1.3	3.0	2,308	1.1
West Midlands	158,731	18.9	20.3	17,828	8.4
North West	55,554	6.6	8.1	9,233	4.4

Source: OPCS (1993), Volume 2, Table 6.

Figure 4.3 *Lorenz curves for distribution of ethnic groups by region*

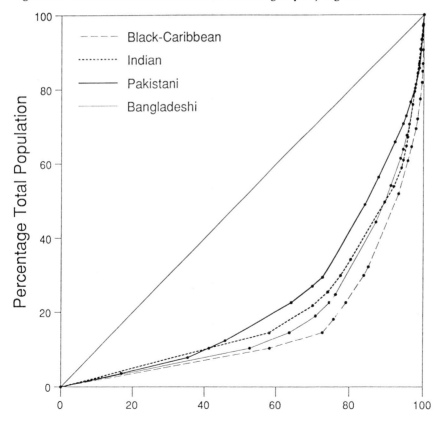

Table 4.3 reduces the spatial scale and focuses only upon the eight largest English conurbations. Column 2 demonstrates how fully two thirds of all Indians in Great Britain live in these cities, a figure well below those for Black–Caribbeans (80.7 per cent) or Bangladeshis (77.3 per cent). A second area where the Indian distribution differs is within London. There, residence in outer London outnumbers residence in inner London (by a factor of 3.7:1), whereas the reverse is true for the other two minority groups. Column 3 compares the 1991 figures with those from the 1981 Census (using the nearest surrogate of people living in households headed by someone born in India), and indicates how the Indian population has been gradually moving out of all the major conurbations, except London. There, there has been a dramatic increase in the number of Indians living in the outer ring, and a decline within the inner boroughs. This national pattern of change is unique to the Indian group (Robinson, 1994) and perhaps hints at trends in social mobility discussed below.

Figure 4.4 reduces the geographical scale further and maps the distribution of Indians at county level. The map underscores how Indians had to undertake greater geographical diffusion on arrival in search of economic opportunities than their precursors, the Afro-Caribbeans, but it also draws attention to the group's presence in areas surrounding major conurbations such as Shropshire, Sussex, Surrey, Derbyshire and Staffordshire. Comparisons with earlier maps reveal significant growth in London, and in areas adjacent to the conurbations of London and the West Midlands (Robinson, 1993b).

England and Wales are divided into 403 census districts but because of the way in which ethnic minority settlement has remained concentrated in certain parts of the country, many of the districts do not have a significant ethnic population. Analysis at this level proves the Indian population to be by far the most spatially dispersed of all the groups. Only 30 districts had

Table 4.3 *Conurban distribution, 1981 and 1991*

	Ethnic Indians 1991 Number	Per cent GB total 1991	Per cent GB total 1991	East African Indians 1991 Number	Per cent GB total 1991	Per cent East African Indians 1991
GB total	840,255	100	100	211,535	100	100
Inner London	74,000	8.8	9.1	17,344	8.2	9.0
Outer London	273,091	32.5	24.1	97,439	46.1	27.9
Greater Manchester	29,741	3.5	4.4	5,922	2.8	3.8
Merseyside	2,646	0.3	0.5	170	0.1	0.4
South Yorkshire	3,526	0.4	0.6	405	0.2	0.5
Tyne and Wear	4,228	0.5	0.6	167	0.1	0.6
West Midlands	141,359	16.8	17.9	15,109	7.1	20.0
West Yorkshire	34,837	4.1	5.2	3,989	1.9	4.9
Conurbation Total	563,428	67.0	62.4	140,545	66.4	67.3

Source: 1981 figures from CRE (1985).
        1991 figures from 1991 Census Small Area Statistics.

Figure 4.4 *Geographic distribution of Indians, by county*

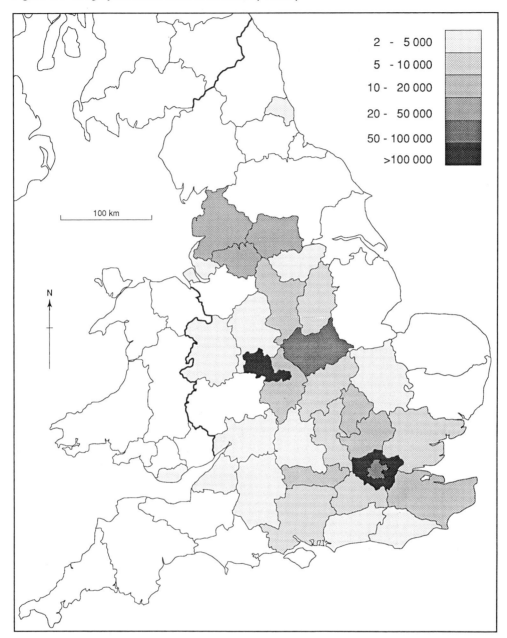

negligible Indian populations (i.e. less than 20 persons), compared with 120 with negligible Black–Caribbean populations, 200 with negligible Pakistani populations and 211 with negligible Bangladeshi settlement. This indicates the significant spatial diffusion which has carried Indians out from their original urban ports of entry. Table 4.4 provides another dimension of ethnic spread: column 1 shows the proportion of Great Britain's Indian population which lives in districts of varying Indian concentration. It is noticeable that

Table 4.4 *Distribution of ethnic Indians by level of concentration, census districts, per cent*

Percentage which Indians form of district population	% of all Great Britain ethnic Indians	% of all Great Britain East African Indians
20%+	7.2	0.0
17.5–19.9	0.0	0.0
15.0–17.4	14.1	0.0
12.5–14.9	8.3	0.0
10.0–12.4	6.1	0.0
7.5–9.9	4.0	28.2
5.0–7.4	16.9	0.0
2.5–4.9	17.6	19.6
2.0–2.4	3.7	6.2
1.5–1.9	5.7	5.3
1.0–1.4	5.5	6.0
0.5–0.9	4.6	13.8
0.1–0.4	6.2	18.6
<0.1	0.1	2.3

Note: Ethnic Indians form 1.54% of Great Britain population, East African Indians form 0.4% of Great Britain population.

Source: 1991 Census, Small Area Statistics.

fully 22 per cent of all Indians live in districts within which they form less than 2 per cent of the total population, and over 6 per cent live in districts where Indians form less than 0.5 per cent of the whole population.

In contrast, Figure 4.5 shows the 20 districts in Great Britain that have the largest Indian populations. It is noticeable that the leading areas of settlement cluster around four foci: London, the West Midlands, Leicester and the North West.

While the geographical location of ethnic minority populations is important, so also is the type of location within which they are settled. Each of the census districts can be allocated to one of 11 categories within a typology of areas. On one level this typology distinguishes between metropolitan London, other metropolitan districts and non-metropolitan districts. On another level, it distinguishes between different types of metropolitan and non-metropolitan districts, such that remoter, largely rural areas are categorised separately from resort and retirement centres.

Figure 4.6 shows the proportion of each of the ethnic minority groups resident in these 11 types of district. It demonstrates how the distribution of both the Bangladeshi and Afro-Caribbean populations closely follows the urban hierarchy, with diminishing proportions of each group being found in progressively smaller/more rural districts. The Pakistani population has avoided London to a much greater extent and is instead more numerous in large cities and their satellites, and industrial areas. Indians have the highest percentage of their population in non-metropolitan districts (over 31 per

Figure 4.5 *Map of twenty districts with largest number of Indians*

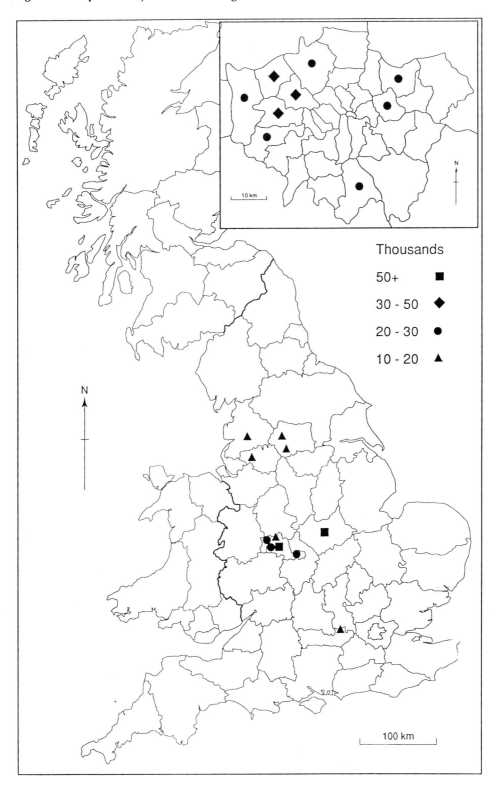

Thousands

50+ ■

30 - 50 ◆

20 - 30 ●

10 - 20 ▲

Figure 4.6 *Distribution of ethnic minorities by district type*

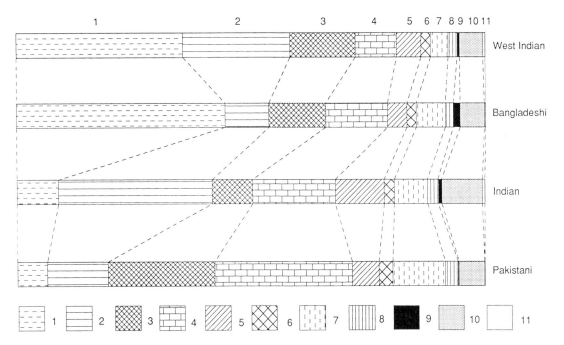

1 Inner London 2 Outer London 3 The principal cities; 4 Others 5 Large cities 6 Smaller cities; 7 Industrial cities;
8 Districts that include new towns; 9 Resort and seaside retirement districts; 10 Other urban, mixed urban rural,
and more accessible rural districts; 11 Remoter, largely rural, districts

cent), are well represented in non-metropolitan cities and have an above average presence in other urban areas and rural areas.

Finally within this section, Figures 4.7 and 4.8 look at the processes that have underlain changes in the geographical distribution of Indians. Figure 4.7 maps variations in the extent to which different counties recorded different levels of Indian spatial mobility within the 12 months prior to the 1991 Census. It shows those counties where a high percentage of the Indian population has moved within the last 12 months. While it has to be acknowledged that percentages of small numbers can be misleading, the Figure does suggest a consistent picture, with relatively static Indian populations within the main centres of settlement, but high proportionate levels of turnover/inmigration in areas away from ethnic cores (e.g. the Scottish Highlands, West and North Wales, Cumbria, Lincolnshire and Norfolk). If this is indicative of a trend, higher turnover might be a product of counter-urbanisation or dissatisfaction with rural living and rural racism (see Jay, 1993; Agyeman, 1990). Figure 4.8 maps the 'flows' of inter-regional migrants of Indian ethnicity over the period 1981–91, as revealed by the Longitudinal Study (see Brown and Fox, 1984). The data reveals the continuation of trends apparent during the 1970s (see Robinson, 1991), namely the movement to the south of the country from the industrial areas of the West Midlands, Manchester and West Yorkshire, the major flow from inner to outer London, and a parallel flow from outer London to the non-metropolitan South East, East Anglia and the South West.

Figure 4.7 Percentage of Indian households changing address in previous 12 months, 1991

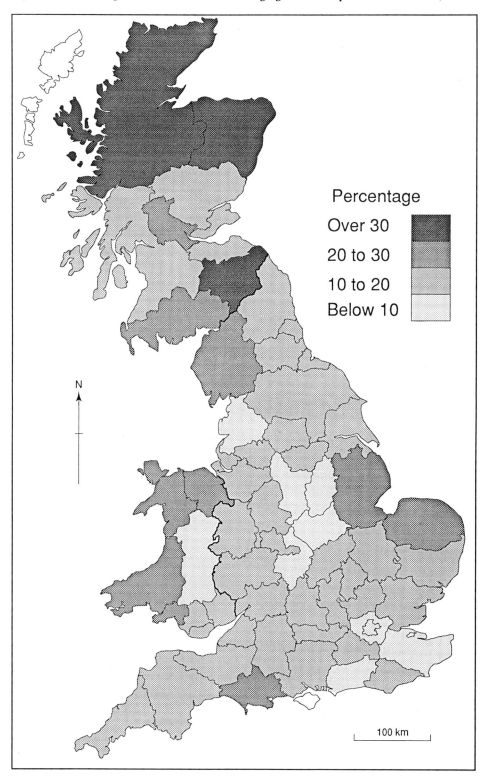

Percentage

Over 30

20 to 30

10 to 20

Below 10

N

100 km

Figure 4.8 *Inter-regional net migration flows, Longitudinal Study 1981-91*

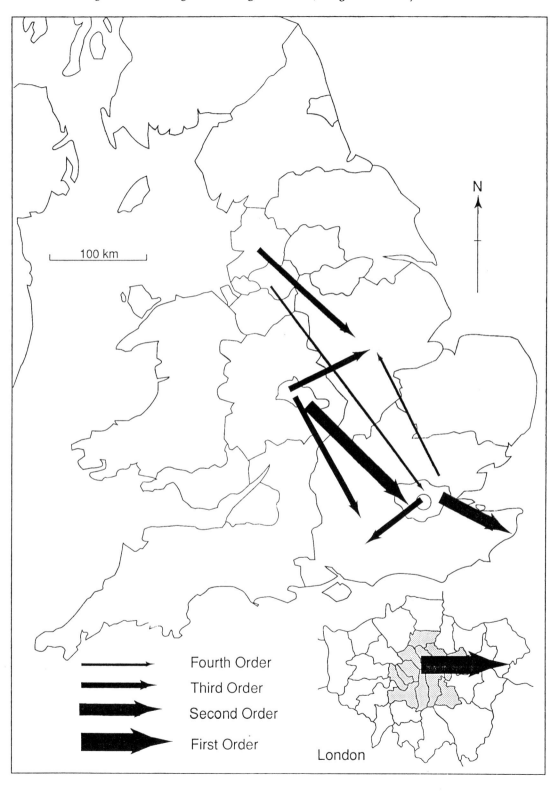

4.4 Social and economic characteristics

Economic status

Geographical location has a direct influence on the economic opportunities available to any individual or group, as does the possession of marketable skills.

Previous research has found the Indian population to have a bipolar educational profile, with an above average percentage of the group having higher qualifications and an above average percentage having no qualifications (Brown, 1984). The 1991 Census confirms this generalisation, since the Indian population has a higher percentage (15 per cent) qualified beyond A-level than any other group except the Chinese. Comparable figures for the White, Pakistani and Bangladeshi populations are 13.3 per cent, 7.0 per cent, and 5.2 per cent respectively. The distribution of these qualifications between different age cohorts is also significant. In the Indian population, those who migrated during the peak of the mass labour migration as adults in their mid-30s, or who have since come as elderly dependants, are less likely to have higher qualifications than their White counterparts. Conversely, those in the 18–29 year age cohort are considerably more likely than their White or Black–Caribbean peers to have qualifications beyond A-level.

There are also notable differences between the economic position of Indians and Whites within Great Britain. As Table 4.5 demonstrates, Indian males are twice as likely as White males to be self-employed (with employees) and also more likely to be own-account workers. Equally they are more likely to be unemployed, though their unemployment levels are much lower than those for Black–Caribbean males (19.1 per cent). These same generalisations apply to Indian women, who, in addition, tend to be full-time workers when many of their White counterparts are part-time employees.

Table 4.5 *Economic status of ethnic Indians, 1991, per cent*

	Males			Females		
	White	Indian	Black–Caribbean	White	Indian	Black–Caribbean
Economically active	*73.2*	*78.0*	*80.0*	*49.7*	*55.4*	*66.9*
Employee – full time	50.8	47.5	50.6	25.9	31.6	43.5
Employee – part time	2.2	2.1	2.4	17.1	9.7	11.7
Self employed – employees	3.7	7.5	1.3	1.1	2.3	0.3
own account	7.6	9.2	4.8	1.9	3.6	0.8
Government scheme	1.0	1.3	1.9	0.5	1.1	1.6
Unemployed	7.8	10.4	19.1	3.1	7.0	9.0
Economically inactive	*26.8*	*21.9*	*19.9*	*50.3*	*44.6*	*33.1*

Source: calculated from 1991 Census Small Area Statistics.

Social class and social mobility

A considerable literature has developed recently about the extent to which colour supplement stereotyping of Asians in the UK as a 'success story' is accurate or helpful (see Robinson, 1990a; Goering,1993; Sunday Times, 1994). Table 4.6 makes a contribution to this debate since it demonstrates clearly that the social class profile of the Indian population in Great Britain is skewed both towards the upper echelons of white collar work (Social Classes I and II) and also towards semi-skilled manual work (Class IV). The corollary of this is a relative under-representation in the intermediate Social Class III (both non-manual and manual) and in the least skilled manual jobs. This lends support to Robinson's (1990b) argument that the bipolar social class profile of Indians has been shaped by the economic restructuring and recession that occurred in Britain in the 1980s, providing opportunities for some while taking them away from others.

Table 4.6 also considers whether the social class profile of the Indian population of England and Wales (as represented by the Longitudinal Study one per cent sample) has changed over time. What the data suggest is that the social class profile has changed in the last 10 years such that the proportions of men and women in Social Class II has risen while the proportion of men in manual work and women in junior white collar work and semi-skilled manual work has fallen.

Finally, Table 4.7 looks at one of the processes which underlie this changing aggregate class profile, namely individual social mobility over the period 1981–91. These data are derived from the Longitudinal Study and therefore chart the progress of a panel of individuals over the decade between censuses. Earlier analysis of the 1971–81 Longitudinal Study demonstrated three points: first, that the main flows of Indian social mobility had been upwards from unemployment and junior white collar work (IIIN non manual) into Social Class II; second, that those who were already employed in white collar work in 1971 tended to retain this position a decade later; and, third, that there had been considerable exchanges between the three manual classes (see Robinson, 1990c for a fuller discussion). The new 1981–91 data suggest that some of these trends have continued into the most recent

Table 4.6 *Social class profile, Indians, 1991*

	Males		Females	
	1981	1991	1981	1991
I	8	8	5	5
II	17	25	15	23
III	12	11	21	18
III	29	27	12	11
IV	27	23	42	38
V	8	5	5	5

Source: Commissioned tables from the Longitudinal Study.

Table 4.7 *Social mobility 1981–91, Indian males: outflow (row) percentages*

Class In 1981	Class in 1991								
	I	II	IIIN	IIIM	IV	V	Unem–ployed	All %	N
I	73	11	5	2	2	0	8	101	125
II	4	73	8	5	5	2	3	100	240
IIIN	4	27	50	5	5	2	7	100	175
IIIM	2	12	3	55	13	5	10	100	445
IV	0	11	5	19	52	5	8	100	407
V	0	10	1	30	23	25	11	100	122
Unemployed	2	18	6	23	18	5	29	100	218
All %	7	22	9	24	20	5	12	99	1,732

Notes: Some figures do not add to 100% because of rounding.
Source: Commissioned tables from the Longitudinal Study.

decade: white collar workers are still likely to retain their relative positions, and this has become increasingly true of employers and managers; and there has been considerable upward movement by manual workers from one social class to the next. Other trends seem to have slackened or been totally replaced. The remarkable movement of people from unemployment in 1971 to professional work by 1981 has all but disappeared, and been replaced by a broader diffusion of the unemployed into Social Classes II, IIIM (manual) and IV. In addition, the unemployed are now much more likely to have remained that way and those in unskilled manual work have become more vulnerable to unemployment.

Household size and type

Table 4.8 looks at the size and composition of Indian households within Great Britain and compares this with those of the White, Black–Caribbean, Pakistani and Bangladeshi populations. The table immediately demonstrates the impact of the different times of arrival of the groups, and therefore the length of time they have had to demographically mature in situ from the very unbalanced labour migrant phase. Each group is at a different point on the transition from youthful male dominance, through family reunion/creation and family building to a balanced demographic state, complete with elders. The average household size, the proportion of households made up solely of people of pensionable age, the proportion of single pensioner households and the percentage of households with children are all related to the concept of 'waves' of migration. Clearly, however, cultural mores also have to be taken into consideration. It is noticeable that extended (mixed sex) households are much more common among the Asian minorities (accounting for around 35 per cent of all households) than they are among

Table 4.8 *Household size or type, per cent*

	White	Black–Caribbean	Indian	Pakistani	Bangladeshi
	%	%	%	%	%
1 adult of pensionable age	15.6	5.3	2.0	0.9	0.7
1 adult	11.5	23.1	7.8	7.2	5.2
1 adult with children	4.0	16.4	3.1	4.8	4.4
2 adults (M+F) no children	29.5	16.0	12.8	7.4	4.4
with children	19.4	14.8	36.4	41.0	43.3
2 adults (same sex) no children	2.8	3.9	1.7	1.6	1.8
with children	0.5	1.7	0.7	1.3	1.4
3+ adults (M+F) no children	11.1	11.4	13.4	7.4	3.9
with children	5.0	5.9	21.2	27.3	32.8
3+ adults (same sex) no children	0.4	0.9	0.6	0.7	1.6
with children	0.07	0.3	0.2	0.4	0.4
Households of pensioners only	25.7	7.2	3.6	1.4	1.0
Average persons per household	2.43	2.51	3.80	4.80	5.33
% with children	28.97	39.1	61.6	74.8	82.3

Source: 1991 Census, Small Area Statistics

Whites or Black–Caribbeans. Similarly, households with single adults are far less common among Asians than among Whites, but relatively common among Black–Caribbeans. Cultural values also influence the choice of whether to have children and the preferred size of family, although there is evidence that this changes over time as a group adjusts to permanent settlement in a different country.

Housing

Table 4.9 addresses the last of the main issues covered by the census, namely housing. Again, time of arrival and cultural values are important variables which help explain differences between groups, but to these must also be added the class position of a group, the degree to which it experiences racial exclusion, and the way in which the housing stock varies markedly between different localities. As relatively recent arrivals in the UK, Indians have not had the same opportunity to inherit or build up equity in the housing market as their White counterparts, yet despite this, they are found to a much greater extent in the owner occupied sector than either Whites or any of the other ethnic minority groups shown in Table 4.9. Conversely they are the least well represented group in social housing. In addition, their housing is comparable to that of Whites on the criteria of shared facilities or presence of central heating, and better than that of other ethnic minorities. However, these two criteria are not comprehensive measures of housing quality.

Table 4.9 *Housing, Great Britain, 1991 (%)*

	White	Black–Caribbean	Indian	Pakistani	Bangladeshi
Tenure[1]					
Owner occupied:					
owned outright	24.4	8.2	16.5	19.4	5.2
buying	42.2	39.8	65.2	57.3	39.3
Private renting	7.0	5.6	6.5	9.6	9.6
Housing Association	3.0	9.7	2.2	2.2	6.1
Local authority	21.1	35.7	7.8	10.4	37.0
Scottish Homes	0.3	-	-	-	-
Facilities[2]					
Lacking/sharing bath shower/WC	0.8	0.9	0.8	1.2	1.6
No central heating	16.8	15.9	11.7	35.2	23.0
Crowding[2]					
1.0–1.49 persons per room	3.1	7.0	16.1	30.6	34.2
1.5+ persons per room	0.6	2.1	4.6	13.2	28.0

1 Households.
2 Residents.
Source: 1991 Census, Small Area Statistics.

The subnational picture

The section above has looked at the characteristics and situation of the Indian population at a national level as if it were an homogenous whole. However, even by the late 1970s analysts were pointing to the fact that the Indian population is an amalgam of different peoples, drawn from different countries and regions, practising different religions and speaking different languages (see for example, Robinson, 1979 and 1986; Helweg, 1980; Tambs-Lyche, 1980). In addition, authors were noting how this diversity of background was being translated into a diversity of trajectories after arrival in Great Britain (e.g. Robinson, 1984). Finally the economic recessions and restructuring of the 1980s reshaped the opportunity structure on offer to all of Britain's population, including the Indian population, providing some places and people with new opportunities while withdrawing them from others.

While the census question on ethnicity does not allow us to decompose the Indian population by religion, mother tongue or region of origin, it is possible to distinguish between those Indians who had substantial links with East Africa and those who came direct from the subcontinent. In addition, it is possible to differentiate segments of the Indian population by area of residence within Great Britain.

East African Indians and subcontinental Indians

Table 4.2 compares the distribution of the subcontinental Indian and East African Indian populations between the countries and regions of Great Britain. It is clear that the two have rather different distributions. East African Indians are less in evidence outside the south eastern part of England, with relative under-representation in Scotland, the North, Yorkshire and Humberside, the North West, the West Midlands, Wales and the South West. Conversely they are over-represented in the South East, the East Midlands and, to a much lesser extent, in East Anglia – all areas which fared better during the economic upheavals of the 1980s. Table 4.3 pursues these differences at the scale of conurbations, by disaggregating the Indian ethnic total into those Indians with East African connections and those without. It is noteworthy that the aggregate Indian ethnic total (discussed earlier in this chapter) actually masks quite significant differences in the distribution of subcontinental and East African Indians between the conurbations. While both groups have around two thirds of their population within the eight English conurbations, East African Indians are much more heavily concentrated in outer London than their subcontinental counterparts. Conversely subcontinental Indians are found to a much greater relative extent in the West Midlands and West Yorkshire.

The finding that subcontinental Indians and East African Indians do not share identical patterns of geographical distribution is underscored by Figure 4.9 which maps the county level distribution of subcontinental and East African Indians and by Figures 4.10 and 4.11 which locate the 20 main centres of concentration for both groups. It is clear that while East African Indians have their main concentrations in Leicester and parts of North West London (Harrow, Brent, Ealing, Barnet), subcontinental Indians have their main cores in the West Midlands (Birmingham, Wolverhampton, Sandwell and Coventry), London (Ealing, Brent, Newham and Hounslow) and parts of West Yorkshire (Kirklees and Bradford).

Having located the main centres of concentration, Table 4.4 addresses the degree of relative concentration. It reveals that very few East African Indians live in districts where that group forms more than 10 per cent of the total population, compared with almost 36 per cent of the subcontinental Indian group. At the other extreme, while 16 per cent of subcontinental Indians now live in districts where that group forms a smaller percentage of the population than they do nationally (i.e. 1.5 per cent of the total population), the same is true of almost 21 per cent of East African Indians (given that they form 0.4 per cent of Britain's entire population).

Regional differences

The census also allows investigation of whether the Indian population has different characteristics in different parts of the country. These differences could be investigated on a variety of spatial scales, but there is always the problem that finer spatial scales progressively reduce sample sizes to the point where sampling errors become unacceptably large. This section

Figure 4.9 *Net movements, Indian population, 1981-91*

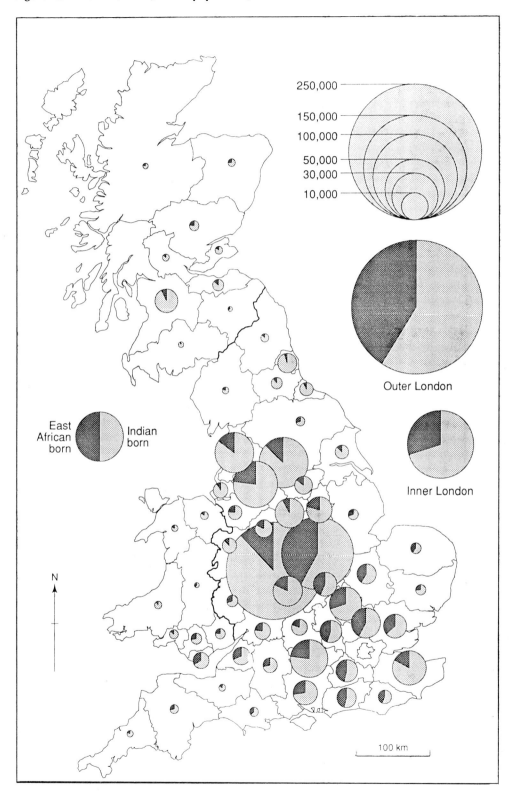

Figure 4.10 *Map of twenty districts with largest number of Indian indians*

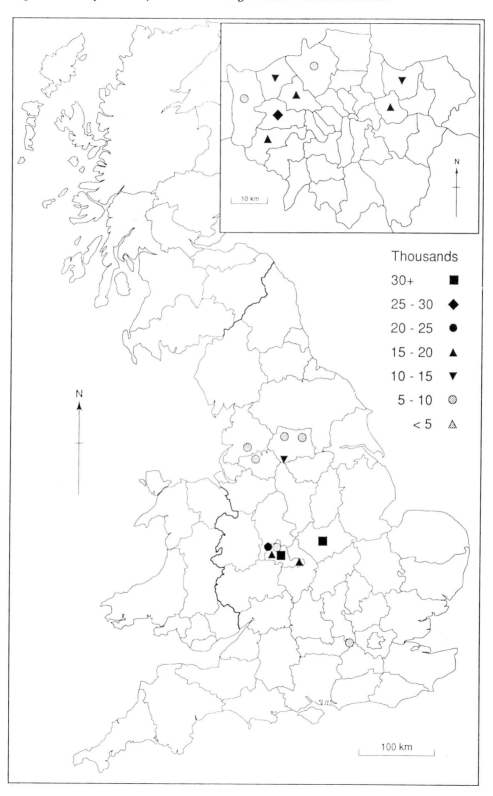

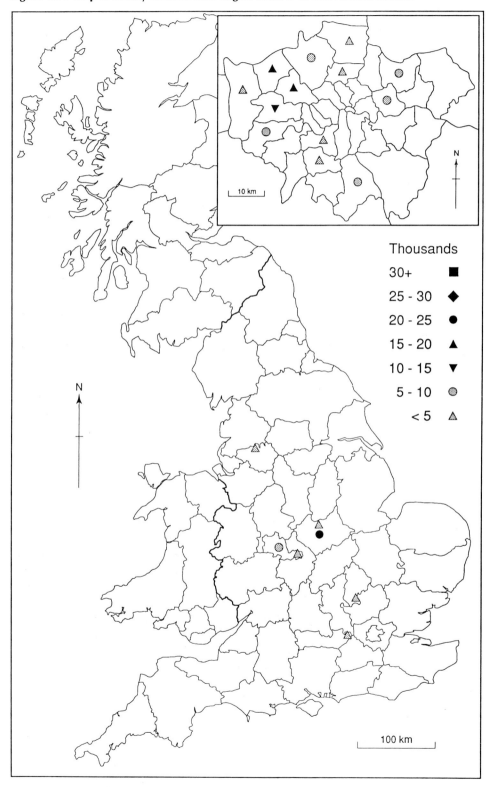

consequently uses county level data, but in some cases particular counties have had to be suppressed or combined where the size of the Indian population was felt to be too small.

Figure 4.12 documents spatial variation within the Indian population in one of the most significant variables, social class. It reveals that there are perhaps seven clusters of counties which have social class profiles that deviate from the national average for Indians, and that these can be divided into two main groups. The first group contains counties with an over-representation of white collar workers. The first cluster within this group has a profile skewed towards professional workers (e.g. Greater Manchester, Merseyside and industrial South Wales); the second has a skew towards both professional workers and those who are employers and managers (e.g. Hereford, non-conurban Scotland and the counties of northern England); the third contains counties skewed towards employers and managers only (e.g. Buckinghamshire, Hertfordshire and the counties of the south west of England); the fourth majors on junior white collar work (e.g. inner and outer London, and Gloucestershire). The second group tends towards manual work. Within this, the first cluster has a skew towards a combination of junior white collar employment and semi-skilled or skilled manual work (e.g. Oxford, Bedfordshire and Wiltshire); the second has a tendency towards skilled and semi-skilled manual employment (e.g. West Midlands, Lancashire and West Yorkshire); and the third tends towards unskilled or semi-skilled work (e.g. Kent and Shropshire).

Parallel analysis of spatial variations in the proportion of the Indian population qualified beyond A-level reinforces the general pattern described above. For example, the counties with an above average percentage of professional workers tend to have around 30 per cent of their population with higher qualifications, while those tending towards junior white collar work have percentages which fall into the mid-teens, and those skewed towards manual work tend towards percentages around or below 10.

This distribution pattern suggests a picture of internal differentiation within Great Britain's Indian population. It suggests that many Indians still fulfil the replacement labour function for which they were originally recruited. They undertake the manual work within manufacturing industry in the major conurbations which had been shunned by Whites in the 1960s. This group are often outright owners of older – and less well specified – properties in places such as the West Midlands, Greater Manchester, the Lancashire mill towns, and the industrial centres of Derbyshire. A second group of Indians is found in locations which have a more diversified and modern economic base (e.g. Oxfordshire, Wiltshire, Northamptonshire, Berkshire and outer London). There, they are either engaged in service work or in more skilled manual employment within the newer, or sunrise, industries. A high percentage tend to be buying a property through a mortgage, and these properties are likely to be better specified (with, for example, central heating) than the national average for the group. Households are also more likely to own a car. A third group is the professionals of the two conurbations of the north west of England, those in the industrial valleys of South Wales and those in Durham. As Anwar and Ali (1987) and Robinson

Figure 4.12 *Social class distribution of Indians, by country*

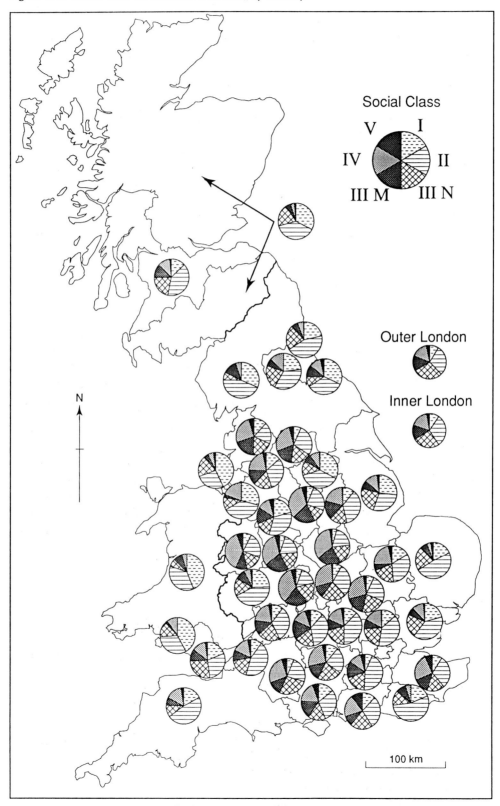

(1988) have shown, this group has as its core, the medical staff of the National Health Service, who are either attracted by the major metropolitan hospitals or have to search out the less desirable lacunae left by White doctors. Medical staff are also important in the fourth grouping, namely those areas which have a preponderance of both professional and managerial employees. The Indian populations in these areas parallel the characteristics of the White population in that they have either engaged in suburbanisation or counter-urbanisation to parallel their social and economic advancement. The Indian populations of rural Wales, rural Scotland, Cheshire, the northern counties of England, Hereford and Stafford thus tend to be purchasers of well-specified properties, have access to cars and to be well qualified. The final group are those Indian communities with an above average percentage of employers and managers, for example those in the counties of south west England and the counties around London. Here again, Indians are following a path well trodden by the White middle class, seeking economic opportunities, economic independence, better housing and a better quality of life.

4.5 Conclusion

Regardless of their present geographical location, many Indians abroad share a set of values, beliefs, aspirations and a clear sense of identity (see Clarke, Peach and Vertovec, 1990 for an international survey). Yet as time passes it is increasingly the diversity within the Indian population of Great Britain that is coming to the fore. The Indian population arrived as a mosaic of groups from different parts of the subcontinent or from East Africa, practising different religions, speaking different languages and drawn from different social and economic backgrounds. Since that time, changes in immigration law, economic restructuring, differential social mobility and the profound impact of locality have ensured that pre-existing differences have been widened as different group fractions drive, or are propelled, along different life trajectories. A concomitant of this is that as fractions head off on divergent paths so the differences which exist between them and their White peers are beginning to narrow.

References

Agyeman, J. (1990) Black people in a white landscape. *Built Environment,* 16,231–6.

Anwar, M. and Ali, A. (1987) *Overseas Doctors; Experience and Expectations.* London: Commission for Racial Equality.

Brown, A. and Fox, J. (1984) Longitudinal Study: ten years on, *Population Trends,* 37: 20–2.

Brown, C. (1984) *Black and White Britain.* London: Heinemann.

Clarke, C., Peach, C. and Vertovec, S. (1990) *South Asians Overseas: Migration and Ethnicity.* Cambridge: Cambridge University Press.

Commission for Racial Equality (1985) Ethnic Minorities in Britain. London: Commission for Racial Equality.

Goering, J. (1993) Reclothing the emperor while avoiding ideological polarisation. *New Community*, 19, 336–47.

Gregory, R. (1993) *South Asians in East Africa*. Oxford: Westview Press.

Helweg, A. (1980) *Sikhs in England*. Delhi: Oxford University Press.

Helweg, A. and Helweg, U. (1990) *An Immigrant Success Story: East Indians in America*. Philadelphia: University of Pennsylvania Press.

Immigrant Statistics Unit (1977) New Commonwealth and Pakistani population estimates. *Population Trends*, 9, 4–7.

Jay, E. (1992) *Keep them in Birmingham*. London: Commission for Racial Equality.

Maan, B. (1992) *The New Scots: Asians in Scotland*. Edinburgh: John Donald.

Marret, V. (1989) *Immigrants Settling in the City*. London: Leicester University Press.

Robinson, V. (1979) *The Segregation of Immigrants in a British City*. Oxford: School of Geography Research Paper 22.

Robinson, V. (1984) Asians in Britain: a study in encapsulation and marginality. In: Clarke, C., Ley D. and Peach C. (eds), *Geography and Ethnic Pluralism*. London: Allen and Unwin.

Robinson, V. (1986) *Transients, Settlers and Refugees:* Asians in Britain. Oxford: Clarendon.

Robinson, V. (1988) The new Indian middle class in Britain. *Ethnic and Racial Studies*, 4, 456–73.

Robinson, V. (1990a) Changing stereotypes of Indians in Britain. *Indo-British Review*, 16, 79–97.

Robinson, V. (1990b) Boom and gloom. The success and failure of Britain's South Asians. In: Clarke, C., Peach, C. and Vertovec, S. (eds), *South Asians Overseas: Migration and Ethnicity*. Cambridge: Cambridge University Press.

Robinson, V. (1990c) Roots to mobility: the social mobility of Britain's black population, 1971–87. *Ethnic and Racial Studies*, 13, 274–86.

Robinson, V. (1991) Move on up; the mobility of Britain's ethnic population. In: Stillwell, J., Rees, P. and Boden, P. (eds), *Migration Patterns and Processes; Population redistribution in the 1980s*. London: Belhaven.

Robinson, V. (1993a) Making waves? The contribution of ethnic minorities to local demography. In: Champion, A. (ed.), *Population Matters: The Local Dimension*. London: Paul Chapman.

Robinson, V. (1993b) The enduring geography of ethnic settlement: first results from the 1991 Census. *Town and Country Planning*, 62, 53–6.

Robinson, V. (1994) The geography of ethnic minorities, 1991. *Geography Review*, 7(4), 10–15.

Robinson, V. (1995) The migration of East African Asians to the UK. In: Cohen, R. (ed.), *The Cambridge World Migration History*. Cambridge: Cambridge University Press.

Rose, E. (1969) *Colour and Citizenship*. London: Oxford University Press.

Smith, D. (1974) *The Facts of Racial Disadvantage*. London: PEP.

Sunday Times (1994) Penniless refugees who moved up to join the millionaires club. May 8, 3.

Tambs-Lyche, H. (1980, *The London Patidars*. London: Routledge Kegan Paul.

Visram, R. (1986) *Ayahs, Lascars and Princes: Indians in Britain*, 1700–1947. London: Pluto Press.

Chapter 5
The Pakistanis: stability and introspection

Roger Ballard

5.1 Introduction

This chapter is primarily concerned with exploring the social and demographic characteristics of those people, 476,555 in total, who identified themselves as Pakistani by ticking the appropriate box in the 1991 Census. But before examining the census data itself, it is worth paying some attention to what the precise significance of the identifier Pakistani might be in the context of contemporary Britain, and also to the extent of the social homogeneity that might be expected among that body of people who so identified themselves. Given that Pakistan is a firmly established nation-state with a current population of more than 100 million, and that the term Pakistani is now in routine use in contemporary English discourse (no less among social scientists than in the everyday vernacular), asking such questions might seem unnecessary, on the grounds that the meaning of this ethnic label is relatively unambiguous. But as a brief historical review soon reveals, this is very far from being the case.

Who are the Pakistanis?

As a national entity, Pakistan only came into existence on 14 August 1947, when the Indian subcontinent was partitioned following independence from British rule. Constituted from (most of) those regions in which the Muslims formed a majority, the new state had two separate wings. West Pakistan, which included the provinces of Sind, Baluchistan, the North-West Frontier and most of Punjab, was geographically the larger, and subsequently the politically and militarily dominant, component of the new state, though East Bengal (separated from the western wing by nearly a thousand miles of Indian territory) was in fact rather more populous. By no means all Indian Muslims became Pakistanis, however. Areas in which Muslims were a minority were not included in the new state, nor indeed were some Muslim majority areas. The most important of these were parts of Hyderabad in the Deccan, and yet more contentiously still, the greater part of Kashmir. Even though the state was contiguous with Pakistan, Kashmir's Hindu ruler decided to accede his entire territory to India rather than to Pakistan.

Partition was also accompanied by a large-scale population exchange, particularly in the west: in Punjab and Sindh virtually all the locally resident Hindus and Sikhs fled to India, while large numbers of Muslim refugees from across the new border replaced them. Yet though Pakistan consequently identified itself as an Islamic homeland for all the subcontinent's Muslims, it does not follow that being a South Asian Muslim and being a

Pakistani are necessarily congruent. Large numbers of Muslims stayed on in India in 1947, and still firmly identify themselves as Indian (as indeed do most of their relatives and descendants who subsequently migrated to Britain, very often by way of East Africa). Nor did Pakistan itself remain united: in 1972 a bloody civil war between the country's eastern and western wings was eventually resolved by second partition, this time between Pakistan and Bangladesh. Those who ticked the box labelled Pakistani in 1991 are therefore those who identify in some way with this much truncated entity.

Beyond this there are further problems about the precise meaning of the term Pakistani when used to identify an ethnic category. While contemporary Pakistan has relatively clear marked external boundaries (except in the case of Kashmir), its population is by no means internally homogeneous. On the contrary regional differences are very substantial, and since 1947 each of its major population components, namely Punjabis, Pathans, Sindhis, Baluchis and Muhajirs (i.e. refugees from India) have all been involved in very vigorous processes of ethnic consolidation. The internal ethnic divisions have now become marked by such severe conflicts that they offer a very serious threat to national unity, and hence to the stability of the Pakistani state (Alavi, 1989).

Pakistanis in Britain

In a British context some of these divisions can, however, be overlooked. Apart from a relatively small number of Pathans, and an even smaller (though socially and politically highly influential) body of Muhajirs, the vast majority of British Pakistanis are of Punjabi descent. Even so, this latter group is far from homogeneous. First, there is a major disjunction between (often well-educated) urbanites from major cities such as Lahore, Sialkot and Faisalabad, and the broad mass of migrants with more rural backgrounds. Second, and in some senses more importantly, there is a further disjunction between those who originate from villages in the prosperous *nehri* (canal-irrigated) regions in the plains of Punjab proper, and those stemming from the less prosperous, and therefore much less economically developed *barani* (rainfall dependent) areas in the Potohar plateau further to the north and west. While the census does not resolve ethnic differences to this level of fineness, my own estimate is that at least two thirds of British Pakistanis are from the Potohar region, and that the great majority of British Potoharis have even more specific origins in the Mirpur district of Azad Kashmir (Ballard, 1983 and 1990).

As was noted earlier, though Kashmir had a Muslim majority, its ruler chose to join his territory to India, not Pakistan. Not only was his decision immediately disputed by Pakistan, but war promptly broke out. Azad Kashmir is a narrow strip of territory adjacent to Pakistan in which the Indian army was unable to enforce its control, and is therefore in principle not part of Pakistan at all, but a fragmentary component of a nominally independent state, albeit one in which all administrative decisions have to be cleared with Islamabad. Until recently such considerations might have wholly arcane, but that is rapidly ceasing to be the case. Although few Mirpuris appear to have taken the opportunity to offer a write-in identification of themselves as Kashmiris in the 1991 Census, an increasing number of Mirpuris, and most especially the rising generation of young people, do now identify themselves as ethnic Kashmiris, and thereby explicitly reject any association with Pakistan.

Does all this matter? Much depends on the analytical perspective one adopts, and on the questions one seeks to answer. To many members of the indigenous majority such issues may seem wholly arcane, on the grounds that any further differentiation beyond the level of 'Pakistani' is of no concern to outsiders. Not surprisingly, however, the insider perspective is quite different: to those who are subsumed under such labels, a refusal to acknowledge either the existence or the significance of internal differentiction is often a source of considerable resentment.

Certainly Pakistanis themselves tend to be acutely conscious of these differences. So, for example, Pathans tend to be most unhappy if misidentified as Punjabis; and Punjabis are just anxious to point out that they are *not* Mirpuris.Mirpuris' growing insistence on being identified as Kashmiris is largely a result of their (well-grounded) belief that Punjabi-dominated Pakistan has given the region a raw deal. Hence they prefer an identification that suggests that they are neither Punjabi nor Pakistani, and which also distances them from the now pejorative label of Mirpuri.

Second, and perhaps even more significantly, the differences to which these arguments point are far more than a matter of mere perception. Given the sharply varying levels of economic development that have been achieved in each of these regions, and that settlers' everyday networks of mutual reciprocity and ethnic solidarity are grounded in the social, religious and cultural specificities of their regions of origin, their trajectories of social, economic and cultural adaptation, and hence the speed and direction of their upward mobility since their arrival in Britain, has varied a great deal from group to group. Had the categories offered in the ethnic group question made space for an expression of these variations, the results could have been used to bring their extent and significance into clearer focus.

But if the data as they stand do not allow these differences to be resolved, it is worth remembering that this is no more than an inevitable consequence of the census methodology. This should also serve to remind us that the social category Pakistani as represented in the data is primarily an artefact of the census procedure itself, and hence that it would be quite wrong to assume that those so categorised form, of necessity, either a real or a homogeneous social group. On the contrary there is plentiful evidence that they do not, however much census procedures may obscure such variations.

Immigration and population growth

The figures themselves show that in 1991 almost exactly 50 per cent of Britain's Pakistani population was locally born. However, it is worth remembering the time depth of the Pakistani presence in Britain is relatively shallow – or to put it another way, the growth of this section of Britain's population has been extraordinarily rapid. The 1961 Census recorded the presence of 24,900 Pakistan-born people, and by 1971 that figure had risen to 127,565. (The figures for 1961 and 1971 include an unknown number of people from East Pakistan who would have identified themselves as Bangladeshi in subsequent censuses.) Come 1981 the number of people living in households with a Pakistan-born head (this was the best available means of estimating the size of Britain's Pakistani population prior to the introduction of a properly formulated ethnic question, see Ballard 1983a) had increased to 285,558, and by 1991 that figure had once again almost doubled to 476,555. Many factors have contributed to this almost exponential pattern of expansion.

While immigration has undoubtedly been one of the most important factors, it is nevertheless worth noting that both the volume and the character of the inflow of Pakistani migrants has varied quite sharply over the years. Prior to the passage of the first Commonwealth Immigration Act in 1961 (a measure whose central purpose was of course to halt the influx of non-European migrants) their entry was virtually uncontrolled. At that stage immigrants from Pakistan, even more than those from India, were almost exclusively male, and the scale of arrival was determined on the one hand by potential migrants' awareness of the possibility of gaining unskilled industrial employment in Britain, and on the other by the extent of those opportunities. Although the inflow from Pakistan consequently declined during periods of economic recession, the demand for unskilled labour in both Midlands engineering companies and the textile mills of Yorkshire and Lancashire (the initial destination of the great majority of Pakistan immigrants) remained high right up until the end of the 1980s, and the inflow never really ceased, despite the passage of increasingly draconian legislation aimed at keeping them out.(Anwar, 1979)

However, after the passage of the first Commonwealth Immigration Act in 1962, the volume and character of Pakistani immigration was increasingly affected by legislative constraints, even if the immediate effects of the new rules were often very different from those which had been expected. So, for example, while the employment voucher system introduced in 1962 was aimed at reducing immigration, the availability of category C vouchers for unskilled workers had the reverse effect, for they actually smoothed the inflow of migrants from rural Pakistan. With hindsight it is easy to see why. While such vouchers could only be issued by employers who were short of labour, most Pakistan immigrants worked in just such contexts. Hence many immediately took the opportunity to obtain vouchers on behalf of kinsmen back home, who promptly made their way to what was effectively a guarantee of employment in Britain.

Largely because of the success with which those involved in chain migration turned the voucher system to their advantage, the scheme was dropped in 1964. Since then adult male labour migrants have been denied free entry to Britain, even if they were Commonwealth citizens. Nevertheless, Britain's Pakistani population has continued to grow very rapidly. Part of this growth came about through illegal immigration, often involving night passages by small boat across the straits of Dover; but although the scale on which this inflow took place is by definition unquantifiable, there is no evidence that it provided anything more than a minor contribution to the rapid rise in numbers. Other factors, and especially a new trend towards family reunion, were far more significant. It is worth remembering that as Commonwealth citizens, Pakistanis became *de facto* British citizens as soon as they had settled in Britain, in sharp contrast to non-Commonwealth aliens, and indeed to the experience of Turkish *Gastarbeiters* in Germany and North African *étrangers* in France, whose experience of migration was otherwise very similar. In addition to gaining some important civil rights, notably the right to vote, from our perspective one of the most important consequences of Commonwealth citizenship was that it offered migrants the right to reunite their families in Britain as and when they chose.

In the longer term, virtually all Pakistani settlers sought to exercise that right, so much so that from the mid-1970s onwards family reunion began to become increasingly commonplace. Even so there was a substantial period after the abolition of the voucher system during which Pakistanis tended to use this provision not so much to reunite their families as a whole, but instead to facilitate a further inflow of male workers. The way in which they achieved this goal is most instructive.

Pakistani responses to immigration control

As already mentioned, during the early period of settlement the Pakistani (and most especially the Mirpuri) presence in Britain was overwhelmingly male. If married – as most were – migrants normally left their wives and children back at home in rural Pakistan. Because their principal objective was to earn and save money to invest in land and housing back home, and as they had no expectation that their wives could or should contribute to the process of capital accumulation, there was no point in bringing them over to Britain, even if they did have the right to do so. Yet though the imposition of ever tighter immigration restrictions nominally brought further adult male migration to an end, careful manipulation of the option for family reunion (British resident fathers could bring their sons over to join them in Britain in their early teens) enabled them largely to circumvent the object of the new rules. This strategy was further facilitated by the fact that wages in the textile industry were only marginally linked to age; thus teenage sons (and sometimes even brother's sons, whom it was easy to pass off as one's own) could expect to earn a full adult income within a year or two of their arrival. Hence just as with the voucher system, the new restrictions had a relatively limited impact on the scale of the inflow of male labour migrants from Pakistan.

However sensible and indeed advantageous this inflow may have seemed from the settlers' perspective, the immigration authorities' perception was quite different: to them such behaviour appeared to be thoroughly reprehensible, and the migrants to be taking advantage of a loophole in the law. Hence in the early seventies the rules were changed once again, such that those seeking to reunite their families were required to bring over all their dependants, rather than just their near adult sons. Yet if the object was to further restrict immigration, its effect was once again largely counterproductive, for instead of leaving everyone back in Pakistan, most settlers began to bring over their wives and daughters as well as their sons. However, this did not necessarily mean that they all became permanent residents: at least some wives (and even more daughters) were sent back to Pakistan once the authorities appeared to have been satisfied.

At the same time other more fundamental changes were also taking place. Pakistani settlements were growing steadily larger and more secure, and as a result most of the migrants' more important social and cultural institutions began to be reproduced within them (for a fuller account see Ballard, 1994, Shaw 1988 and Werbner 1991). As ethnic colonisation grew more active, Britain (or rather the small areas in which Pakistanis had chosen to settle) became a steadily less alien place, and hence settlers' fears that their wives and daughters would be morally corrupted by exposure to English ways if they took up the option of family reunion began to carry less and less force. And that was not all. By this time stories about some men's involvement with English women had begun to circulate back in Pakistan, leading many wives to conclude (often with good reason) that it was their husbands who needed protection from moral corruption. Moreover the remedy was obvious: to take a flight to Heathrow at the earliest possible opportunity. Hence during the 1970s there was a marked shift towards comprehensive family reunion, often led by the women themselves.

Since each male settler was usually joined by a number of children in addition to his wife, the shift towards family reunion further increased the total migrant inflow, sharpening yet further the intensity of popular demands to reduce the scale of the inflow. The result has been a complicated game of cat and mouse. While their British citizenship meant that male settlers' rights to reunite their families could not be gainsaid, all sorts of administrative obstacles which hindered their ability to exercise those rights began to be introduced, and by the late 1970s lengthy queues had developed at each of the many stages in the process of gaining leave to enter. Yet although this was an effective way of reducing the headline figures in the short term, it did not prevent the eventual arrival of persistent applicants, especially when they took their cases to the courts. Thus while the process of family reunion took much longer to complete among the Pakistanis than it had among the Indians (see Ballard, 1983b and 1990), by 1991 the overwhelming majority of families had been reunited.

Even so this has not brought further immigration to a complete halt; the reasons are instructive. As in the rest of South Asia, Pakistani marriages are normally arranged, most usually by the couple's parents; but in northern Pakistan, and most especially in Mirpur, close kin marriage, particularly between cousins, is also much preferred. This preference is continuing to have a substantial effect on the migratory process. While settlement overseas has divided many *biraderis* (extended Kinship groups), close kin marriage provides an excellent means of bridging the gap, while also facilitating further entry into Britain. Hence British-based parents, and especially those from Mirpur, still routinely receive offers of marriage for both their sons and their daughters from Pakistan-based kin, and often feel honour bound to accept them. And although large obstacles have now been placed in their path, (for example, such couples are now required to demonstrate that the marriage was not contracted with the 'primary purpose' of entering Britain), many still succeed in gaining entry.

5.2 Social and economic characteristics

Fertility and population growth

Other than immigration, the second, and currently far more significant, source of British Pakistani population growth is their relatively high fertility rate. Fertility rates in rural Pakistan are among the highest in the world, and Mirpur is no exception; even though they often had to endure long periods of separation from their husbands during the early phase of settlement, Mirpuri women's fertility was not significantly reduced. Prior to the reunion of their families, most Mirpuri men acted as inter-continental commuters, regularly returning home on extended holidays which could last for a year or more before returning to another spell of work in Britain. Nor did subsequent reunion in Britain lead to a decline in fertility. Older women rejoining their husbands often produced more children soon after their arrival, while the arrival of a new generation of women married to their British-born cousins means that many mothers continue to approach fertility within the context of a mind-set which suggests that the birth of additional children – and especially male children – is by definition an asset to the family.

In these circumstances it is hardly surprising that the second generation of Pakistani mothers (the daughters and daughters-in-law of the original generation of settlers who are now reaching the childbearing age) also tend to raise large families, if not necessarily quite so large as those of their mothers. And thus though the mean fertility of the Pakistani population is dropping steadily, it could be argued that it will not be until the majority of Pakistani mothers are British-born that their fertility rate will begin to approach the average for the population as a whole.

The age profile of Britain's Pakistani population

Since raw statistics need to be read in context if they are to be properly interpreted, there is good reason to suppose that it will be difficult, if not impossible, to make much sense of the ethnic dimensions of the census in the absence of a broad qualitative awareness of the basic features of the population itself. Nowhere is this more obvious than with respect to the current distribution of British Pakistanis across the age spectrum, which is manifestly an essential starting point in any assessment of the demographic character of this section of the British population, let alone its likely pattern of future growth.

As Figure 5.1 shows, and Figure 5.2 confirms, not only has the gender imbalance of Britain's Pakistani population now virtually disappeared, but both its male and female components exhibit a very sharp skew across the age spectrum. Hence the number (and even more so the proportion) of Pakistanis who have reached retirement age remains very small, while the two school-age cohorts are very much larger than any other. This is, of course, very much the pattern that would be expected in a population of relatively recent migrants with a high fertility rate.

Nevertheless there are several features in Figure 5.1 that deserve further comment. First of all, the age skew is far from smooth, for it includes some marked population peaks: among men in their fifties, those in their thirties, and finally among schoolchildren, with more or less clearly marked troughs between them. Given the earlier discussion, this pattern can best be explained as a consequence of the impact of immigration control. The peak of men currently in their fifties is primarily composed of those who made their way to Britain as young adults in the period immediately before entry was seriously restricted in the mid-1960s, 30 years ago. In like manner the trough of among men currently in their forties provides an indication that immigration control was at least partly successful: when men in these two age cohorts reached their twenties, the obstacles to entry were substantially greater than those encountered by men a few years older than themselves.

Figure 5.1 *Age profile of Pakistani men by place of birth, Great Britain, 1991*

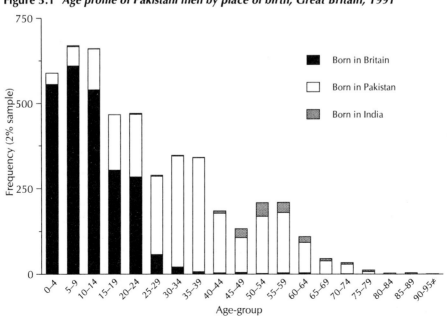

Source: 2% SARs

Figure 5.2 *Age profile of Pakistani women by marital status, Great Britain, 1991*

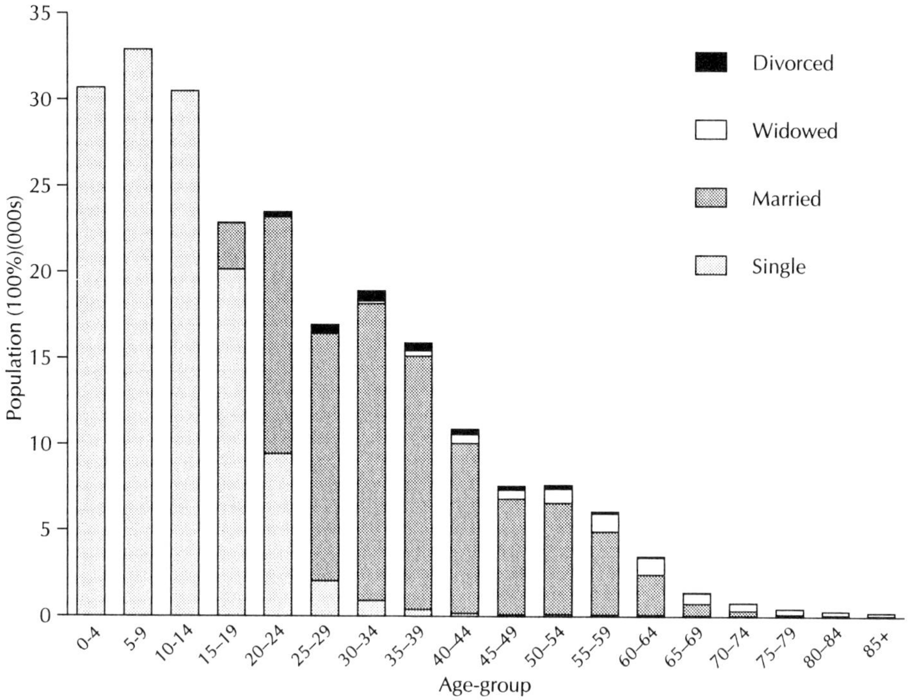

Source: OPCS/GRO(S) 1993, Volume 2, Table 6

However, the peak of men aged between 30 and 39 in 1991, itself substantially greater than the peak of men in their fifties, provides a clear indication that the new restrictions had only a temporary impact on the scale of the inflow. Since virtually everyone in this age cohort was born in Pakistan, there can be little doubt that it is overwhelmingly composed of the sons of the men who make up the earlier peak, and who entered Britain in their early teens as their fathers' dependants. This peak is followed by a rather shallower dip, a generation later than the dip amongst the 45-49-year-olds, and is followed by a further peak in the two school-age-groups. However, by now the peak has begun to broaden very considerably, which is much as one would expect since the offspring of any one father are likely to be born across a period of at least 10 years. Finally it is worth noting that among the youngest age cohorts the vast majority of children are British-born.

A second very obvious feature of the pattern in Figure 5.1 is the steady growth in the height of successive peaks, such that each is approximately double the height of its predecessor. This pattern is a clear indication of the Pakistanis' high level of fertility, such that to date their birth rate has been running at approximately double replacement level. Whether this will be sustained, or whether fertility rates will fall to levels closer to the average for Britain as a whole is a crucial issue for the future. While the slight fall in the size of the very youngest age cohort is manifestly a significant development, it would nevertheless be unwise to jump to the conclusion that this is anything more than another temporary dip without very careful scrutiny of the demographic characteristics of the population that will produce such children – Pakistani women.

As Figure 5.2 shows, while the pattern of Pakistani women's distribution across the age spectrum is broadly congruent with that for men, in their case the pattern of peaks and troughs is a good deal less clearly marked. Once again qualitative considerations can help in understanding why this should be so. Although Pakistani men have tended (like most others) to marry wives a few years younger than themselves, the width of that gap can vary a great deal; and because immigration restrictions were directed largely at men, this has led to a smoothing of the pattern of peaks and troughs among Pakistani women. While birthplace patterns vary little by gender, and hence have not been shown in Figure 5.2, what has been highlighted instead is the issue of marital status. Here, once again, some important trends can be detected. First of all, in comparison with the indigenous majority, Pakistani women not only marry relatively early, but rarely remain unmarried beyond the age of 30, while divorce is still extremely rare. However, comparison with the British majority is by no means necessarily the most appropriate yardstick, especially when looking at change: comparison with the situation in rural Pakistan may well be the more revealing measure. In this respect some further important differences can be detected. While marriage is just as popular and divorce just as rare in Pakistan, the age at which marriage is contracted is rising in Britain. Thus while the great majority of women in rural Pakistan marry before they reach the age of 20, in Britain a substantial number of women in the 20-24 age-group are still unmarried. This suggests that in the British context, marriage is beginning to be delayed, a trend which may well be further reinforced in future.

While such a prospect is as yet little more than a straw in the wind, it makes a good deal of intuitive sense as well as being congruent with ethnographic experience. Even so it is still too early to say whether such changes are the principal cause of the current slight dip in the size of the very youngest age cohort (and hence a harbinger of impending demographic stability) or whether this is nothing but a temporary trough. A number of other factors can provide an equally plausible explanation of the current pattern. First, the downward blip could be an aspect of the wave effect which has already been noted, as the number of women in the most fertile age cohort, the 25-29-year-olds, is itself in temporary decline. Second, the current blip could be the result of *delayed*, rather than reduced fertility: it is only in the last few years that a British-raised generation of Pakistani women, most of whom will also have married rather later than their Pakistan-raised counterparts, have come on stream as mothers. Last but not least it could reflect a real and substantial decline in Pakistani women's preferred completed family size. Much more data will be required before it becomes possible confidently to disentangle the relative impact of each of these factors.

What is undeniable, however, is that the number of Pakistani women reaching childbearing age will continue to rise quite substantially for at least a decade; and that even if their level of fertility was to drop to no more than a replacement level (which is the most that can reasonably be expected), there is every reason to expect that future Pakistani five-year age cohorts will be at least 30,000 strong for both males and females. Assuming an average life expectancy of 80 years, this suggests that if everything else were to remain equal, Britain's Pakistani population could be expected eventually to stabilise at around one million, or more than double its present size.

One further dimension of Figure 5.1 deserves some comment, namely the patterns of birthplaces that it reveals. First while British-born Pakistanis only begin to make their presence felt in the 25-29 age cohort, they become a clear majority among the 20-24-year-olds, reflecting the rapid development of family reunion from the early 1970s onwards. Second, it is worth noting that while only a very small minority of those who identified themselves as Pakistanis indicated that their birthplace was in India, those who did so were almost all over the age of 45. Again this is very much as might be expected, because almost all such persons would have belonged to families that fled to Pakistan as a result of Partition in 1947. Finally while 13,225 Pakistanis indicated that their birthplace was in India, a further 6,089 indicated an East African connection. This latter figure is also most instructive, because no less than 142,702 East African-born people identified themselves as ethnic Indians. Although the majority of East African Asians were either Hindu or Sikh, the Muslims undoubtedly made up a good deal more than 1 per cent of that population. Hence it would appear that most of South Asian Muslims with East African roots chose to identify themselves as Indians rather than Pakistanis in 1991. Given that the great majority of East African Asian Muslims originally migrated from India's Gujarat province, it follows that in their case at least historical regional origins rather than religion was the prime determinant of their choice of a categorical ethnic identifier.

5.3 Geographical distribution

Over and above its very uneven distribution across the age spectrum, the regional distribution of Britain's Pakistani population is also far from uniform. Again this is very much to be expected: like all the other visible minorities, Pakistanis came to fill a series of gaps in Britain's labour market, which were heavily concentrated in those towns and cities which benefited from the post-war industrial boom. Hence relatively few settled either in rural areas, or in those cities, such as Liverpool, Newcastle and Glasgow, which were largely bypassed by economic growth. But though post-war migrants were consequently concentrated in and around London, and the cities of the industrial Midlands and the textile towns of the Pennine region, inter-ethnic variations between the minorities were, and remain, considerable.

As Figure 5.3 shows, while the distribution of Britain's Pakistani population broadly conforms to this pattern, its members are nevertheless particularly heavily concentrated in the West Midlands, West Yorkshire and Greater Manchester regions, and to a rather lesser extent in outer London and the south east; elsewhere their presence is almost negligible. But as Figure 5.4 shows, while the Indians and Bangladeshis have also congregated in the same areas, the proportional scale of their presence varies a great deal from region to region. Thus while the Bangladeshis are particularly heavily concentrated in inner London, the Indians predominate in outer London, the East and West Midlands and in south east England; by contrast the Pakistani population comes to the fore in West Yorkshire, Greater Manchester, Lancashire and Scotland.

Figure 5.3 *Regional distribution of the Pakistani population, Great Britain, 1991*

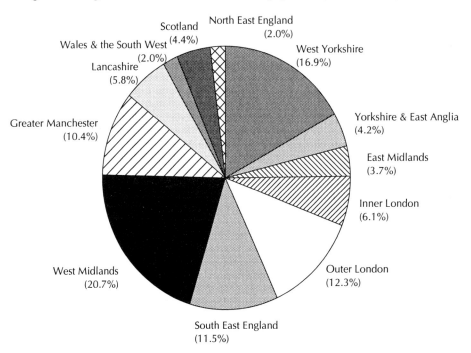

Figure 5.4 *Regional distribution of South Asian population, Great Britain, 1991*

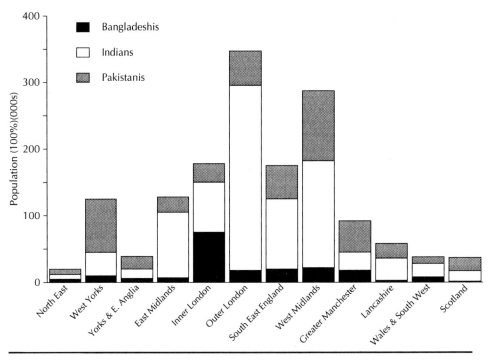

Although the census data alone provides no explanation for these differential spatial distributions, a knowledge of the process of South Asian settlement in Britain, together with an awareness of the social and economic objectives, and above all the differential distribution of skills, between different subsections of the South Asian population enables a good deal of light to be thrown on these variations. As argued elsewhere (Ballard, 1982 and 1990), immigrants from India tended to have better educational qualifications, a greater knowledge of English, more immediately marketable skills and a considerably greater commitment to upward social mobility in their new context than did most of those arriving from Pakistan and Bangladesh. This was not because the Pakistanis and Bangladeshis were more intrinsically 'backward' than the Indians, but rather a consequence of the restricted level of economic development in Mirpur and Sylhet Districts, most especially as compared with Punjaband Gujarat, two of India's most prosperous regions. These differences had a far-reaching impact on patterns of settlement in Britain.

Above all the inflow from India contained a substantially larger leaven of professionally qualified people than did that from either Pakistan or Bangladesh. Moreover this tendency was further reinforced by the inflow from East Africa. Not only do most East African Asians identify themselves as Indian, but they were also particularly likely to be professionally qualified or commercially experienced. Such migrants were particularly likely to settle in and around London, not least because the more cosmopolitan character of the job market in the capital offered better chances of gaining professional employment. Meanwhile the Indians of more rural origins (in fact the vast majority) tended to find their way into semi-skilled (but often physically demanding) manual jobs, many of which were located either in the industrialised suburbs of west London, or in the cities of the East and West Midlands. While at least some Pakistanis and Bangladeshis sought out much the same jobs, most tended to set their sights rather lower down the market, partly because of their lack of skills and experience, but also because they were often prepared to take jobs with relatively low hourly rates, but where the weekly wages of those who worked long hours of overtime, most usually on the night shift, were often quite respectable. Hence Pakistanis congregated in particularly large numbers in the textile towns of West Yorkshire, Greater Manchester and Lancashire, which the Indians for the most part avoided. Prior to the collapse of the textile industry, the Bangladeshi presence in the Pennine region was considerably more substantial than it is today. However, given that the community had a substantial base in Tower Hamlets, many Bangladeshis moved down to London during the 1980s. Housing was exceedingly difficult to find, but employment was much more readily available than in the north.

Patterns of industrial employment

For the reasons outlined above, most Pakistani settlers initially found employment either in the textile industry or in the heavy engineering sector; and because the demand for their labour in this sector of the employment market appeared to be stable, and the jobs available provided a reasonable weekly income, albeit in return for working long and very anti-social hours, migrants might change employers, but rarely sought work in any other sector of the employment market. However, during the early eighties Britain's employment market suffered a radical change, and nowhere was the shake out more intense than in the long established, labour intensive, and generally under-capitalised industries in which the Pakistanis were almost exclusively employed. In addition to motor manufacturing in the Midlands, the textile industry in Yorkshire and Lancashire was particularly hard hit. In the short period between 1979 and 1982 the majority of mills in the Pennine region closed, and the few that did stay in business were only able to do so by installing new and much less labour intensive machinery. As the total number of jobs available in the textile industry plummeted, workers who were unskilled, on the night shift, and especially those who had taken an extended holiday in Pakistan expecting to be re-employed on their return (as they always had been hitherto) were acutely vulnerable to redundancy. Moreover their prospect of finding alternative industrial employment was necessarily remote. It is against that backdrop that the employment and occupational patterns of economically active Pakistanis revealed by the 1991 Census need to be understood. Perhaps the most striking aspect of Table 5.1 is the extent to which Pakistani men have retreated from work in the manufacturing sectors in which they had previously been overwhelmingly concentrated. With the exception of the very oldest age-group, only 30 per cent of Pakistanis are now active in this sector of the labour market. Instead they have found alternative employment in the service sector, and most particularly in the distribution, catering and transport sector; by contrast their participation in other industrial sectors is close to minimal.

Table 5.1   *Industrial distribution of employed and self-employed Pakistani men (10% sample)*

	18–29		30–44		45–59		60–64	
	Per–sons	% of age group	Per–sons	% of age group	Per–sons	% of age group	Per–sons	%of age group
Metal manufacturing	223	10.7	336	11.5	183	12.3	24	15.9
Other manufacturing	390	18.7	543	18.5	275	18.5	38	25.2
Banking and finance	176	8.4	200	6.8	106	7.1	9	6.0
Other services	183	8.8	278	9.5	188	12.6	13	8.6
Distribution and catering	712	34.1	799	27.3	365	24.5	33	21.9
Transport	235	11.2	531	18.1	241	16.2	21	13.9
Construction	37	1.8	46	1.6	25	1.7	2	1.3
Agriculture and fishing	1	0.0	0	0.0	2	0.1	1	0.7
Energy and water	7	0.3	15	0.5	6	0.4	0	0.0
Mining	55	2.6	98	3.3	63	4.2	7	4.6

Source: OPCS/GRO(S) (1993) Ethnic Group and Country of Birth Report, Volume 2, Table 14.

Some form of comparison is obviously essential in order to assess the extent to which these patterns are ethnically specific, so while Table 5.2 has the same basic format as Table 5.1, it also includes data about the White majority and the two other South Asian groups. Against that background it becomes apparent that despite the extent of Pakistani men's retreat from the earlier condition of overwhelming involvement in manufacturing, they are still slightly over-represented in this sector compared with the White majority and indeed with their Indian and Bangladeshi compatriots. However, they are strikingly over-represented in distribution and catering compared with the White majority (though not with the Bangladeshis), and equally strikingly under-represented in the construction, agriculture and energy sectors.

It is also worth considering what the census can reveal about patterns of employment among Pakistani women, though in considering the figures it should be remembered that the census is notoriously poor at identifying activities in the domestic sector, in which women's contribution to economic activity tends to be heavily concentrated. Hence while Table 5.3 highlights the industrial sectors in which Pakistani women are active, a comparison with Table 5.1 shows that a large proportion of Pakistani women are classified as inactive (or in other words as being primarily domestically engaged). However, it is also worth emphasising that apart from regular domestic tasks, many Pakistani women are involved in home working, most usually by stitching up clothing for local manufacturers. Such activities seem rarely to have been recorded in census returns. Nevertheless Table 5.3 also shows that there is a strong trend towards extra-domestic employment among younger Pakistani women. However an examination of Table 5.4 suggests that their distribution between the various industrial sectors is less ethnically distinctive than among Pakistani men, and that their activities are thus quite closely congruent with those of the majority.

Table 5.2 *Percentage distribution between industrial sectors of White, Pakistani, Indian and Bangladeshi men*

	18–29				30–44				45–59			
	White	Paki–stani	Indian	Bang–ladeshi	White	Paki–stani	Indian	Bang–ladeshi	White	Paki–stani	Indian	Bang–ladeshi
Metal manufacturing	12.4	10.7	12.3	1.4	12.7	11.5	16.1	1.0	14.2	12.3	13.6	7.4
Other manufacturing	9.8	18.7	12.2	8.3	8.8	18.5	13.1	12.2	9.4	18.5	10.6	14.5
Banking and finance	12.1	8.4	14.2	3.5	11.7	6.8	9.1	4.9	9.7	7.1	8.3	6.7
Other services	15.7	8.8	11.2	5.3	20.0	9.5	11.9	9.9	18.9	12.6	20.0	14.7
Distribution and catering	20.6	34.1	32.2	75.6	14.9	27.3	29.2	66.1	14.4	24.5	25.2	45.8
Transport	7.2	11.2	9.2	1.0	9.3	18.1	10.3	1.9	9.8	16.2	12.5	5.8
Construction	13.5	1.8	3.9	0.6	12.1	1.6	4.9	0.3	12.1	1.7	3.9	0.7
Agriculture and fishing	2.6	0.0	0.1	0.0	2.3	0.0	0.1	0.0	3.0	0.1	0.1	0.0
Energy and water	2.1	0.3	0.5	0.5	3.5	0.5	0.7	0.1	3.1	0.4	0.8	0.2
Mining	3.2	2.6	2.2	0.0	4.0	3.3	3.1	0.4	4.4	4.2	3.1	1.1

Source: OPCS/GRO(S) (1993) Volume 2, Table 14.

Table 5.3 *Industrial distribution of employed and self-employed Pakistani women (10% sample)*

	18–29		30–44		45–59		60–64	
	Persons	% of age group	Persons	% of age group	Persons	% of age group	Persons	% of age group
Metal manufacturing	39	3.5	29	4.3	19	6.9	1	10.0
Other manufacturing	218	19.7	95	14.2	44	16.0	1	10.0
Banking and finance	164	14.8	59	8.8	8	2.9	1	10.0
Other services	279	25.2	218	32.5	93	33.8	4	40.0
Distribution and catering	292	26.4	203	30.3	84	30.5	3	30.0
Transport	48	4.3	28	4.2	15	5.5	0	0.0
Construction	3	0.3	3	0.4	0	0.0	0	0.0
Agriculture and ishing	4	0.4	4	0.6	1	0.4	0	0.0
Energy and water	7	0.6	1	0.1	1	0.4	0	0.0
Mining	13	1.2	4	0.6	1	0.4	0	0.0

Source: OPCS/GRO(S) (1993) Volume 2, Table 14.

Table 5.4 *Percentage distribution between industrial sectors of White, Pakistani, Indian and Bangladeshi women*

	18–29				30–44				45–59			
	White	Pakistani	Indian	Bangladeshi	White	Pakistani	Indian	Bangladeshi	White	Pakistani	Indian	Bangladeshi
Metal manufacturing	5.1	3.5	5.1	0.5	3.9	4.3	8.2	5.6	4.5	6.9	9.5	9.6
Other manufacturing	8.7	19.7	12.9	22.9	7.1	14.2	20.3	12.1	7.7	16.0	23.4	7.7
Banking and finance	18.7	14.8	19.8	9.3	12.8	8.8	9.0	7.3	9.0	2.9	4.7	1.9
Other services	33.3	25.2	26.1	29.4	44.5	32.5	25.3	39.5	46.1	33.8	30.4	61.5
Distribution and catering	24.4	26.4	25.1	28.0	23.2	30.3	28.1	25.0	24.2	30.5	23.3	13.5
Transport	4.1	4.3	6.1	1.9	3.0	4.2	4.5	0.8	2.6	5.5	3.1	1.9
Construction	1.5	0.3	0.8	0.9	1.6	0.4	0.6	0.8	1.6	0.0	0.3	0.0
Agriculture and fishing	0.5	0.4	0.1	0.0	0.9	0.6	0.2	0.0	1.3	0.4	0.6	1.9
Energy and water	1.0	0.6	0.8	0.0	0.8	0.1	0.4	0.0	0.7	0.4	0.5	0.0
Mining	1.9	1.2	1.2	0.0	1.5	0.6	1.7	0.8	1.5	0.4	2.0	0.0

Source: OPCS/GRO(S) (1993) Volume 2, Table 14.

Occupational distributions

Further insights into the Pakistanis' position in the employment market can be gained from an examination of their occupational distributions, with the further benefit that the routinely published census data also provides information on levels of employment and unemployment. Leaving aside the latter issue for the moment, the figures in Table 5.5 not only provide further confirmation of Pakistani men's retreat from industrial employment, but also offer information on the alternative activities into which they have moved, such as sales and services and driving. There has also been a small but highly significant move into technical occupations and office work among younger men.

Table 5.5   Occupational distribution of employed status of economically active Pakistani men

	18–29			30–44			45–59		
	Per–sons	% of age group	% unem–ployed	Per–sons	% of age group	% unem–ployed	Per–sons	% of age group	% unem–ployed
Professionals	144	5.4	4.2	212	5.8	5.7	107	5.5	3.7
Teachers	8	0.3	25.0	30	0.8	3.3	25	1.3	8.0
Technicians	112	4.2	17.0	108	2.9	12.0	62	3.2	22.6
Office workers	220	8.2	18.2	160	4.4	15.0	115	6.0	13.0
Skilled craftsmen	340	12.6	19.4	518	14.1	24.1	247	12.8	27.1
Sales and services	464	17.2	22.8	332	9.1	17.8	129	6.7	18.6
Industrial workers	435	16.2	27.1	700	19.1	29.1	394	20.4	30.7
Drivers	177	6.6	10.7	528	14.4	12.5	197	10.2	17.8
Other	336	12.5	28.3	344	9.4	29.1	239	12.4	32.2
On a government scheme	94	3.5	0.0	68	1.9	0.0	33	1.7	0.0

Source: OPCS/GRO(S) (1993) Volume 2, Table 15.

Looking next at levels of unemployment, it is clear that these are particularly high among those still committed to the industrial occupations in which Pakistani settlers initially specialised, but a good deal lower in their 'new' occupations of driving, and sales and services. They are higher among both skilled craftsmen and (semi- and unskilled) industrial workers right across the age spectrum.

Taking a comparative perspective, Table 5.6 shows that while rates of unemployment among Pakistanis in virtually all occupational sectors are substantially higher than among White workers, there is a good deal of variation among the South Asians. While Bangladeshis appear to be experiencing very similar difficulties to the Pakistanis, the Indians' position is very much closer to that of the White majority.

While an exploration of the sources of this inter-ethnic variation among South Asians is beyond the scope of this chapter, it is nevertheless worth emphasising that although high levels of unemployment do indeed point to the very real difficulties that South Asians are encountering in the employment market, it is by no means necessarily the case that their condition can be straightforwardly understood as one of failure and deprivation. It is instructive to note that rates of unemployment are lowest in both absolute and relative terms in precisely those occupational sectors which offer the best prospects either of self-employment or of working in a small family business. Thus it could well be that the greater difficulties in which Pakistanis and Bangladeshis appear to find themselves arise not so much because they encounter a more intense level of exclusionism, but rather because they have not yet honed up the entrepreneurial skills needed to counter exclusionism quite as effectively as have their Indian peers.

Because the categories which OPCS routinely uses to classify patterns of employment are much better attuned to identify the differential experience

Table 5.6 *Percentage unemployed by occupation and ethnicity of White, Pakistani, Indian and Bangladeshi men*

	18–29				30–44				45–59			
	White	Paki–stani	Indian	Bang–ladeshi	White	Paki–stani	Indian	Bang–ladeshi	White	Paki–stani	Indian	Bang–ladeshi
Professionals	3.1	4.2	4.5	16.0	2.2	5.7	3.0	4.2	3.0	3.7	3.0	6.1
Teachers	5.1	25.0	3.6	0.0	1.6	3.3	5.1	0.0	2.3	8.0	4.8	25.0
Technicians	6.3	17.0	7.3	11.1	4.5	12.0	5.6	18.2	5.2	22.6	8.7	0.0
Office workers	8.8	18.2	11.2	18.5	6.8	15.0	8.6	16.0	7.3	13.0	10.7	22.2
Skilled craftsmen	12.9	19.4	14.4	33.0	9.2	24.1	11.6	48.6	8.8	27.1	13.8	55.8
Sales and services	11.4	22.8	12.1	11.6	6.9	17.8	10.4	19.9	6.8	18.6	7.2	39.7
Industrial workers	15.1	27.1	19.4	20.0	8.7	29.1	10.9	38.1	8.4	30.7	15.1	46.6
Drivers	12.5	10.7	12.2	50.0	9.7	12.5	10.2	37.5	8.1	17.8	9.9	45.5
Other	24.9	28.3	15.8	23.4	17.7	29.1	15.2	29.4	13.7	32.2	10.4	49.1
On a govt scheme	0.0	0.0	0.0	0.0	0.0	0.0	0.0	0.0	0.0	0.0	0.0	0.0

Source: OPCS/GRO(S) (1993) Volume 2, Table 15.

of those who work for others rather than those who are self-employed, and are particularly poor at providing information about those who are self-employed, but not in a professional occupation of some kind, it follows that the census data will not necessarily be structured in such a way as to make it easy to explore the extent to which the South Asian minorities are using such entrepreneurial routes to upward mobility. That said, the figures in Table 5.7, in which those socio-economic categories involving self-employment are highlighted, are most instructive because they very clearly indicate the extent to which South Asians in general, and the Pakistanis in particular, appear to be following this route towards upward mobility. Of course, self-employment covers a very wide range of occupations and statuses, and it is clear that within that broad pattern the Indians are particularly heavily represented among what is in all probability the most prosperous area as self-employed professionals. Even so the Pakistanis are also manifestly pressing forward in this area, for the proportion so employed is not far behind the figure for the White majority. Where all the South Asian groups are well ahead of the White majority is as small-scale employers, and where the Pakistanis stand out among South Asians is in the sphere of non-professional self-employment: taxi driving would be a typical example of an occupation in this category.

Looking at the remainder of the table, it is clear, once again, that the Indians have been fairly successful in moving into professional and managerial roles (though their success in this area is not nearly as dramatic as it is in their move into self-employment), and that though the Pakistanis lag some way behind, their proportionate presence in most of these areas is broadly akin to that among the indigenous majority. One further point worth making with respect to the Bangladeshis is that the high frequency of those classified as personal service workers on the one hand, and as small-scale employers on the other, is almost certainly a reflection of their extensive involvement in the restaurant trade.

Table 5.7 Percentage distribution between socio-economic groups by age and ethnicity for men

	18–29				30–44				45–59			
	White	Paki–stani	Indian	Bang–ladeshi	White	Paki–stani	Indian	Bang–ladeshi	White	Paki–stani	Indian	Bang–ladeshi
Employer (large scale)	0.0	0.0	0.1	0.0	0.0	0.0	0.2	0.1	0.1	0.2	0.1	0.0
Self-employed professional	0.3	0.2	1.2	0.0	1.8	1.4	3.6	1.0	1.9	3.3	6.0	4.0
Employer (small scale)	1.4	5.0	4.4	9.2	4.4	10.3	8.5	21.2	5.0	10.9	7.9	17.2
Non-professional self-employed	7.5	11.7	8.2	2.4	9.9	17.9	13.4	6.1	10.3	14.6	12.1	6.3
Total self-employed	**9.2**	**17.0**	**14.0**	**11.6**	**16.1**	**29.6**	**25.6**	**28.5**	**17.3**	**29.0**	**26.0**	**27.5**
Manager (large scale)	3.3	1.5	2.4	0.5	7.9	1.9	3.4	1.3	8.0	2.0	3.3	1.8
Employed professional	5.5	6.3	9.9	2.8	6.4	5.3	8.4	2.7	5.3	4.0	8.8	6.5
Manager (small scale)	6.7	5.7	7.6	3.4	10.8	5.5	7.7	7.2	10.1	5.3	7.1	5.4
Semi-professionals	8.8	4.7	8.3	2.5	10.7	4.0	6.2	4.5	8.7	4.2	6.9	3.8
Supervisors	2.4	1.6	2.1	0.6	4.3	1.8	2.8	0.4	4.8	2.6	2.7	0.0
Junior non-manual	13.8	15.9	19.5	5.4	7.3	6.9	7.8	3.6	6.2	6.5	9.1	5.4
Personal service workers	2.5	3.7	1.8	56.6	0.8	1.8	1.0	34.3	0.6	1.0	0.7	17.4
Skilled manual workers	24.3	15.6	15.1	2.7	19.3	18.8	17.3	3.7	20.0	18.1	14.4	6.9
Semi-skilled manual workers	13.2	19.0	13.6	6.8	9.3	17.2	14.9	8.7	11.3	18.3	15.1	14.7
Unskilled workers	4.7	4.8	2.9	2.5	2.8	4.2	2.7	1.9	3.6	6.3	3.7	7.1
Agricultural workers	2.1	0.0	0.1	0.0	1.9	0.0	0.0	0.0	2.5	0.1	0.1	0.0
Armed forces	2.7	0.1	0.2	0.1	1.4	0.0	0.1	0.1	0.4	0.0	0.0	0.0
Inadequately described	0.9	4.1	2.5	4.3	0.9	2.9	2.0	3.0	1.1	2.7	2.1	3.6

Source: OPCS/GRO(S) (1993) Volume 2, Table 16.

While Table 5.7 provides clear confirmation of the move in to self-employment taking place among South Asian men (reflecting, in the author's opinion, the fact that racial exclusionism is much less of a handicap for those trading goods and services directly in the market place than it is for those relying on the willingness of others to allocate them waged employment), these tendencies are even more salient among South Asian women, and most particularly among the Pakistanis: no less than 26.5 per cent of Pakistani women aged between 45 and 59 are self-employed, and of those a significant number (proportionately far higher than among the White majority) are self-employed professionals (see Table 5.8). While these figures may seem on the face of things to wholly contradict almost everything that has been said about Pakistani women so far, this contradiction is more apparent than real. If it is remembered that Britain's Pakistani population is a far from homogeneous social category, it seems plausible to suggest that while it is indeed the case that older women of rural origin have for the most part shunned the local employment market, and are therefore very unlikely to have moved into self-employment, the same is much less true of women of urban origin. While women drawn from the country's urban elite may only make up a small proportion of the Pakistani population as a whole, the very low levels of overt economic activity among those of rural origins means that given a high level of activity among the former, their success in moving into business activities stands out with particular clarity. Meanwhile Pakistani

Table 5.8 Percentage distribution between socio-economic groups by age and ethnicity for women

	18–29				30–44				45–59			
	White	Paki–stani	Indian	Bang–ladeshi	White	Paki–stani	Indian	Bang–ladeshi	White	Paki–stani	Indian	Bang–ladeshi
Employer (large scale)	0.0	0.0	0.0	0.0	0.0	0.0	0.1	0.0	0.0	0.0	0.0	0.0
Self-employed professional	0.1	0.3	0.5	0.0	0.5	1.2	1.0	0.8	0.2	4.4	1.5	5.8
Employer (small scale)	0.6	2.6	1.6	1.9	2.1	8.5	4.4	2.4	2.5	9.1	4.0	0.0
Non-professional self-employed	1.8	5.6	2.7	3.3	3.4	12.1	8.4	3.2	3.1	13.1	8.3	5.8
Total self-employed	**2.5**	**8.5**	**4.8**	**5.1**	**6.0**	**21.8**	**13.9**	**6.5**	**5.8**	**26.5**	**13.9**	**11.6**
Manager (large scale)	3.4	2.1	2.6	0.5	3.6	1.3	1.6	2.4	2.7	0.0	0.9	1.9
Employed professional	2.3	2.9	5.1	0.9	1.7	2.5	3.0	6.5	0.8	1.8	2.9	11.5
Manager (small scale)	6.3	3.7	4.1	1.9	6.2	3.9	3.6	2.4	5.0	3.3	3.3	3.8
Semi-professionals	15.1	9.3	10.3	10.7	19.8	15.1	10.8	19.4	16.2	15.6	11.6	28.8
Supervisors	2.1	1.6	2.0	0.0	2.3	0.7	1.6	0.8	2.3	1.1	0.8	0.0
Junior non-manual	42.9	41.3	48.4	36.0	33.6	20.9	26.9	17.7	33.2	12.4	17.9	17.3
Personal service workers	8.5	3.9	2.8	15.0	8.0	6.3	3.5	14.5	8.4	5.8	3.4	5.8
Skilled manual workers	3.1	3.1	1.8	3.7	2.3	3.0	4.0	2.4	2.6	2.5	4.8	3.8
Semi-skilled manual workers	9.2	18.6	14.5	16.8	8.3	17.5	26.0	15.3	10.2	21.5	31.8	5.8
Unskilled workers	3.0	1.1	1.5	0.9	6.7	2.2	3.2	2.4	11.0	4.0	6.0	7.7
Agricultural workers	0.6	0.4	0.1	0.5	0.7	0.3	0.1	0.0	0.9	0.7	0.3	0.0
Armed forces	0.4	0.0	0.0	0.0	0.0	0.0	0.0	0.0	0.0	0.0	0.0	0.0
Inadequately described	0.7	3.6	2.0	7.9	0.7	4.5	1.9	9.7	0.8	4.7	2.5	1.9

Source: OPCS/GRO(S) (1993) Volume 2, Table 16.

women at the younger end of the age spectrum are still heavily concentrated in semi-skilled manual and junior non-manual jobs (as indeed are most White women), but are nevertheless achieving a considerable degree of success, though less dramatically so than among the Indians, in gaining access to professional employment.

Given the vigour with which all three South Asian minorities have engaged in entrepreneurial activity, the summary figures for ethnicity and social class presented in Tables 5.9 and 5.10, revealing a considerable degree of congruence between patterns of social class distribution among the Pakistanis on the one hand and the White majority on the other, should not come as a great surprise. What these figures suggest is that although they started out at the bottom of the employment market, (as indeed do almost all immigrants, whatever their circumstances), and though they have undoubtedly encountered considerable handicaps of racial exclusionism along the way, Pakistani men and women have now achieved a position of near parity with the White majority in the social class hierarchy (at least as measured by OPCS). Furthermore, if Tables 5.10 and 5.11 are examined with an eye to comparisons among South Asians, it is clear that the Indians have achieved a considerably greater degree of upward social mobility than the Pakistanis, and the Bangladeshis rather less.

Table 5.9 Percentage distribution of men by social class and ethnicity

	18–29				30–44				45–59			
	White	Paki–stani	Indian	Bang–ladeshi	White	Paki–stani	Indian	Bang–ladeshi	White	Paki–stani	Indian	Bang–ladeshi
Professionals	5.8	6.5	11.1	2.8	8.2	6.8	12.0	4.2	7.3	7.2	14.8	10.5
Managers	20.4	19.2	25.4	7.2	33.3	23.4	30.4	14.3	32.3	25.2	30.8	14.7
Skilled non-manual	14.8	18.3	21.1	14.0	9.5	9.7	10.3	21.2	8.5	10.8	12.0	20.5
Skilled manual	32.7	23.7	20.9	31.7	31.3	32.7	25.6	33.0	32.3	27.0	20.2	21.0
Semi-skilled	17.1	23.3	15.9	37.3	11.9	20.2	16.8	22.2	14.0	20.6	16.3	22.5
Unskilled	5.5	4.8	3.0	2.5	3.4	4.3	2.8	1.9	4.2	6.4	3.8	7.1
Armed Forces	2.7	0.1	0.2	0.1	1.4	0.1	0.1	0.1	0.4	0.0	0.0	0.0
Inadequately specified	0.9	4.1	2.5	4.3	0.9	2.9	2.0	3.0	1.1	2.7	2.1	3.6

Source: OPCS/GRO(S) (1993) Volume 2, Table 16.

Table 5.10 Percentage distribution of women by social class and ethnicity

	18–29				30–44				45–59			
	White	Paki–stani	Indian	Bang–ladeshi	White	Paki–stani	Indian	Bang–ladeshi	White	Paki–stani	Indian	Bang–ladeshi
Professionals	2.4	3.2	5.6	0.9	2.2	3.7	4.0	7.3	1.0	6.2	4.4	17.3
Managers	25.5	20.1	20.2	14.0	32.2	34.3	26.1	27.4	27.5	35.3	26.1	34.6
Skilled non-manual	45.1	42.7	49.9	37.9	36.2	23.0	28.6	17.7	35.4	14.5	19.0	17.3
Skilled manual	7.7	6.2	3.7	10.3	6.1	6.4	6.3	8.1	7.3	6.5	6.7	5.8
Semi-skilled	15.2	22.9	17.1	28.0	15.8	25.8	30.0	27.4	16.9	28.7	35.3	15.4
Unskilled	3.0	1.2	1.5	0.9	6.8	2.2	3.2	2.4	11.1	4.0	6.0	7.7
Armed Forces	0.4	0.0	0.0	0.0	0.1	0.0	0.0	0.0	0.0	0.0	0.0	0.0
Inadequately specified	0.7	3.6	2.0	7.9	0.7	4.5	1.9	9.7	0.8	4.7	2.5	1.9

Source: OPCS/GRO(S) (1993) Volume 2, Table 16.

However, it should by now be obvious that any attempt to assess British Pakistanis' current socio-economic position, and most particularly any attempt to understand how they achieved that condition, which relied solely on this summary view would in all probability be most misleading. It is only by looking behind the summary figures and exploring the industries and occupations into which Pakistanis have moved that their heavy reliance on self- and family-based employment (which is in all probability even more extensive than the census figures suggest) springs into focus. And that is not all. What the detailed figures also reveal is how varied the strategies of each ethnic category that the census identifies have proved to be. Hence the detection of ethnic variety involves much more, in the author's view, than a pursuit of exoticism. It is precisely because the Pakistanis have pursued their own distinctive agenda that they have not only traced their own distinctive trajectory through the employment market, but have also been able to circumvent to a very significant degree the obstacles placed in their path by White exclusionism.

With a mean size of 4.81 persons, Pakistani households are substantially larger than those of the Indians (3.80 persons) and even more so the Whites (2.43 persons), though they are still slightly smaller than those of the Bangladeshis (5.34 persons). In explaining these variations a number of factors need to be borne in mind. First, the much larger proportion of elderly people among the indigenous majority, together with the fact that the English propensity for nuclear residence, means that most elderly Whites live in small or very small households, goes some considerable way towards explaining the larger mean size of households in all three South Asian groups. Likewise the relative high fertility rates of South Asians, which are particularly strongly marked among Pakistanis and Bangladeshis, and hence the comparatively high proportion of school-age children in this section of the population, has exactly the same effect.

The larger mean size of Pakistani households has some paradoxical consequences, for as Table 5.11 shows, the proportion of households that conform to the indigenous nuclear ideal of a married couple supporting their dependent children is almost three times higher in their case than among the English majority. By contrast single person households are much less frequent among Pakistanis (and indeed among the Indians and Bangladeshis) than among the Whites, while households with two families (or in other words extended families from a South Asian perspective) are very much more frequent.

How are these patterns best explained? The high frequency of nuclear households which can now be observed among all three South Asian minorities has led many external commentators to conclude that traditional patterns of kinship reciprocity, and hence the practice of extended family residence, is rapidly being eroded as a result of living in Britain. However, not only would all those who have conducted ethnographic research within South Asian settlements strongly challenge that hypothesis, but a closer examination of the census data, together with a more careful consideration

Table 5.11   Percentage of households by household membership and ethnicity

	White	Pakistani	Indian	Bangladeshi
Single person	26.6	7.6	9.5	6.2
Lone parent, with dependent child(ren)	5.0	7.3	4.4	8.3
Lone parent, non-dependent child(ren) only	3.7	1.9	2.6	0.8
Married couple, no children	24.8	7.4	12.7	4.7
Married couple, with dependent child(ren)	21.8	58.3	49.7	63.6
Married couple, non-dependent child(ren) only	8.7	4.1	8.1	2.4
Cohabiting couple, no children	3.4	0.5	0.8	0.3
Cohabiting couple, dependent child(ren)	1.7	0.5	0.5	0.4
Cohabiting couple, non-dependent child(ren)	0.2	0.0	0.0	0.0
Two or more unrelated persons	3.2	2.9	2.7	4.3
Households with two or more families	0.8	9.5	8.9	9.0

Source: OPCS/GRO(S) (1993), Volume 2, Table 18.

of the constraints which the very nature of the housing stock in Britain imposes upon South Asian domestic arrangements provides ample grounds for questioning its plausibility.

Returning to Table 5.11, it is noticeable that cohabitation (or in other words household formation in the absence of marriage) occurs much less frequently among all the South Asian groups than among the White population. That said, one set of figures may still seem puzzling: the relatively high frequency of households consisting of a lone parent supporting dependent children among both the Pakistanis and the Bangladeshis. Since lone parenthood is routinely regarded as a prime indicator of family breakdown in White majority contexts, should not the same conclusion be drawn here? Again care is needed, for though some South Asian wives have indeed been deserted by their husbands, it is the author's suspicion that a substantial proportion of these households are those in which the husband (and sometimes the wife) has left on an extended visit to Pakistan or Bangladesh. If so their identification as one parent families is largely an artefact of the census process.

A further very significant aspect of Table 5.11 can be observed in the bottom row, which shows that among all three sections of the South Asian population the frequency of households containing two or more families is extraordinarily high, at least by indigenous standards. The interpretation of such patterns raises large conceptual problems, most especially with regard to the meaning and significance of the term family as against household. In line with the cultural expectations of the indigenous majority, most analyses of the census results – and indeed the way in which those results are themselves categorised – give as much emphasis to the family (i.e. a unit based on either a formally married or a cohabiting couple, together with their unmarried offspring) as they do to the household (i.e. a group of people who share the same set of domestic facilities, and who may therefore include more than one such family). This not only reflects the indigenous cultural assumption that the idea of a family and of a conjugal partnership is virtually coterminous, but also implicitly accepts the view that families in this sense should also normally be households. From this it follows that households containing more than one such family are in some sense aberrant, and that its members will in all probability have entered into that arrangement because they were unable to find, or to afford, suitable accommodation. In other words any kind of deviance from the conjugal/nuclear norm – whether towards over-largeness or over-smallness – tends to be perceived as unfortunate and hence as potentially pathogenic.

It should be obvious, however, that South Asians have very different expectations about the organisation of kinship reciprocities, and hence about the way in which their domestic affairs should be arranged. Yet though all South Asian migrants stem from a cultural tradition where households based on corporate extended families are very much the ideal norm, by no means all households are actually so structured. Decisions about residence are never a matter of free choice, for they are always constrained by personal considerations and family politics, and above all by the shape, size and cost of the housing units available. Therefore, in Britain no less than in the subcontinent, any analysis of housing and households needs to take all these factors into account. That said, what does the census data reveal about the way in which Britain's Pakistani population has housed itself?

As Table 5.12 shows, no less than 77 per cent of Pakistani households are composed of owner-occupiers and, despite the relative youth of this section of the population, nearly one in five of these own their property outright. How, though, are these figures best understood? At the extreme, two radically contrasting explanations have been advanced. On the one hand there is the position which can conveniently be described as sociological orthodoxy: this suggests that these outcomes are above all a consequence of the exclusionism encountered by the visible minorities in the housing market, such that their entry into rented local authority accommodation as well as good standard (and therefore mortgageable) private housing has been rendered intensely problematic. By contrast the ethnographic consensus, based largely on qualitative observation, suggests that while racial exclusionism is only too real, the South Asian preference for purchase, and even more so for outright purchase, is largely the outcome of culturally grounded choices rather than structurally determined constraints. Now that the results of the census are available they are well worth examining in terms of these two radically contrasting perspectives.

Table 5.13 shows, Pakistanis are still overwhelmingly concentrated in terraced housing. Given that this is precisely the kind of property found at the cheapest end of the owner-occupied market, this pattern appears, on the face of it, to confirm the deprivationist hypothesis.

Moreover the argument that Pakistanis enjoy a substantially inferior quality of housing compared with that occupied by the indigenous majority appears to be further confirmed by Tables 5.14 and 5.15, which suggest that Pakistanis (and even more so the Bangladeshis) are far more likely than anyone else to be living in overcrowded circumstances, as well as in houses in which lack central heating.

Table 5.12 *Percentage of households by tenure and ethnicity*

	White	Pakistani	Indian	Bangladeshi
Owner occupied – owned outright	24.44	19.41	16.51	5.17
Owner occupied – buying	42.21	57.32	65.23	39.33
Rented privately – furnished	3.32	7.32	4.80	6.92
Rented privately – unfurnished	3.67	2.25	1.67	2.73
Rented with a job or business	1.93	1.06	1.82	2.75
Rented from a housing association	3.02	2.24	2.16	6.09
Rented from a local authority	21.42	10.42	7.81	37.01

Source: OPCS/GRO(S) (1993), Volume 2, Table 11.

Table 5.13 Percentage of households by household type and ethnicity

	White	Pakistani	Indian	Bangladeshi
Detached house	20.5	13.0	6.1	3.8
Semi-detached house	30.1	26.7	18.3	9.6
Terraced house	28.6	41.6	60.2	44.8
Purpose-built flat	14.9	9.5	8.6	31.1
Flat in commercial building	1.1	4.8	3.2	5.3
Converted flat	3.2	3.0	2.1	3.7
Converted flatlet	0.2	0.4	0.2	0.4
Non-self-contained flat or bedsit	0.9	1.0	1.2	1.3
Non-permanent accommodation	0.4	0.0	0.0	0.1

Source: OPCS/GRO(S) (1993), Volume 2, Table 18.

Table 5.14 Mean household size by housing density and ethnicity

	White	Pakistani	Indian	Bangladeshi
Over 1.5 persons per room	3.93	8.01	6.49	7.84
Over 1 and up to 1.5 persons	5.43	6.77	6.06	6.53
Over 0.75 and up to 1 persons	3.87	5.03	4.56	4.79
Over 0.5 and up to 0.75 persons	3.37	3.93	3.75	3.68
Up to 0.5 persons per room	1.78	2.01	2.10	1.94

Source: OPCS/GRO(S) (1993), Volume 2, Table 11.

Table 5.15 Percentage of households lacking amenities by ethnicity

	White	Pakistani	Indian	Bangladeshi
Lacking or sharing bath and/or inside WC	1.22	1.69	1.14	2.03
No central heating	18.92	34.24	12.36	23.61
No car	33.04	36.29	23.22	60.90

Source: OPCS/GRO(S) (1993), Volume 2, Table 11.

Even so, it is by no means the case that this constitutes conclusive evidence that Pakistanis have been pushed into a condition of severe adversity in the housing market. In the first place, any population that includes many large families will almost inevitably show up as having a large number of persons per room; likewise a population heavily concentrated in terraced housing will tend, with an almost equal degree of inevitability, to be less likely to have the benefit of central heating than those occupying more recently constructed council or housing association properties. Given all this, a comparative examination of Table 5.16, which shows mean household size by tenure and ethnicity, and Table 5.17, showing the proportion of households in each ethnic group occupying accommodation of various sizes, is

Table 5.16 Mean household size by tenure and ethnicity

	White	Pakistani	Indian	Bangladeshi
Owner occupied – owned outright	1.96	5.25	4.01	5.51
Owner occupied – buying	2.90	5.04	3.98	5.39
Rented privately – furnished	1.89	3.54	2.68	4.70
Rented privately – unfurnished	1.95	4.04	3.13	4.79
Rented with a job or business	2.66	3.43	3.35	3.23
Rented from a housing association	1.88	3.66	2.66	5.16
Rented from a local authority	2.28	4.16	3.12	5.61

Source: OPCS/GRO(S) (1993), Volume 2, Table 11.

Table 5.17 Mean household size by number of rooms occupied and ethnicity

	White	Pakistani	Indian	Bangladeshi
1 room	1.20	1.62	1.43	2.30
2 rooms	1.31	2.21	1.91	3.03
3 rooms	1.57	3.29	2.71	4.17
4 rooms	2.01	4.04	3.31	5.02
5 rooms	2.61	4.74	3.82	5.57
6 rooms	2.76	5.25	4.12	5.96
7 or more rooms	3.21	5.85	4.62	6.42

Source: OPCS/GRO(S) (1993), Volume 2, Table 11.

most instructive, above all because they provide no evidence at all of an association between large households and either poverty or housing stress. Not only is the mean size of Pakistani households largest among those who own their property outright, but a substantially larger proportion of Pakistanis (and indeed of Indians) live in properties with six or more rooms than do the indigenous majority. Thus while the conundrum cannot be finally resolved without a far more accurate measure of housing quality than that available from the census, all the evidence suggests that though Pakistani households do indeed tend to be larger than average, and therefore place particularly acute demands on available resources, they have nevertheless made considerable efforts to seek out larger houses. Given that only a relatively small proportion of the housing stock includes seven or more rooms (not least because of the indigenous preference for residence in small-scale nuclear households) there is good reason to suppose that if more larger houses were available, the Pakistanis (and their Indian and Bangladeshi peers) would in all probability be eager to occupy them.

Conclusion

What lessons can be drawn from all this? Despite the richness, and above all the greatly improved reliability of the data associated with the new ethnic group question, the results of the 1991 Census by no means answer all the questions that one might wish to ask for it. So, for example, while the data just examined breaks a great deal of new ground, it is still neither sufficiently detailed nor sufficiently well structured to generate a conclusive response to questions about the relative impact of cultural preference as against structural constraint in patterns of household formation, or indeed with respect to the many other variables discussed in this chapter.

Even so what the results do undoubtedly demonstrate is that despite the South Asians' exposure to all sorts of social and economic handicaps, there is no evidence that either this population as a whole or its Pakistani components in particular have been relegated to an underclass, such that they fill the least attractive jobs and live in the lowest quality of housing. Although this chapter's exploration of patterns of inter-ethnic difference may have produced a good deal of evidence to suggest that the minorities have unequal access to scarce resources, the analysis has also repeatedly revealed that the size of these inequalities is less extensive than might have been expected, as well as the far reaching effects of qualitative differences, both between South Asians and the White majority, and between the various components of the South Asian presence. Hence in virtually every sphere explored here (whether in terms of patterns of immigration, age, fertility or employment, let alone with respect to their preference for self-employment, house purchase and living in extended households) it is quite clear that the differences uncovered cannot be satisfactorily explained solely in terms of the negative impact of racial discrimination. What the census serves to highlight is that new minorities are *ethnic* groups, each with their own specific set of culturally grounded values and expectations.

If only because the implications of such conclusion can so easily be mistaken, I should emphasise that this cannot be used as evidence to suggest that either Britain's visible minorities in general, or its Pakistani components in particular, do not suffer from the effects of racial exclusionism. Quite the contrary: there is now such plentiful evidence which demonstrates that exclusionism is such a routine part of the minority experience that the adoption of such a position would manifestly be absurd. However in emphasising the impact of cultural and ethnic distinctiveness on Census outcomes – as the data leaves us with no alternative but to do – we should take care to avoid falling into a similar trap at the opposite extreme, by adopting an equally naive form of cultural determinism which reduces ethnicity to fixed and primordial quality which dictates how all those involved will behave in all possible circumstances.

What the Census results suggest is that both these deterministic extremes must be rejected in favour of a more moderate and multi-dimensional perspective. Thus while exclusionism is a very real constraint, it is *not* the sole determinant of all outcomes, for however intense such constraints may grow, its victims will always seek to resist them. Moreover as soon as one steps beyond the patronising vision of black people as nothing but helpless pawns to bring the minorities' manifest capacity to act on their own behalf more clearly into focus, it is immediately apparent that their ability to access an alternative set of cultural resources offers a particularly effective means of subverting the worst of those constraints, and thus of avoiding the condition of unalloyed deprivation to which they might otherwise have been consigned. However, these ethnic strategies are by their very nature neither given nor pre-determined. Rather their effectiveness is centrally grounded in their flexibility: those involved routinely revise and where necessary to reinvent their ethnic and cultural resources to make the best in their own terms of changing contexts, no matter how adverse their situation may seem at first sight. So it is that members of each of Britain's many ethnic minorities have drawn on their own specific heritage to devise their own distinctive trajectories of adaptation.

Hence my central aim in this chapter has not just been to describe outcomes, but to seek to establish how they arose. In doing so my central interpretative assumption has been that in establishing themselves in Britain, Pakistanis have sought to press their way forward on their own terms through a social order containing many opportunities, but where access to all the most favourable of these is more or less jealously guarded by members of the indigenous majority, who much preferred to reserve these for themselves. Yet despite the exclusionism which Pakistani settlers and their offspring have consequently encountered, most especially when they began to compete for more sought-after opportunities, the Census results provide emphatic confirmation of the extent to which they have nevertheless managed to circumvent those constraints to achieve a considerable degree of upward mobility; and although I have managed to plot their progress through the employment and housing markets in this chapter, had space allowed, much the same could also be shown to be true of their educational experience.

How, though, has this been achieved? While data on outcomes provide little or no explicit information on the processes that generated them, contextual evidence gives a good indication how this came about; above all through the flexible and creative character of the settlers' responses to the challenges they faced. Thus when immigration restrictions were introduced as an obstruction to halt further settlement, they promptly utilised the resources of their kinship networks to organise further chain migration. And while the precipitate collapse of the industries on which they had long relied, for employment was an even more severe blow, the results of the census show that Pakistanis have not waited for alternative forms of waged industrial employment to turn up (the reaction of the majority of their indigenous working class peers), but have stepped sideways into the service sector. Moreover there is now plentiful evidence that their success in starting a huge range of small-scale business enterprises has been greatly facilitated by their skilled utilisation of their own internal resources and traditions. In just the same way they have responded to the equally vigorous forms of exclusionism that they encountered in the housing market by ploughing their own course through it, in pursuit, once again, of their own distinctive goals and objectives.

Once recognised (and there are many commentators who are still intensely resistant to doing so), the existence of ethnic diversity in this sense poses all sorts of challenges for social analysis, above all because it forces us to ask questions about the cultural groundings of the analytical categories that we routinely deploy. Unless the issue has been both carefully and explicitly considered, such categories will inevitably tend to reflect the cultural assumptions of Britain's dominant majority, and therefore may well be ill-suited to the analysis of minority behaviours.

For example, it was suggested at the outset that however commonsense the label Pakistani may seem to the indigenous majority, this population category is a great deal less homogeneous than is commonly supposed. Indeed many of the patterns explored in this chapter are best understood not so much as Pakistani, but as characteristic of the unasked about (and therefore undetected) Mirpuri population who form a clear majority among British Pakistanis. Yet although it is impossible, by definition, to disaggregate the categorical labels around which the ethnic group question was structured, it is still most illuminating to compare the similarities and the differences between the three South Asian population categories. On the one hand there are many similarities, such that the South Asians can be seen to differ not just from the indigenous majority, but also from the Chinese, the Africans and the Afro-Caribbeans. But at the same time there are also some very considerable differences between them, most particularly with respect to the speed and precise direction of their upward social mobility. For example, while a large number of Pakistani men have become taxi drivers, an even higher proportion of Bangladeshis have made for the catering industry, where they are overwhelmingly employed in their own restaurants and take-aways. But while social and cultural change as well as upward social mobility is becoming ever more rapid, the census provides little evidence that this is associated with an erosion of ethnic distinctiveness. Not only are the roots of mobility often grounded in ethnic resourcefulness, but once achieved, minority behaviour shows little sign of becoming comprehensively congruent with majority expectations. Since households with two or more families are no less frequently found among the more affluent Indians than among the significantly less successful Pakistanis and Bangladeshis it would seem that such 'deviant' residential patterns are much more a matter of *choice* than the unfortunate consequence of either poverty or deprivation.

References

Alavi, H. (1989) Ethnic conflict in Pakistan. In: Alavi, H.and Hariss, J. (eds), *The Sociology of Developing Societies: South Asia.* London: Macmillan.

Anwar, M. (1979) *The Myth Of Return.* London: Heinemann Educational.

Ballard, R. (1982) South Asian families. In: Rapaport, Fogarty and Rapaport, *Families in Britain.* London: Routledge.

Ballard, R. (1983a) Race and the census: what an 'ethnic question' would show. *New Society* 12 May, 212–14.

Ballard, R. (1983b) Emigration in a wider context: Jullundur and Mirpur compared. *New Community,* **11**.

Ballard, R. (1990) Migration and kinship: the impact of marriage rules on Punjabi migration to Britain. In: Clarke, Peach and Vertovec (eds), *South Asians Overseas* Cambridge: Cambridge University Press.

Ballard, R. (1991) New clothes for the emperor? The conceptual nakedness of Britain's race relations industry. New *Community,* 18.

Ballard, R. (1994) *Desh Pardesh: The South Asian Presence in Britain.* London Hurst and Co.

Ballard, R. and Kalra, V. (1994) *The Ethnic Dimensions of the 1991 Census.* Manchester Census Group.

Shaw, A. (1988) *A Pakistani Community in Britain.* Oxford: Blackwell.

Werbner, P. (1991) *The Migration Process.* London: Berg.

Chapter 6
The Bangladeshis: the encapsulated community

John Eade, Tim Vamplew and Ceri Peach

6.1 Introduction

The Bangladeshi community of Great Britain is the youngest and fastest growing of all the ethnic populations recorded in the 1991 Census of Great Britain. The census enumerated a Bangladeshi resident population of 162,835. This represents a growth of two and a half times its estimated 1981 population. It is difficult to give precise measures of the growth before this time, because Bangladesh had not been an independent state. Between 1947 and 1971 Bangladesh had constituted the eastern wing of Pakistan, formed from the partition of British India. However, at the end of 1971, the East seceded from West Pakistan and became an independent state. The United Kingdom did not recognise the secession until 1972. Thus, Bangladeshis living in Britain up to and including the 1971 Census were counted as Pakistanis. An estimate of growth of the Bangladeshi population in Britain between 1961 and 1991 is shown in Table 6.1.

Bangladeshi migration to Britain dates back to the time of the East India Company in the 18th and 19th centuries, when lodging houses were set up for 'Lascars' as they were known, (in the London docklands) (Robinson, 1986, 26; Adams, 1987). The current Bangladeshi community, however, is of very recent origin, although its statistical history is difficult to chart before

Table 6.1 *Estimates of the growth of the Bangladeshi population in Great Britain 1961-1971*

Year	Bangladeshi born	UK born Bangladeshis (estimates)	Total ethnic Bangladeshi population
1961	6,000		6,000
1971	21,000	1,000	22,000
1981	48,517	16,000	64,561
1985/87	79,000	32,000	111,000
1991	105,012	59,679	162,835

Source: 1961, 1971, 1981 based on Peach (1990).
     1985/87 <u>Labour Force Survey 1987,</u> Tables 5.29 and 5.38
     1991 from OPCS (1993) Volume 1, Table 1, 24; Table 3, 304; OPCS/GRO(S) (1993) Volume 2, Table 7, 636
Note: The sum of the Bangladesh born and the UK born Bangladeshis in 1991 is higher than the total ethnic Bangladeshi population because not all Bangladesh born persons are ethnically Bangladeshi

1981. The 1991 Census is the most important source of information on the group available, but it is worth noting two facts which the census itself is not designed to elicit. The first is that the Bangladeshi community originates overwhelmingly from a single district, Sylhet, in the north east of Bangladesh (Eade, 1990; Bentley, 1972/3; Carey and Shukur, 1985/6; Gardner, 1995, Choudhury, 1993; Barton, 1986; Chatterjee and Islam, 1990). The second is that the Bangladeshi population is overwhelmingly (over 80 per cent) Muslim (Brown, 1984). The census does not ask questions about religion. However, to understand the socio-economic position of the community in Britain it is important to understand the constraints which traditional religious values place on female employment.

The Bangladeshi population is distinct from the rest of the ethnic groups covered in the 1991 Census. Bangladeshis in this country are, as a whole, an exception to many of the generalisations that can be made about South Asian ethnic minority populations. This distinctiveness relates to the rapid and continuing growth of the Bangladeshi population, the very high proportion of young people, the large family size, the concentration of residents within Greater London, and especially Tower Hamlets, the high degree of segregation, the low socio-economic status and the dependence on local authority housing. Combined with these characteristics are a high proportion of self-employment in the catering trade, high unemployment rates and low levels of female employment in the formal sector. When comparisons between Bangladeshis and other ethnic minority groups are considered it might be argued that Bangladeshis have more in common with Black–Caribbean residents than with Indians and Pakistanis. They are predominantly working class, waged labour, state educated and council housed. They face what Peach (see Introduction) characterises as an 'Irish' rather than a 'Jewish' future.

Whereas the Black–Caribbean, Indian and Pakistani populations in Britain grew rapidly during the 1950s and 1960s, the rapid expansion of the Bangladeshi population came during the 1980s when wives and dependants joined their husbands or new unions were forged with female partners in Bangladesh and children were born in this country. The familiar pattern emerged of male workers migrating to the UK and later forming family groups, as wives, often much younger than themselves, joined them from Bangladesh. Peach (1990) suggests that the numbers of Bangladeshi children born in Britain doubled from 16,000 to 32,000 between 1981 and 1985–87 and doubled again between 1985–87 and the 1991 Census (see Table 6.1). In 1991, 59,337 or 36.4 per cent of the total Bangladeshi population was born in the UK.

6.2 Social and economic characteristics

Age sex ratio

The age and sex pyramid of the Bangladeshi population, shown in Figure 6.1, is the most irregular of all of the ethnic groups in the 1991 Census. It distinguishes between the overseas-born Bangladeshis, shown in light grey on the diagram and the British-born, shown in a darker shade. Compared with the broadly cylindrical shape of the total population, characteristic of a mature society, Bangladeshis demonstrate a youthful, triangular pattern, typical of Third World countries. The British-born Bangladeshis show an even younger second generation population nested within the overseas-born pattern. The British-born Bangladeshis have their largest proportion aged 0 to 4; they decrease monotonically in proportions until there are very small numbers above the age of 30.

The Bangladeshi population as a whole is highly male dominated, with an overall ratio of males to females of 100:64. The sex ratio of the British-born Bangladeshis is more or less symmetrical so that the gender imbalance is a feature of the overseas-born. The gender imbalance within the Bangladesh born population is of two contrasting kinds. The male dominance is particularly marked in the 50 years and older age-group (see Figure 6.1). However, the sex ratio in the 35 to 50-year-olds reverses the overall male dominance, with female dominance being sharpest in the band aged between 40 and 44. One possibility is that the earlier arriving males who came to the UK in the 1960s selected wives from Bangladesh who were younger than themselves. This seems to be born out by the Samples of Anonymised Records (SAR) which show that the average age of Bangladeshi husbands is 10 years older than Bangladeshi wives (45.6:36.7). Certainly, Bangladeshi females aged 20 to 24 are three times more likely to be married than Bangladeshi men of the same age (71.3 per cent to 23.6 per cent).

Figure 6.1 *Comparison of Bangladeshi and total population age/sex pyramids, Great Britain, 1991*

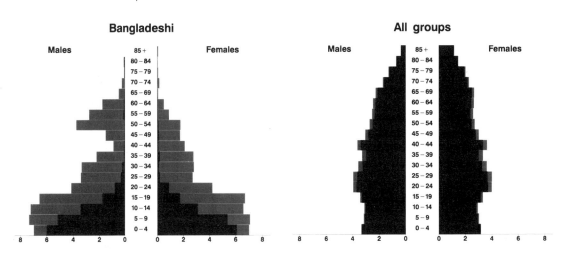

Dark shading represents British-born population; light shading represents overseas-born on both diagrams.

The rapid rise in population is forecast to continue for some time, given the very young character of the Bangladeshi population. Already the third generation of young Bangladeshis is moving through the school system and will be approaching marriageable age in large numbers during the next 10 years.

The imbalance between genders will have an impact on the source areas for female partners at this later stage. There appears to be a preference at the moment for Bangladeshi males in Britain to seek partners in their country of origin. There have been anecdotal claims that some young females are sent back to Bangladesh before they can be 'spoilt' by living within Britain. However, it seems likely that marriages will be increasingly contracted between males and females born in Britain and that such a tendency will be strengthened by the difficulty of gaining entry to this country from Bangladesh.

Household size

The average household size of Bangladeshis is relatively large at 5.3 persons. Figure 6.2 shows household size for households in which the head was born in Bangladesh (rather than for the ethnic population). This shows that over 60 per cent of Bangladeshi households were of five persons or more (these figures do not take account of the British-born Bangladeshi household heads). By comparison, less than 8 per cent of total households were of this size and the average size (2.5) is less than half of that of the Bangladeshis.

Coupled with large household size come very poor living conditions; there is a high degree of crowding and overcrowding. Nearly a fifth (19 per cent) of Bangladeshi households lived at the highest density given by the census

Figure 6.2 *Percentage distribution of household size for selected groups, by birthplace of head, Great Britain, 1991*

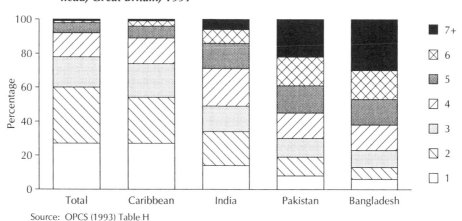

Source: OPCS (1993) Table H

of over 1.5 persons per room compared with less than half of one per cent of the total resident population and only 8 per cent of Pakistani households. Nearly a quarter of Bangladeshi households (24 per cent) lacked central heating (compared with the average of 19 per cent). Over 60 per cent of Bangladeshi households had no car compared with one third of all households (OPCS/GRO(S) 1993, Volume 2, Table 11). Perhaps as a reflection of these living conditions, a striking proportion of Bangladeshis is permanently sick: 9 per cent of men aged 16 and over are in this position and 2 per cent of women. Nationally, 5 per cent of men and 3 per cent of women aged 16 and over are permanently sick (OPCS/GRO(S) 1993, Volume 2, Table 10)

Family structure

Bangladeshi households are not only large, but like the Indian and Pakistani populations, possess significant number of multi family households. For all three South Asian groups 9 per cent of households are in this category. This figure is about ten times the national average. Lone parent households are at the national average, accounting for 9 per cent of Bangladeshi and Pakistani and 7 per cent of Indian households, whereas they form 28 per cent of Black–Caribbean households. Cohabitation scarcely exists among Bangladeshi, Indian or Pakistani households (OPCS/GRO(S) 1993, Volume 2, Table 18), while the national average for such households is 5 per cent. Thus, Bangladeshi households show a conservative traditional pattern of nuclear and extended families with relatively little manifestation of Western patterns of cohabitation (see Figure 6.3).

Figure 6.3 *Comparison of household type for selected groups, Great Britain, 1991*

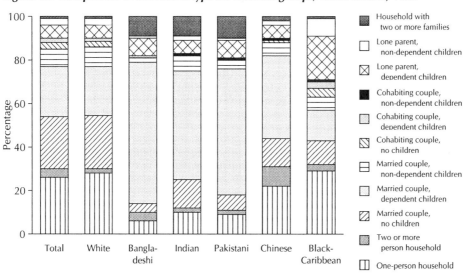

Ethnically mixed households

Unlike the Black–Caribbean households, there are very few mixed marriages in Bangladeshi households. In particular, there are almost no Bangladeshi females in non-Bangladeshi male unions (see Table 6.2).

Socio-economic class

Bangladeshis occupy a poor economic position. Although their overall rate of economic activity is the same as the national average (61 per cent), it is low compared with the Indian (67 per cent) and Black–Caribbean (73 per cent) populations. This can be partly explained by the very low participation in the formal labour market of Muslim women; only 22 per cent of Bangladeshi women aged 16 and over are economically active compared with the national average of 50 per cent. Pakistani women have a similarly low participation rate of 27 per cent. Indian women, by comparison, are 55 per cent economically active and Black–Caribbean women are two thirds involved. Unemployment rates among the Bangladeshi population are massively high, indeed the highest of all ethnic groups. Over a third of the Bangladeshi economically active women (35 per cent) are unemployed and just under one third (32 per cent) of Bangladeshi men. By comparison 19 per cent of Black–Caribbean men and 14 per cent of Black–Caribbean women are in this position. For the Pakistani population the rates are 30 per cent for women and 29 per for men (OPCS/GRO(S) 1993, Volume 2, Table 10).

The socio-economic class of economically active men is strongly skewed towards the manual end of the distribution (see Table 6.3). Nearly two thirds (63 per cent) of Bangladeshi men aged 16 and over are in manual employment (socio-economic classes III(Manual), IV and V). This compares with just over half (55 per cent) for the Pakistanis and 41 per cent for the total male population (OPCS/GRO(S) 1993, Volume 2, Table 16). At the other end of the scale, 16 per cent of Bangladeshi men are in the professional and managerial classes (socio-economic classes I and II combined). This is less than half of the national average of 36 per cent and the lowest of all of the ethnic groups in the 1991 Census. Only the Black–Caribbean men have a

Table 6.2   Ethnic marriage partners of Bangladeshi men and women, Great Britain, 1991

Male	Female	Number	Per cent
Bangladeshi	Bangladeshi	203	74.1
Bangladeshi	White	3	1.1
Bangladeshi	Black African	2	0.7
Bangladeshi	Other–Other	2	0.7
Bangladeshi	Pakistani	1	0.4
Bangladeshi	(None)	32	11.7
Other–Asian	Bangladeshi	1	0.4
(None)	Bangladeshi	23	8.4

Source: 1991 Census, Crown Copyright.

Table 6.3 *Ethnic group for men aged 16 and over, by socio-economic class,*
Great Britain, 1991

	Economically active	In employment	I	II	III Non Manual	III Manual	IV	V
Total	73.3	87.4	6.8	27.4	11.5	32.2	16.4	5.7
White	73.2	88.0	6.7	27.6	11.3	32.4	16.3	5.7
Black – Caribbean	80.1	73.8	2.4	14.2	12.2	38.9	23.6	8.7
Black – African	69.0	66.8	14.3	24.5	17.5	17.6	17.3	8.9
Black – Other	81.9	70.5	3.2	24.8	17.2	30.2	17.6	7.1
Indian	78.1	84.9	11.4	27.2	14.4	23.8	18.1	4.0
Pakistani	73.3	68.9	5.9	20.3	13.5	29.9	24.1	6.3
Bangladeshi	72.4	67.3	5.2	8.5	12.9	31.5	35	6.8
Chinese	70.1	88.1	17.6	23.3	19.3	29.5	8	2.4
Asian – Other	76.2	83.0	15.9	34.3	18.2	16	12.3	3.3
Other – Other	75.4	77.7	14.5	30.5	16.1	19.8	14	5.1
Irish–born	70.1	84.3	6.9	23.3	7.7	34.3	16.9	10.9

Source: GB LBS, Table 9 and two per cent SAR © Crown copyright.

similarly low figure (19 per cent). Figure 6.2 compares the socio-economic class of Bangladeshi men with that of the total population, the Irish-born, Indian and Pakistani populations, illustrating its unfavourable concentration in the non-skilled, manual occupations.

Given the very low participation rates of Bangladeshi women in the workforce, it is not meaningful to analyse their socio-economic position in any depth. It appears that their distribution is bipolar in professional and skilled manual work. The proportion in class 1 (4.7 per cent) is the highest of all of the South Asian groups and two and a half times the national average. Like the Indian and the Pakistani ethnic groups, there is also an above average representation in the skilled manual class (27 per cent in III(Manual) as opposed to the average of 16 per cent), which would include clothing manufacture and restaurant work (see Table 6.4).

Housing tenure

Bangladeshi housing tenure shows a relatively high dependence on the public sector and differs substantially from both the national average and from that of the other South Asian groups. Bangladeshi housing tenure is 50 per cent below the national average for owner occupation and 50 per cent higher than the national average for social housing (council housing and housing association property).

Nationally, 66 per cent of all households own or are buying their homes and a quarter live in council or housing association accommodation. Indian and Pakistani home ownership is even higher at 82 per cent and 77 per cent

*Table 6.4   Ethnic group for women aged 16 and over, by socio-economic class,
Great Britain, 1991*

	Economically active	In employment	I	II	III Non Manual	III Manual	IV	V
Total	49.9	92.1	1.7	25.9	38.8	7.6	18.0	7.9
White	49.7	92.6	1.7	25.9	39.0	7.6	17.8	8.0
Black – Caribbean	66.9	84.1	1.0	30.3	33.7	6.9	19.5	8.5
Black – African	60.1	71.0	3.0	31.8	30.8	5.6	16.9	12.0
Black – Other	62.9	77.9	1.3	25.2	40.6	9.3	19.1	4.6
Indian	55.4	85.3	4.4	20.9	34.9	6.4	29.2	4.1
Pakistani	27.1	65.5	2.7	22.3	34.2	6.5	31.7	2.6
Bangladeshi	21.8	57.6	1.8	22.9	35.8	6.4	26.6	6.4
Chinese	53.1	90.0	7.6	28.5	31.6	13.0	13.9	5.4
Asian – Other	53.9	84.9	6.0	30.7	33.8	7.0	16.6	6.0
Other – Other	53.9	82.5	4.5	30.8	38.4	6.2	15.1	4.9
Irish–born	49.9	92.4	2.6	33.2	26.8	6.3	18.5	12.6

Source: GB LBS, Table 9 and two per cent SAR © Crown copyright.

respectively, while dependence on public housing is about half the national average (10 and 13 per cent respectively live in council or housing association property) (OPCS/GRO(S) 1993, Volume 2, Table 11). The Bangladeshi population, by comparison, has a much lower level of home ownership and a much higher representation in local authority and housing association tenures: 45 per cent own or are buying their homes and 43 per cent live in council or housing association houses. The Bangladeshi pattern is much closer to that of the Black–Caribbean population than to the other South Asian groups.

Part of the explanation of tenure is due to geographical location. Tower Hamlets, for example, has until recently had very little owner occupation and the large proportion of the Bangladeshi population concentrated in this single borough would be affected by this fact, irrespective of social class. Howes and Mullins (1994) have attempted to control for this factor (see Chapter 10, Volume 4 of this series). They conclude that, allowing for location, Bangladeshis are somewhat over-represented in local authority housing (about 17 per cent more than would be expected). They show that their degree of under-representation in owner occupation is only about 5 per cent (Howes and Mullins, 1995, Table 10).

6.3   Geographical distribution

The Bangladeshi population is overwhelmingly located in England (97 per cent). Three quarters are found in the four Metropolitan counties (see Introduction to Volume 2) and over half (53 per cent) in Greater London.

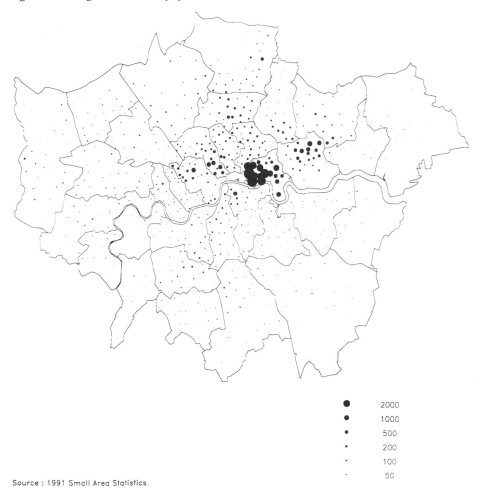

- ● 2000
- ● 1000
- • 500
- · 200
- · 100
- · 50

Source : 1991 Small Area Statistics

Nearly half (43 per cent) of the London Bangladeshis are found in the single borough of Tower Hamlets (see Figure 6.4). This means that nearly a quarter (23 per cent) of the British total of Bangladeshi residents live in a single London borough. The combination of recent arrival, young age structure, large and extended families and poor economic situation has led to high levels of segregation of the Bangladeshi community in most of the cities in which they have located. The Index of Segregation which measures the percentage of the population which would have to shift its area of residence in order to be the same as that of the rest of the population, shows that, on average, two thirds of the Bangladeshi population would have to shift their wards of residence in order to accomplish this distribution (see Chapter 3, Volume 3 of this series). Analysis of change in the Bangladesh-born population in London between 1981 and 1991 indicates that it is simply a reflection of the existing settlement pattern. As yet, little dispersal is taking place in London. In fact, London's share of the Bangladesh born population also increased in 1981–1991 from 46 to 53 per cent.

It is, however, a very young and recently arrived community and may well develop some of the entrepreneurial activities shown by other South Asian groups (Alam, 1988). This is particularly true of the catering trade, where survey evidence shows the Bangladeshis to be important. Nearly 8 per cent of the all Bangladeshi males aged 16 and over are self-employed with employees, compared with 5 per cent of Pakistanis, 7 per cent of Indians and 4 per cent of the total population (OPCS/GRO(S) 1993, Volume 2, Table 10). Eleven per cent of economically active Bangladeshi males are managers or proprietors, slightly more than Pakistanis. There is little evidence that Bangladeshis are beginning to disperse from their original node of settlement.

All in all, however, the Bangladeshi population still shows strong signs of traditional values and encapsulation. A very low proportion of women is engaged in the formal employment sector, single person households are rare, ethnically mixed unions are very few and extended families are significant. The 1980s were a difficult time for the British population as a whole in terms of the economic restructuring of the economy and the difficulties were even more strongly marked for those groups who were marginalised within the economy. It will be a matter of considerable interest to see whether the Bangladeshi population follows what Peach characterises as a 'Jewish' or an 'Irish' route of development in the 1990s.

References

Alam, Fazlal (1988) *Salience of Homeland: Salience of polarization within the Bangladeshi population in Britain*, Research papers in Ethnic Relations, no.7. University of Warwick

Adams, C. (1987) *Across Seven Seas and Thirteen Rivers: Life Stories of Pioneer Sylhetti Settlers in Britain*. London: Thap Books.

Balarajan, R. and McDowall, M. (1990) Mortality from congenital malformations by mother's country of birth. *Journal of Epidemiology and Community Health*, 39, 102–6.

Barton, S. (1986) *The Bengali Muslims of Bradford*. University of Leeds: Community Religions Project.

Bentley, S. (1972/3) Intergroup relations in local politics: Pakistanis and Bangladeshis. *New Community*, 2(1), 44-7.

Brown, C. (1984) *Black and White Britain: The Third PSI Survey*. London: Heinemann.

Carey, S. and Shukur A. (1986/6) A profile of the Bangladeshi community in East London. *New Community*, 12(3), 405–17.

Chatterjee, D. and Islam, R. (eds) (1990) *Barbed Lines*. Yorkshire Arts Circus.

Choudhury, Y. (1993) *Roots and Tales of Bangladeshi Settlers*. Birmingham: Sylhet Social History Group.

Eade, J. (1990) Bangladeshi Community Organisation and Leadership in East London. In: Clarke, C., Peach, C. and Vertovec, S. (eds) *South Asians Overseas*. Cambridge: Cambridge University Press.

Gardner, K. (1995) *Global Migrants, Local Lives: Travel and Transformation in Rural Bangladesh*. Oxford: Clarendon Press.

Howes, E. and Mullins, D. (1994) Ethnic Minority Tenants. Paper given at the OPCS conference on Ethnic Minorities in the 1991 Census, University of Leeds, 5-6 September, 1994. (To be published as Chapter 10 of OPCS Volume 4 in this series, *Employment, education and housing among the ethnic minority populations in Britain*, edited by Valerie Karn).

Howes, E. and Mullins, D. (1996) Ethnic Minority Tenants. Chapter 10 in OPCS Volume 4, *Employment, education and housing among the ethnic minority populations in Britain*, edited by Valerie Karn. To be published by HMSO, 1996.

Khaum, S. (1994) We just buy illness in exchange for hunger. Experience of health care and illness among Bangladeshi women in Britain. Unpublished PhD thesis, University of Keele.

OPCS/GRO(S) (1993) 1991 Census, *Ethnic Group and Country of Birth, Great Britain*. Two Volumes. London: HMSO.

Peach, C. (1990) Estimating the growth of the Bangladeshi population of Great Britain. *New Community*, 16(4), 481–91.

Raleigh, S. V, Botting, B. and Balarajan, R. (1990) Perinatal and postneonatal mortality in England and Wales among immigrants from the Indian subcontinent. *Indian Journal of Pediatrics*, 57, 551–62.

Robinson, V. (1986) *Transients, Settlers and Refugees: Asians in Britain*. Oxford: Clarendon Press.

Chapter 7
The Chinese: upwardly mobile

Yuan Cheng

7.1 Introduction

Before the 1991 Census, the information about the size of the Chinese population in Britain was based on estimates of local councils (Home Affairs Committee, 1985) or from the country of birth of the head of household figures given in the census. The figures obtained from either source provided inaccurate and therefore unsatisfactory information about the Chinese community in Britain. The census of 1991 gave the number of the Chinese in the UK as 156,938. This was the first time that an accurate number of the Chinese in Britain had been reported by official statistics.

It can be seen from Table 7.1 that the Chinese form the smallest ethnic group identified in the census. They are fewer in number even than the Bangladeshsis, whose population is 1.04 times that of the Chinese. Other ethnic minority groups are much more populous than the Chinese. For example, the group size of the Pakistanis is 3 times bigger than the Chinese, the Black–Caribbeans 3.18 times, persons born in Ireland 5.34 times and the Indians 5.35 times. For every 1,000 persons in this country, there are less than three persons of Chinese origin.

Table 7.1   Ethnic distribution in the 1991 Census

Ethnic group	Number	Per cent
White	51,873,792	93.09
Black–Caribbean	499,964	0.96
Black–African	212,362	0.38
Black–Other	178,401	0.32
Indian	840,255	1.51
Pakistani	476,555	0.86
Bangladeshi	162,835	0.29
Chinese	156,938	0.28
Other–Asian	197,534	0.35
Other – Other	290,206	0.52
Persons born in Ireland	837,464	1.50
Total	55,726,306	100.00

Source: OPCS/GRO(S) (1993) Volume 2.

7.2 Country of birth

The Chinese ethnic minority group is a young one. Table 7.2 shows that only 28 per cent of this group were born in the UK. The percentage of the British-born population of the Chinese is smaller than those of all other ethnic groups identified in the census, except Other– Asians, of whom 22 per cent are British-born.

An additional 34 per cent of the Chinese came from Hong Kong, which is the single largest area sending Chinese immigrants to Britain. Malaysia and Singapore supplied another 13 per cent, as did China (including Taiwan). Six per cent of the Chinese migrated from Vietnam. The rest – about 12 per cent – came from about 80 other countries all over the world. Table 7.3 presents the distribution of Chinese by country of origin.

Table 7.2   Percentage of ethnic minorities British–born

Ethnic group	Per cent British–born
Chinese	28.44
Black–Caribbean	53.67
Black–African	36.41
Black–Other	84.44
Indian	41.95
Pakistani	50.48
Bangladeshi	36.65
Other–Asian	21.90
Other – Other	59.79

Source: OPCS/GRO(S) (1993) Volume 2, Table 5, pp. 403-6.

Table 7.3   Country of origin of Chinese, Great Britain ,1991

Country	Number	Per cent
UK	44,635	28.44
Hong Kong	53,473	34.07
Malaysia/Singapore	20,001	12.75
China (and Taiwan)	20,141	12.83
Vietnam	9,448	6.02
Other parts of the world	9,240	11.91
Total	156,938	100.00

Source: OPCS/GRO(S) (1993) Volume 2, Table 5, pp 403–6.

It should be pointed out that the Sample of Anonymised Records (SAR) variable on the country of birth is a highly collapsed one. For instance, it does not distinguish the Chinese born in China (including Taiwan) from those born in Vietnam. This prevents further disentanglement of the differences in the profiles of these two groups, which had quite different experiences of migration.

7.3 Migration history

Large-scale migration of the Chinese to Britain is fairly recent. Despite more than a hundred years' presence, there were fewer than 5,000 Chinese in Britain up to the end of the second world war (Shang, 1984). The first wave of Chinese migration to Britain started in the second half of the 19th century. The opening up of the China trade to British merchants after China's defeat in the Opium Wars increased the need for Chinese seamen. The British East India Company recruited cheap labourers from villages in Southern China to work on British ships. Some Chinese seamen jumped ship to work in better paid jobs in the British ports, and became the first Chinese settlers in Britain. Towards the end of the century, Chinese communities in port cities, such as Liverpool, Cardiff and London, began to take shape. Provision stores and restaurants were opened up to cater for the consumption needs of the Chinese seamen, dock workers and students who had come to study in Britain (Shang, 1984). The early 20th century saw the Chinese move away from the dockland occupations into laundries and the catering trade. But up until the second world war, migration, which consisted mainly of males, remained a trickle.

The second wave of migration brought the majority of today's Chinese population into Britain. The post-war British demand for ethnic cuisine coupled with deteriorating economic conditions in rural Hong Kong formed the major pull-push factors of this migration (Baxter, 1988). While the second wave of immigration in Britain took place as early as the 1950s, the large influx of Chinese did not follow until the 1960s.

The second wave was characterised by chain migration and employment concentration in the catering trade. Many Hong Kong Chinese who came in the 1950s and 1960s relied on contacts already established in Britain to find employment. These contacts were often brothers, uncles, cousins, fellow villagers or friends. The foothold established by these relatives and friends facilitated the passage of the newcomers (Watson, 1977).

It has been pointed out by some researchers that the Chinese chain migration and concentration in catering were heavily shaped by the admission requirements imposed by the Commonwealth Immigration Act of 1962. The Chinese came under the work voucher system, which demanded that prospective immigrants be issued with an employment voucher for a specific job for a single named employer in Britain (Baxter, 1988). It was a time when a big number of Chinese already in Britain had moved into the catering industry, boosted by the changing diet and conventions about eating out in Britain. Therefore, kinship network and employment in catering became the natural channel through which the Hong Kong Chinese migrated to Britain.

The South East Asian Chinese in Britain were mainly drawn from the Chinese communities in Malaysia and Singapore. For many decades, the Chinese in those countries were only familiar with the traditional way of life they had brought with them from China. The introduction of western technology and ideology in the 1950s, however, modernised both material and social life among the Chinese community in those countries. Education in English schools was highly valued because of its vital role in obtaining highly rewarded jobs. Western life-style was copied and western consumer goods were pursued Under these circumstances, migration to Britain was a means towards better western education, greater career opportunities and aspirations for wealth that could not be fulfilled at home.

The rest of the Chinese in Britain came from China, Taiwan and Vietnam. Only a very small minority came from other parts of the world. Migration from China to Britain started as early as the late 19th century. The pioneers of today's immigrants from China, however, migrated during and after the civil war, which came to an end in 1949. Since the 1980s, there has been a resurgence of immigration from mainland China. Various categories of students and scholars arrived in Britain, after mainland China was opened to the western world. Many stayed on after completing their education. This group, which is small in number but rapidly growing, comprises the most highly qualified Chinese migrants Britain has ever received. The expansion of this group will impact the socio-economic composition of the Chinese community in Britain in due course.

The Vietnamese Chinese came to Britain as political refugees. After the fall of Saigon in 1975, the Chinese in Vietnam were persecuted and many had to flee the country. Britain received 20,000 Vietnamese refugees as part of an international settlement effort (Jones, 1982). Because of a relatively non-selective system of admittance, few of the British Vietnamese possess trans-ferable skills and their knowledge of English is poor. As a result, only a few are employed casually within the Chinese catering business, or consigned to other areas of menial work. Most of them remain unemployed due to lack of qualifications or deficiencies in governmental resettlement policies (Peach et al, 1988).

7.4 Gender

The Chinese have a balanced gender distribution. Of 156,938 Chinese identified in the census, 77,669 are males and 79,269 are females. This is equivalent to 102 women for every 100 men. Table 7.4 presents sex ratios for the Chinese and a few other ethnic groups. Compared with the British-born Whites, for whom there are 107 women for every 100 men, the Chinese have a higher proportion of males. But compared with South Asian groups, the

Chinese have a much lower proportion of men. Excess of male members, which is normally expected from minority groups with many economic immigrants, is a result of male migration followed by female migration with a marked time lag. There is little evidence that this is the case for the Chinese when the group is examined as a whole.

However, the Chinese population is not a homogeneous one. It is known from their migration history that nearly all voluntary migrants of Chinese origin came to Britain to improve their economic opportunities, but there was already a marked difference in their economic status at the time of migration and hence different expectations. The Chinese from Hong Kong, for instance, consist primarily of economic immigrants in the traditional sense. But those from South East Asia are more likely to be second time migrants, whose forebears left China a long time ago. These people, who were more economically prosperous than the former group, came to Britain for better education and greater career opportunities, which their first country of settlement could not provide. Such a difference is bound to have a bearing over the demographic composition of the various subgroups of the Chinese population in Britain. Therefore, in Table 7.4, the sex ratios for four subgroups of Chinese, distinguished by their country (or place) of origin, are also calculated.

It is evident that there are substantial differences in sex distributions within the Chinese population. The Chinese from Hong Kong are the only group marked by an excess of men – 100 men for 99 women. The British-born Chinese have a sex ratio of 100:108, an obvious excess of females. The Chinese from South East Asia and other parts of the world also have more female than male members. The sex ratio is the lowest for those born in Malaysia and Singapore, for whom there are 161 women for every 100 men. Chinese migration from South East Asia is clearly dominated by the migration of women. Many of these women had fairly good qualifications and came to work in the British health profession (Cheng, 1994).

Table 7.4   Sex ratio for selected ethnic groups, Great Britain, 1991

Ethnic origin	Sex ratio
Chinese	100:102
Chinese born in UK	100:108
Chinese born in Hong Kong	100: 99
Chinese born in South East Asia	100:161
Chinese born in other parts of the world	100:139
Indian	100: 98
Pakistani	100: 94
Bangladeshi	100: 92
Whites	100:100

Source: OPCS/GRO(S) (1993) Volume 2, Table 7, pp. 636–7.

7.5 Age

The Chinese are a young population. The average Chinese person in Britain is 29 years old – nine years younger than the average White person. The mean age of an immigrant Chinese is 36, and that of a British-born Chinese, 13. Among immigrant Chinese, there is little difference in the average age level. The mean age is a summary statistic, which indicates an overall age level. It is not informative as far as the age structure is concerned. Population pyramids allow us to observe the age profile and foresee the future demographic trajectory of a particular population. In Figure 7.1, the population pyramids for the Chinese compared with the total population are presented.

These pyramids represent the age-sex-origin composition of the Chinese and the total population. The bars represent age-groups in ascending order from the lowest to the highest. The bars for males are given to the left of the central vertical axis and those for females to the right. The number of males or females of a particular age-group is indicated by the length of the bar measured from the central axis. In each graph, two overlapping pyramids are presented, with that of the native-born given in black and that of the foreign-born in grey. It can be seen that the pyramid of the White population has a gentle slope, with a narrow base gradually expanding in the middle portion and tapering at the top. It illustrates a situation where there are few children and few older people, although the age cohorts do not differ very much in the number of people they contain.

Figure 7.1 *Comparison of Chinese and total population age/sex pyramids, Great Britain, 1991*

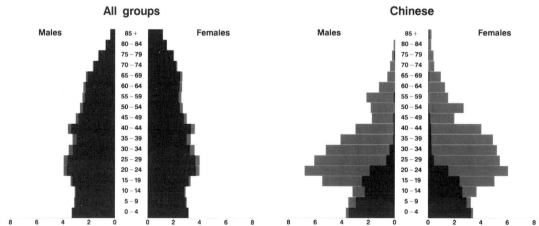

In contrast, the slopes for the two pyramids representing the Chinese are more rugged. In the case of Chinese immigrants, the pyramid has a narrow base, a very wide middle portion and a tapering top. It shows concentration in the intermediate age cohorts, especially among the cohorts aged from 20 to 55. It can also be seen that the gender distribution is balanced in the intermediate age cohorts. There is no indication of more men than women engaged in the work-force in this age span.

The pyramid for the second generation Chinese presents a different shape. It has a wide base that sharply narrows into a tapering top. It is a group which primarily consists of youths and children. Only a tiny proportion of this group are above age 20 and even fewer above age 35. Therefore, the great majority of this group are likely to be engaged in full-time education and a small number of them at the early stage of their career.

7.6   Region

The regional distribution of the Chinese is characterised by the concentration in the South East and wide dispersion in other parts of Britain. It can be seen in Table 7.5 that altogether 53 per cent of the Chinese live in the South East whereas 30 per cent of Whites live in this region. The percentage of the Chinese living in inner London is much higher than that of Whites: 17 per cent of the Chinese versus only 3 per cent of Whites. In all the other regions, the Chinese are under-represented compared with the White population. Even in the North West, where the second largest concentration of the Chinese is found, the number of Chinese living there as a proportion of the total Chinese population in Britain is still lower than the proportion of the White population, 10.5 per cent versus 11.3 per cent.

Table 7.5   Regional distribution of Chinese of different regional origin, Great Britain, 1991

Region	Whites	Chinese total population	Chinese UK– born	Chinese Hong Kong–born	Chinese SE Asia– born	Chinese born elsewhere
North	5.6	2.8	3.5	3.9	0.9	1.7
Yorkshire and Humberside	8.7	6.0	5.6	6.1	4.0	7.4
East Midlands	7.5	4.6	4.2	5.3	4.3	4.2
East Anglia	3.9	2.3	1.6	2.4	3.8	2.2
Inner London	3.3	17.2	15.9	12.6	22.3	22.5
Outer London	6.4	17.7	17.0	13.9	25.7	19.4
Rest of South East	20.1	17.7	18.4	19.4	18.1	14.1
South West	9.1	5.3	4.7	6.1	5.1	4.7
West Midlands	9.0	6.3	7.0	6.7	4.9	5.6
North West	11.3	10.5	13.4	11.1	3.8	10.2
Wales	5.3	3.1	2.5	4.6	2.8	2.0
Scotland	9.8	6.5	6.2	8.0	4.3	5.9
Total	100.0	100.0	100.0	100.0	100.0	100.0

Source: Two per cent individual SAR. © Crown copyright.

The regional distribution of the Chinese varies with the country (or place) of origin and is affected by employment patterns. The Hong Kong Chinese, who have the highest percentage of caterers, are most widely dispersed across the country. Their level of concentration in the South East (46 per cent) is the lowest among all Chinese immigrants. The demand for ethnic cuisine, which started in the 1960s, encouraged the gradual diffusion of the Chinese into progressively smaller towns and even villages across the country (Livesey, 1988).

The Chinese from South East Asia have the highest level of concentration in the South East. Altogether 66 per cent live in this region. This pattern might be explained by the fact that many people from this group are either professionals or have technical skills. Therefore, they are more likely to work in the South East where such jobs are more readily available than in other parts of the country. The concentration in the South East is also notable for the Chinese from other parts of the world. This group is mixed. Their pattern of settlement is due to a combination of the Vietnamese refugees who, in spite of the government's intention of dispersal, came to live in London (Peach et al, 1988), and the qualified Chinese from China who hold professional or skilled jobs.

After the South East, the North West has the largest Chinese concentration. It attracts 11 per cent of the Hong Kong Chinese and 10 per cent of the Chinese from other parts of the world. However, only 4 per cent of the South East Asian Chinese are found in this region, a pattern reminding us again of the differences in employment patterns.

7.7   Household size and family structure

The average Chinese household contains 3.9 persons. It is slightly larger than the average household of the White population, which has 3.2 persons. It can be seen in Table 7.6 that while 59 per cent of Whites live in households with three or fewer people, only 43 per cent of the Chinese live in households of the same size. Similarly, only 6 per cent of Whites live in households with five or more people, whereas 19 per cent of Chinese live in such households. Two factors are likely to account for the relatively larger household size of the Chinese: multi-family households and the presence of dependent children.

The one per cent household sample allows calculation of the percentage of people living in single family households versus multi-family households. This reveals that nearly all White people live in single family households (99.2 per cent) and few live in multi-family ones (0.8 per cent). The Chinese, however, display a slightly greater inclination to live in multi-family households, 2.8 per cent. The SARs also provide us with further information on household formation. Of those people living in multi-family households, 63 per cent of the Chinese versus 46 per cent of Whites reported the presence of extended families.

*Table 7.6   Percentage distribution of persons per household, Chinese and Whites,
Great Britain, 1991*

Number in household	Chinese	Whites
1	6.5	10.5
2	15.8	28.1
3	20.6	19.9
4	25.4	26.0
5	12.9	10.6
6	12.5	3.7
7	3.4	0.8
8	1.1	0.4
9	0.9	0.1
11	0.8	0.0
Total	100.0	100.0

Source: One per cent household SAR. © Crown copyright.

Presence of dependent children also contributes to household size. While 53.2 per cent of the White population live in families with dependent children, 71.3 per cent of the Chinese population do so. This reflects on the earlier finding on the different age structures between the Chinese and host populations. The Chinese are on the average younger than the host population. Therefore, they are more likely to have young children living in the households and less likely to have grown up children who live elsewhere.

7.8   Housing tenure

The Chinese have a lower level of home ownership than the indigenous population. Sixty four per cent of the Chinese are home owners compared with 70 per cent of Whites (see Table 7.7). While 20 per cent of Whites own their homes outright, only 14 per cent of Chinese are in this position.

The Chinese have a lower level of rented housing from the public sector than the White population. Fifteen per cent of the Chinese versus 20 per cent of Whites live in rented accommodation from the local authority, although housing association accommodates a similar proportion (2 per cent) of both the White and Chinese populations.

The Chinese display a higher level of rental from the private sector than Whites. Private sector tenants make up 17 per cent of the Chinese population, but only 8 per cent of the White population. This reflects the fact that the Chinese have a higher proportion of students (Chan, 1994).

There is substantial difference in housing tenure among the Chinese population itself. Among immigrants, the level of home ownership is highest among those from Hong Kong (69 per cent) and lowest among those from 'other parts of the world' (49 per cent). As most Hong Kong Chinese run

Table 7.7   Housing tenure for Chinese, by regional origin, Great Britain, 1991

Tenure	Whites	Chinese total population	Chinese UK– born	Chinese Hong Kong–born	Chinese SE Asia– born	Chinese born elsewhere
Owner occupier–outright	19.9	13.7	13.1	16.4	11.7	11.7
Owner occupier–buying	49.9	50.4	56.8	53.0	54.2	36.9
Rented private furnished	2.9	11.5	4.9	11.3	20.6	15.0
Rented private unfurnished	2.8	2.1	2.8	1.8	1.2	2.3
Rented job/business	2.1	4.2	2.4	6.5	4.0	3.4
Rented housing association	2.4	2.6	2.3	13.1	16.4	11.7
Rented LA/NT E+W	16.6	14.8	17.4	9.0	6.7	24.3
Rented LA Scotland	3.0	0.5	0.2	0.5	0.5	1.1
Rented New Town Scotland	0.1	0.0	0.0	0.0	0.0	0.0
Rented Scottish homes	0.4	0.1	0.1	0.1	0.0	0.0
Total	100.0	100.0	100.0	100.0	100.0	100.0

Source: Two per cent individual SAR. © Crown copyright.
Note: Figures from the SARs differ slightly from those in the published volumes, e.g. OPCS/GRO(S) (1993)
          Volume 2, Table 11, 769.

their own business in catering, they may be more likely than other groups to accumulate wealth, which gives them greater housing security. The bulk of the Chinese from other parts of the world are either Vietnamese refugees, among whom the unemployment rate is high, or those from mainland China, for whom immigration is a new phenomenon. It is not surprising, therefore, that the level of rental from public sector is the highest among this group. For instance, 31 per cent of the Chinese from 'other parts of the world' are accommodated by either local authorities or housing associations.

7.9   Highest qualifications

The variable in the SARs which directly measures the level of education is the highest qualification. Foreign qualifications have been translated into those of UK standard. Therefore, it is possible to compare directly the educational qualifications of the Chinese with those of the White population. The highest qualification refers to those qualifications which are generally obtained at 18 and above. It includes higher degrees of UK standard, first degree and all other qualifications of UK first degree standard and other qualifications that are generally obtained at 18+. The highest qualification only reflects the educational level of the qualified and does not provide information on the educational level of those without any of these qualifications. In order to present educational distribution of the whole population, people without such qualifications are included, labelled as unqualified.

As shown in Table 7.8, the Chinese as a whole are better educated than the White population. Among the Chinese, 2.3 per cent have higher degrees.

Table 7.8   Academic qualifications by regional origin

Qualification	Whites	Chinese total population	Chinese UK–born	Chinese Hong Kong–born	Chines SE Asia–born	Chinese born elsewhere
Higher degree	0.6	2.3	0.9	2.0	4.0	3.2
First degree	4.6	8.4	2.8	8.3	18.3	9.2
A-level	5.0	6.3	2.0	4.4	18.7	6.7
Below A-level	89.9	83.1	94.2	85.3	58.9	80.8
Total	100.0	100.0	100.0	100.0	100.0	100.0

Source: Two per cent individual SAR. © Crown copyright.

This compares with only 0.6 per cent of the White population. The proportion of the Chinese with first degrees and above is 10.7 per cent, and that of Whites, 5.2 per cent. At the other end of the spectrum, a higher proportion of the White population than the Chinese is unqualified, 90 per cent versus 83 per cent. It should be noted that the highly collapsed categories of the SARs do not allow examination of the unqualified in more detail. It has been shown in a previous study that the White population is more represented at GCSE level, whereas the Chinese have a greater proportion of people without any qualifications at all (Cheng, 1994).

There is substantial differentiation among the Chinese with regard to educational level. Of all immigrant groups, the Chinese from South East Asia are the best qualified and those from Hong Kong the least qualified, with those from other parts of the world somewhere in the middle. Over 22 per cent of the South East Asian Chinese hold first degrees and above. This compares with 11 per cent of the Hong Kong Chinese. At the other end of the spectrum, 85 per cent of the Hong Kong Chinese have lower than A-level qualifications versus only 59 per cent of the South East Asian Chinese.

The British-born Chinese display the lowest level of qualification among all subgroups of the Chinese. Only 4 per cent have attained first degrees and 94 per cent have qualifications lower than A-level. This is the only Chinese subgroup that is less qualified than the White population. One explanation might be that this group is fairly young and most may still be engaged in continuous full-time education. If this is the case, the difference in qualification level compared with the White population should disappear once the age effect is removed. If the group difference persists given the same age, another possible explanation would be ethnic disadvantage in educational attainment. To test these two competing hypotheses, a simple age control can be introduced by selecting those at and above age 16 and below age 30 from the White and British-born Chinese groups, given that 16 is the minimum school leaving age and 30 is the age when continuous full-time education should already be completed. The results are reported in Table 7.9. The Chi-squared test gives a likelihood ratio of 8.1 given three degrees of freedom. It shows that the qualification distribution varies with ethnic groups. Further examination of qualification distribution of the two groups

Table 7.9   Educational distribution for Chinese and Whites aged 16–30

Qualification	Whites	Chinese
Higher degree	0.5	1.8
First degree	5.5	7.3
A-level	4.1	5.5
Below A-level	90.0	85.4
Total	100.0	100.0

Source: OPCS/GRO(S) (1993) 1991 Census, Ethnic Group and Country of Birth, Volume 2, Table 17, pp 825-827.

reveals that within the age span of 16–30, the British-born Chinese actually display some ethnic advantage over the White population in becoming qualified. The analysis here provides no support for the educational disadvantage of the Chinese youths in Britain (see Parker, 1994).

7.10   Industry

It is common knowledge that the Chinese are over-represented in the catering and related industries. But the estimated proportion of the Chinese working in catering has varied from about 90 per cent (Home Affairs Committee, 1983) to around 67 per cent (Cheng, 1994). The census, which covers the whole Chinese population in Britain, shows that about 55 per cent of the Chinese work in distribution. Within this group, the Chinese are markedly concentrated in a single industry – restaurants, snack bars, cafes and other eating places. Altogether 41 per cent of the Chinese work in this single industry. Moreover, the industrial distribution varies with ethnic origins. For instance, 58 per cent of the Hong Kong-born Chinese and 42 per cent of the Chinese born in other parts of the world work in this industry. However, only 10 per cent of the South East Asian Chinese fall into this category. Outside distribution, the Chinese are also concentrated in the other services and banking, which employ 20 per cent and 12 per cent of the Chinese population respectively.

7.11   Socio-economic class

Seventy per cent of Chinese men aged 16 and over are economically active, which is slightly lower than that of the White population, at 73 per cent. Of those men who are economically active, 88 per cent of both the Chinese and the Whites are in paid work. Compared with White women, the percentage of economically active women is slightly higher among the Chinese, 53 per cent versus 50 per cent. But a greater proportion of economically active White women than Chinese women are in paid work, 93 per cent versus 90 per cent.

There is marked ethnic difference in the distribution of socio-economic class between the Chinese and the British. Table 7.10, presents socio-economic class by gender for the two groups. Chinese men are over-represented in Class I and Class III, i.e. professional occupations and non-manual skilled occupations. Nearly 18 per cent of Chinese men are professionals versus 7 per cent of White men. Nineteen per cent of Chinese men work in non-manual skilled occupations, compared with 11 per cent of White men. However, compared with White men, Chinese men are under-represented in managerial and technical occupations, 23 per cent to 28 per cent. At the other end of the spectrum, the Chinese are less likely than Whites to work in partly skilled or unskilled jobs.

Like Chinese men, Chinese women are over-represented in professional occupations and under-represented in partly skilled or unskilled jobs. Nearly 8 per cent of Chinese women work as professionals compared with only 2 per cent of White women. Unlike Chinese men, Chinese women are over-represented in managerial and technical occupations. Nearly 29 per cent of Chinese women work in such occupations compared with 26 per cent of White women. Compared with White women in skilled occupations, Chinese women are more likely to work in manual skilled jobs and are less likely to work in non-manual skilled jobs. It is interesting to note that the opposite is true for Chinese men.

Table 7.10 Socio-economic group for males and females, Whites and Chinese, Great Britain, 1991

Socio-economic group	Male		Female	
	Whites	Chinese	Whites	Chinese
Economically active	73.2	70.1	49.7	53.1
Employed	88.0	88.1	92.6	90.0
I	6.7	17.6	1.7	7.6
II	27.6	23.3	25.9	28.5
IIIN	11.3	19.3	39.0	31.6
IIIM	32.4	29.5	7.6	13.0
IV	16.3	8.0	17.8	13.9
V	5.7	2.4	8.0	5.4

Source: OPCS/GRO(S) (1993) Volume 2, pp. 811–824.

7.12 Occupational returns to education

The issue of Chinese occupational returns to education in comparison with the British-born Whites was first examined by Cheng and Heath using a collapsed sample of the Chinese from the national Labour Force Survey (Cheng and Heath, 1993; Cheng, 1994). The study was about Chinese immigrants only. More recently, another study was conducted by Heath and McMohan in an effort to extend the analysis of immigrants to the second generation minority members in Britain using the 1991 Census data (Heath and McMohan, 1994). Unfortunately, the British-born Chinese were left out of the discussion because the sample of the employed second generation Chinese was too small for sensible analyses to be carried out.

The aim of this section is to examine the occupational attainments of the Chinese immigrants in detail. The cross-tabular analyses above have revealed that Chinese immigrants are far from being a homogeneous group. Country of origin affects the migratory experience, demographic profile, industrial distributions and educational qualifications of Chinese subgroups. It follows that the Chinese immigrants may also have differentiated levels of occupational returns to education, depending on their country of origin. This exercise compares the British-born White population with three subgroups of the Chinese population: Chinese from Hong Kong, Chinese from South East Asia and Chinese from other parts of the world.

It can be seen from previous analyses that all Chinese, except the British-born, have greater propensity than Whites to work in professional occupations and lower propensity to work in partly skilled or unskilled occupations. An explanation is that the Chinese are generally better educated than the White population and that their higher levels of qualification account for their greater occupational attainments (Cheng and Heath, 1993; Cheng, 1994; Heath and McMohan, 1994). But is this still the case when the Chinese immigrant population is split by country of origin and each subgroup is compared with the British-born Whites? The Chinese immigrants as a whole may not show ethnic differences from Whites in translating education into equitable occupational success, but this does not mean that the rate of return is the same for the Chinese from Hong Kong as for the Chinese from the South East Asia or from other parts of the world. Therefore, the first hypothesis to test is whether country of origin makes a difference in access to the salariat once the effect of education is taken into consideration. An issue related to the occupational attainments of the Chinese is the level of success. While previous research used highly collapsed categories of socio-economic class, occupational success was very often described as access to rather crude salariat that ranged from high level managerial to foremen of non-manual workers. Recently, there has been mounting concern (especially in the American literature; see Duleep 1988) over the issue of the glass ceiling. It has been found that although some ethnic minority groups (including the Chinese) are as successful as Whites in gaining access to the more privileged occupational groups, such as professional occupations, they are more likely to concentrate towards the lower end of the hierarchy within these occupational groups whereas their White counterparts are more likely to end up with jobs at the top of the hierarchy. To test this hypothesis, the higher salariat must be distinguished from the lower salariat. Therefore, the second hypothesis to test is whether ethnicity makes a difference in access to the higher salariat regardless of educational background, for the Chinese population and for the different subgroups.

The concentration of the Chinese in catering is an established fact (Cheng, 1994; Parker, 1995). Previous case studies have shown that recruitment into the catering business largely depends on kinship network and is not necessarily related to educational background (Ng, 1968). If this is the case, it is likely that an encapsulated labour market will be identified, where education has little effect on the taking up of a small business, but being Chinese, especially Hong Kong Chinese, is highly related to employment in small business at all levels of education.

The Chinese are known to have a lower unemployment rate than Whites (Cheng, 1994). An explanation is that the family oriented catering business serves as a safety net, which creates jobs for its own members during hard times. It could also be the fact that a greater proportion of the Chinese have above A-level qualifications. Therefore, they are more likely to be employed in the expanding service sector, which generally requires good skills from employees. On the other hand, Whites with lower qualifications on average, may have a greater propensity to work in manufacturing industries, which suffered from more job losses in the 1980s. If this hypothesis is true, ethnic differences would be expected to disappear once education is held constant.

However, if ethnic differences persist, the safety net hypothesis would be true. Chinese achievement was examined in comparison with White achievement in four levels of occupation: higher salariat, salariat, petty-bourgeoisie and unemployment. While ethnic differences in occupational returns to education between the Chinese and Whites have been thoroughly discussed in the past (Cheng and Heath, 1993; Cheng, 1994; Heath and McMohan, 1994), this analysis concentrates on the differences between various sub-groups of the Chinese and the Whites.

The four dependent variables are derived from the socio-economic status (SEG) in the SARs and are recoded following the Goldthorpe Class Schema (Goldthorpe, 1987). The professional and managerial occupations, which are also called the salariat, include seven categories in SEG: employers in large establishments, managers in large establishments, managers in small establishments, professionals who are self-employed, professionals who are employees, ancillary workers or artists, and foremen and supervisors of non-manual workers. This is the class of people who generally enjoy more favourable conditions of employment, such as autonomy, security and good pay, compared with the rest of the work-force.

To test the glass ceiling effect, a variable that represents the higher salariat was derived. This variable covers four categories from the SEG: employers in large establishments, managers in large establishments, professionals who are self-employed and professionals who are employees. It should be pointed out that even this distinction is not satisfactory, especially for the analysis of the Chinese. From previous analyses it is known that the Chinese are especially more likely to become professionals than Whites, but the higher salariat so defined bands all levels of professionals together and does not provide any information on the hierarchy within the professional occupations. For example, it does not differentiate between a full tenured professor from a post-doctorate researcher working on a short-term contract. Unfortunately, the census does not give further information on the employment relations of the population. It is to be hoped that this gap will be filled by the availability of more detailed employment data from the fourth PSI survey of British ethnic minorities.

The third variable concerns the taking up of small business and it consists of two categories in the SEG: employers in small establishments and own account workers (excluding the professionals). This class of people is called the petty bourgeoisie. The fourth variable concerns unemployment. It is derived from the economic activity of the main job and refers to people who are either unemployed or on a government scheme.

In Table 7.11 the results from four multivariate logistic regressions are presented. The coefficients represent the ethnic effect of being in a particular subgroup of the Chinese, given the same age and education. They are presented in the form of both log odds ratios and exponentiated values. The base category is the British-born Whites, which is set to be 0 in the log form and 1 when exponentiated.

There is no ethnic difference in access to the salariat between the Chinese from South East Asia and Whites. This is also the case for the Chinese from other parts of the world. The Hong Kong Chinese have significantly worse chances of gaining access to this class. Compared with a White person of the same age and with the same qualifications, the odds of a Hong Kong born Chinese person getting into the salariat rather than not is only 46 per cent. Chances of access to the salariat are even worse when Hong Kong-born Chinese men are compared with White men. The ethnic difference may partly be explained by the fact that many Hong Kong Chinese migrated to the UK through the voucher system. They came with guaranteed jobs offered by their family members or relatives who had already settled and started Chinese restaurants. The route of employment, which was secured by the family, encapsulated the Chinese in the traditional catering trade and prevented them from competing for more highly regarded jobs in the wider labour market.

There is considerable ethnic differences in access to higher level salariat jobs. The Chinese from other parts of the world, both men and women, have a greater propensity for holding jobs in this category. For example, comparing people of similar age and education, the odds of a Chinese person being in the higher level salariat rather than not is 1.8 times that of a White person; it is 1.7 times for men and 2.2 times for women. The Chinese from South East Asia also display ethnic advantage in entering the higher salariat, but the advantage is mainly confined to men. A somewhat different pattern applies to the Chinese from Hong Kong. When compared with the White population as a whole, the Hong Kong Chinese show lower (but statistically insignificant) chances of access to this class. When men and

Table 7.11 Logistic regression: ethnic effects in occupational attainments

	All	Male	Female
Salariat			
Whites	0.	0.	0.
Chinese/United Kingdom	0.2247 (1.25)	0.4896 (1.63)	-0.0975 (.91)
Chinese/Hong Kong	-0.7846 (.46)*	-0.6351 (.53)*	-1.043 (.35)*
Chinese/South East Asia	.0.2481 (1.28)	0.3797 (1.46)	0.1158 (1.12)
Chinese/Other	-0.1514 (.86)	-0.2360 (.79)	-0.0745 (.93)
Higher salariat			
Whites	0.	0.	0.
Chinese/United Kingdom	-0.2821 (.75)	-0.3269 (.72)	-0.3441 (.71)
Chinese/Hong Kong	-0.2459 (.78)	-0.5648 (.57)*	0.2674 (1.31)
Chinese/South East Asia	0.3222 (1.38)*	0.6281 (1.87)*	0.3201 (1.38)
Chinese/Other	0.5933 (1.81)*	0.5513 (1.74)*	0.7755 (2.17)
Petty bourgeoisie			
Whites	0.	0.	0.
Chinese/United Kingdom	0.2743 (1.32)	0.0243 (1.02)	0.7648 (2.15)
Chinese/Hong Kong	1.754 (5.78)*	1.600 (4.95)*	2.062 (7.86)*
Chinese/South East Asia	-0.0461 (.95)	-0.6608 (.52)	0.6796 (1.97)*
Chinese/Other	0.8883 (2.43)*	0.6012 (1.82)*	1.413 (4.11)*
Unemployed			
Whites	0.	0.	0.
Chinese/United Kingdom	0.2926 (1.34)	0.1427 (1.15)	0.5525 (1.74)
Chinese/Hong Kong	-0.3063 (.74)*	-0.6559 (.52)*	0.2439 (1.28)
Chinese/South East Asia	-0.2039 (.82)	-0.0063 (.99)	-0.2910 (.75)
Chinese/Other	0.7129 (2.04)*	0.7105 (2.04)*	0.7129 (2.04)*

* Significant at the 0.05 level.
The figures in brackets are exponentiated values of the estimates.
Source: Two per cent individual SAR. © Crown copyright.

women were examined separately, it was found that it was really the Hong Kong-born Chinese men who suffered from ethnic disadvantage when compared with their White male counterparts. There was little difference in the chance of becoming higher salariat between Hong Kong Chinese women and White women.

Petty bourgeoisie is predominantly a characteristic of the Hong Kong-born Chinese, and to a less extent, the Chinese from other parts of the world. The analysis on access to petty bourgeoisie suggests that compared with Whites of same age and qualifications, the odds of a Hong Kong-born Chinese person entering this class rather than not is 5.7 times. It was 4.9 times for the Hong Kong-born Chinese men and 7.8 times for the women. The ethnic difference is somewhat smaller (but statistically significant) between the Whites and the Chinese born in other parts of the world. Of all immigrants, the South East Asian Chinese are the only group that shows no difference from the Whites in becoming petty bourgeoisie. Moreover, there were gender differences among the South East Asian Chinese. While men have a lower (though statistically insignificant) propensity to be in this class, their female counterparts display a greater propensity to do so, when compared with Whites of the same age with the same qualifications. These results refute the common perception that the Chinese in Britain are typically employed in the catering trade. They suggest the need to distinguish the South East Asian Chinese men from the rest with regard to catering.

There is considerable internal differentiation among the Chinese with regard to the risks of unemployment. At the one end of the spectrum, the Hong Kong-born Chinese are sheltered from unemployment by their family oriented catering business, where jobs can be created for all members during hard times (Runnymede Trust, 1985). For example, the odds of a White person being unemployed rather than not is 1.4 times that of a Chinese person born in Hong Kong. It is twice when men are compared and 1.3 times when women are compared. At the other end of the spectrum, the Chinese born in other parts of the world display greater risks of unemployment than Whites. For example, the odds of the Chinese born in other parts of the world being unemployed rather than not are twice those of the Whites. The size of ethnic difference is the same for men and women. Previous research has shown that the Chinese born in Vietnam came to Britain as refugees. They possessed poor language and technical skills. They were marked by high rates of unemployment (Jones, 1982). Although the SARs do not allow the Vietnamese Chinese to be distinguished from the rest within the category of Chinese born in other parts of the world, it is likely that a high risk of unemployment is primarily a characteristic of the Vietnamese Chinese.

7.13 Conclusion

The profile of the Chinese in Britain is one of a successful ethnic minority. It is small in size, young in age, balanced in gender and its arrival was one of the most recent on the British scene. The Chinese are well educated, the proportion of college educated and above surpassing that of the White population. They have a lower unemployment rate and are disproportionately over-represented in professional and skilled occupations. In education and occupation, the Chinese have out-performed the Whites and present a socio-economic profile reminiscent of the Chinese in the United States. Given that the Chinese have been successful in getting into the top occupational groups, it remains to be researched in the future whether they are also successful in obtaining the most desirable jobs within the top occupational groups.

The Chinese are not a homogeneous group. The analyses suggest the need to differentiate the Chinese into various subgroups, which present different demographic and socio-economic profiles. The restaurateur image is true for only 40 per cent of the working Chinese population and is mainly characteristic of the Hong Kong-born Chinese. Immigration from South East

Asia and more recently from mainland China is characterised by the selected migration of the well educated, who aspired for greater career opportunities. They come at the top of the Chinese socio-economic profile, followed by the Hong Kong Chinese and Vietnamese refugees, who come at the bottom.

There is little knowledge about the socio-economic profile of the British-born Chinese. One concern over their future occupational integration in Britain is they may be trapped in the traditional catering trade (Home Affairs Committee, 1985) in spite of their expressed aspirations for top professional jobs (Chan, 1986). Unfortunately, we do not have the appropriate data to test this hypothesis. However, the analysis on the educational attainments of the British-born Chinese shows that at least in education, the Chinese outdo the Whites. Given the present level of occupational attainments of the immigrant generation, more successful occupational integration of the second generation Chinese in Britain is predicted.

References

Baxter, S.C.C. (1988) *A Political Economy of Ethnic Chinese Catering Industry*. Unpublished Ph.D. Thesis, University of Aston.

Chan, A. (1986) *Employment Prospect of Chinese Youths in Britain*. London: Commission for Racial Equality.

Chan, Y. M. (1994) The Chinese in Greater Manchester: a demographic profile. *New Community*, 20, 655–9.

Cheng, Y. and Heath, A. (1993) Ethnic origins and class destinations. *Oxford Review of Education*, 19, 151–65.

Cheng, Y. (1994) *Education and Class: Chinese in Britain and the United States*. Aldershot: Avebury Press.

Duleep, H. (1988) *Economic Status of Americans with Asian Descent: An Exploratory Investigation*. Washington: The United States Commission of Civil Rights.

Heath, A. and McMohan, D. (1996) Educational and Occupational Attainments: The Impact of Ethnic Origins. In: Karn, V. (ed.), *Employment, education and housing among the ethnic minority populations of Britain*. To be published by HMSO, 1996.

Home Affairs Committee (1985). *Chinese Community in Britain*. London: HMSO.

Jones, P. (1982) *Vietnamese Refugees: a study of their reception and resettlement in the UK*. London: Home Office Research and Planning Unit.

Goldthorpe, J. (1987) *Social Mobility and Class Structure in Modern Britain*. Oxford: Clarendon Press.

Livesey, C. (1988) *The Residential Dispersal and Social Isolation of Chinese in Greater Manchester*. Unpublished BA Thesis, Oriel College, University of Oxford.

Ng, K.C. (1968) *The Chinese in London*. London: Oxford University Press. OPCS/GRO(S) (1993) *1991 Census Ethnic Group and Country of Birth*. *Great Britain* London: HMSO.

Parker, D. (1995) *Through Different Eyes*. Aldershot: Avebury Press.

Peach, C., Robinson, V., Maxted, J. and Chance, J. (1988) Immigrants and ethnicity. In: Halsey, A. H. (ed.), *British Social Trend Since 1900: A Guide to the Changing Social Structure of Britain*. London: Macmillan.

Runnymede Trust (1985) The Chinese community in Britain: background paper. *Runnymede Trust Bulletin*, 178, 8–15.

Shang, A. (1984) *The Chinese in Britain*. London: Batsford Academic and Educational.

Watson, J.L. (1977) The Chinese Hong Kong villagers in the British catering trade. In: Watson, J. L. (ed.), *Between Two Cultures: Migrants and Minorities in Britain*. Oxford: Basil Blackwell.

Chapter 8
The Other–Asians: the salad bowl

David Owen

8.1 Introduction

The Other–Asian ethnic grouping is a novel feature of the 1991 Census ethnic group classification. Previous official ethnic group classifications focused on the major ethnic groups present in the UK and included large undifferentiated 'Other' and 'Mixed' categories (Sillitoe and White, 1992; Bulmer, 1995). This is one of three 'Other' categories among the 10 ethnic groups that contain people who would have been included in either the mixed or the other ethnic groups in the Labour Force Survey (but unlike the Black–Other and Other–Other ethnic groups, it does not contain people of mixed parentage).

As such, the Other–Asian group is inevitably heterogeneous, since it lumps together people from numerous small ethnic groups, merged together on the basis of ultimate ethnic origin within the same very large region of the world, rather than on common characteristics or cultural affinity. Hence, the average characteristics of Other–Asians revealed by the published census data may not be typical of any of their constituent ethnic groups. There are a number of Asian ethnic groups now present in Britain whose members would have been recorded as being from 'Any other ethnic group' on the census form. These include people from a wide range of smaller New Commonwealth countries (e.g. Mauritius or Nepal) and ethnic minority groups from larger countries (such as Indo-Caribbeans), who have arrived as refugees, as students, or as people who have come to the UK as a result of changing patterns of economic activity. Each different category of people will tend to exhibit distinctive characteristics, and this chapter aims to provide more specific information about the characteristics of these groups (though much is already known about the larger components).

The Vietnamese and many Sri Lankans came to the UK as refugees from the late 1970s onwards. The former tended to be manual workers with little education and high reliance on council accommodation (Robinson and Hale, 1989). East African Asians also arrived as refugees in the early 1970s, but had the advantages of greater wealth and higher levels of education, and have therefore been more economically successful than many other ethnic minority groups (Brown, 1984; Jones, 1993). Increased teaching of overseas students has resulted in growth in the numbers of South East Asian people living in Great Britain (particularly from countries such as Malaysia and Singapore), mostly engaged in higher education and thus forming a mostly youthful transient population living in rented accommodation. The increasing integration of the UK into the European Union made it an attractive location for overseas investment during the 1980s, most of which originated in the United States and Japan. Consequently, the number of Japanese-born people resident in Great Britain more than doubled during the 1980s (Owen, 1993), most being managers of Japanese-owned firms or employees in financial services companies. Such people would probably stay for a limited period as part of their career progression within the organisation. They would be relatively affluent and some would bring their families with them, but would be less inclined to buy their own houses. Another substantial South East Asian ethnic group is the Filipinos, many of whom are women (Filipinas) working in domestic service.

This chapter uses census data to identify the experience of some of these Asian ethnic groups. It starts by identifying the ethnic and national origins of people classified as being Other–Asians, and then contrasts the demographic, social and economic characteristics of a number of the larger national groupings within the ethnic group. Finally, the extent to which census data can provide useful information on the smaller Asian ethnic groups present in Great Britain is assessed.

Ethnic composition and national origins

The category Other–Asian was constructed by OPCS from the written answers provided to the ethnic group question. Answers provided in both the 'Black–Other' and 'Any other ethnic group' boxes were allocated to this category if the description of the individual's ethnic group indicated an origin associated with Southern and South-Eastern Asia, including people describing themselves as East African Asians or Indo-Caribbeans. Consequently, the category includes both people whose ultimate national origin lay in and around the Indian subcontinent and those originating in the countries of South East Asia (excluding the Chinese), who would probably have very different social and economic characteristics.

It is therefore important to be aware of the detailed composition of this ethnic group. Table A of the *Ethnic Group and Country of Birth Report* (OPCS/GRO (S), 1993) provides a more detailed breakdown of the category, which is summarised in Figure 8.1. It shows that a small part of this ethnic group (3.7 per cent) was accounted for by Indo-Caribbeans, and a further fifth by people from the Indian subcontinent. More than three quarters were from the very broad category of Other–Asians. None of the census reports provide a more detailed ethnic breakdown of this subgroup, but Table 5 in the *Ethnic Group and Country of Birth report* disaggregates the Other–Asian category by country of birth, which provides important information on the 'national' ethnic groups making up the census ethnic group.

Table 8.1 lists those countries in which more than 500 Other–Asian people living in Great Britain in 1991 had been born. This contrasts strongly with other ethnic minority groups in having a relatively large share (49 per cent) of its overseas-born population born outside the New Commonwealth. The largest countries of origin were Sri Lanka, Japan, the Philippines, Mauritius, Malaysia and Vietnam, while a further 11,245 Other–Asian people had been born in East Africa. The relatively large shares of the population from Sri Lanka and East Africa and the presence of Vietnamese people are expected,

Figure 8.1 *Composition of the Other–Asian ethnic group*

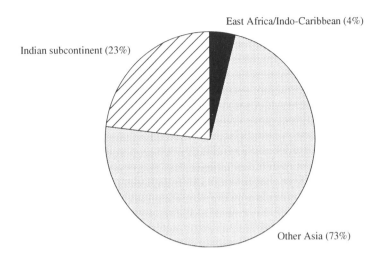

East Africa/Indo-Caribbean (4%)

Indian subcontinent (23%)

Other Asia (73%)

but the novel feature of this table is perhaps the substantial number of Japanese-born people, who comprised an eighth of all Other–Asian people living in Great Britain in 1991, reflecting the rapid expansion of Japanese inward investment and the location of Japanese financial institutions in Britain during the 1980s.

People from other South East Asian countries also formed a significant part of the Other–Asian ethnic group, possibly resulting from increased numbers of overseas students from these countries coming to the UK to receive higher education during the 1980s, but perhaps also reflecting increased migration to fill low status service sector jobs in the case of Filipinas. Though this table illustrates the great diversity of the ethnic group in national terms, it still fails to identify subnational ethnic groups who may have filled in the 'Any other ethnic group' box, such as Parsis originating in India or Pakistan and smaller national groups, such as Afghans and Nepalese, which were aggregated into Other–Asian.

The final column of Table 8.1 presents the percentage of all persons born in a given country and resident in Great Britain in 1991 who were classified as being from the Other–Asian ethnic group. This may be interpreted as an indicator of how good the country of birth is as an ethnic indicator. Thus, more than 80 per cent of all persons born in Japan and the Philippines and three quarters of the Sri Lankan born were Other–Asians, showing a close correspondence between nationality and ethnicity. However, Other–Asians formed a minority of persons born in Malaysia, Mauritius and Vietnam; this partly reflects the number of White people born in former colonies (as in East Africa), the presence of other significant ethnic groups (e.g. the Chinese in Vietnam) and ethnic diversity (the Mauritian-born boasted a very broad range of ethnic groups in 1991).

Table 8.1 *Geographical distribution of Other – Asian people born outside the UK, in 1991: origins of more than 500 people*

Country of birth		% of all Other – Asians	% of non– UK born Other – Asians	% of all born in country of origin
All countries of birth	197,534	100.0	-	0.4
United Kingdom	43,265	21.9		0.1
Outside United Kingdom	154,269	78.1	100.0	4.1
New Commonwealth	78,665	39.8	51.0	4.7
Sri Lanka	29,474	14.9	19.1	74.8
Japan	24,482	12.4	15.9	86.7
Phillippines	17,634	8.9	11.4	80.7
Mauritius	11,352	5.7	7.4	48.4
Malaysia	9,614	4.9	6.2	22.1
Vietnam	9,561	4.8	6.2	47.5
Kenya	6,161	3.1	4.0	5.5
India	5,996	3.0	3.9	1.5
Thailand	4,882	2.5	3.2	66.4
Pakistan	3,280	1.7	2.1	1.4
Uganda	2,901	1.5	1.9	5.7
Burma (Myanmar, Union of)	2,322	1.2	1.5	21.9
Tanzania	2,183	1.1	1.4	7.3
Singapore	1,122	0.6	0.7	3.3
Iran	1,111	0.6	0.7	3.4
Bangladesh	993	0.5	0.6	1.0
Seychelles	766	0.4	0.5	25.8
Guyana	746	0.4	0.5	3.6
United States of America	724	0.4	0.5	0.5
Trinidad and Tobago	673	0.3	0.4	3.8
Malawi	642	0.3	0.4	6.0
Hong Kong	611	0.3	0.4	0.8

Source: OPCS /GRO(S) (1993) Ethnic Group and Country of Birth Report, Volume 1, Table 5.

In the remainder of this chapter, the average results for the Other–Asian group as a whole will be broken down where possible by country of birth. However, while the Samples of Anonymised Records (SARs) (Marsh and Teague, 1992) have great value in enabling more detailed analyses of census data on ethnic groups to be undertaken than is possible using the standard outputs from the census, the need to preserve confidentiality means that the level of detail available is restricted for some variables. The condensed country of birth classification (into 42 categories) used in the SARs greatly restricts the analysis of the Other–Asian category which can be undertaken, since countries such as Vietnam and Japan have been combined into a very broad 'Other Asia' category. A five-fold classification of national origins into East Africa, the Caribbean, Sri Lanka, Malaysia/Singapore and Other Asia is thus adopted for the analyses presented in the remainder of this chapter, in order to provide some indication of the contrasting characteristics of the ethnic groups corresponding to these national origins, while recognising that this obscures important contrasts, for example between the Japanese and the Vietnamese.

8.2 Geographical distribution

The distribution of Other–Asian people across the regions, countries and metropolitan counties of Great Britain is summarised in Table 8.2. Overall, 142,900 of the total ethnic group population of 197,500 lived in south east England, where it formed 0.8 per cent of the population. However, this disguises the marked concentration of Other–Asian people in Greater London (mostly in outer London), where the ethnic group's share of the resident population was 4.25 times greater than its share of the population of Great Britain. Outside London, Other–Asian people mainly lived in and around the larger cities, with the Other–Asian share of the resident population greatest in the West Midlands, West Yorkshire and Greater Manchester

Table 8.2 *Regional distribution of the Other–Asian ethnic group, 1991*

Region or metropolitan county	Other–Asians	% of pop–ulation	Regional share of				
			East Africa	Carib–bean	Sri Lanka	Malaysia Singapore	Other Asia
South East	142.9	0.8	67.4	85.2	89.5	52.7	75.9
Greater London	*112.8*	*1.7*	*54.5*	*69.3*	*74.3*	*36.9*	*60.5*
Inner London	45.4	1.8	11.1	17.3	21.5	16.6	27.7
Outer London	67.4	1.6	43.4	52.0	52.8	20.3	32.8
East Anglia	3.8	0.2	4.3	-	1.2	1.9	2.5
South West	4.5	0.1	3.1	-	0.8	2.5	3.0
West Midlands	11.5	0.2	5.7	3.6	1.1	6.0	3.3
West Midlands	*8.9*	*0.3*	*4.6*	*-*	*0.3*	*5.4*	*2.1*
East Midlands	7.2	0.2	9.1	8.2	2.5	4.7	2.6
Yorkshire and Humberside	7.3	0.2	2.6	-	1.9	9.0	1.9
South Yorkshire	*1.4*	*0.1*	*0.8*	*-*	*0.5*	*3.1*	*0.7*
West Yorkshire	*4.6*	*0.2*	*1.5*	*-*	*1.5*	*3.1*	*0.9*
North West	8.9	0.1	4.2	-	1.1	6.3	4.3
Greater Manchester	*4.9*	*0.2*	*2.7*	*-*	*0.3*	*2.7*	*2.5*
Merseyside	*1.3*	*0.1*	*-*	*-*	*1.8*	*1.2*
North	3.1	0.1	-	-	0.5	6.3	2.0
Tyne and Wear	*1.6*	*0.1*	*-*	*-*	*0.2*	*4.9*	*0.9*
Wales	3.7	0.1	1.0	-	0.5	5.3	1.9
Scotland	4.6	0.1	2.4	3.0	0.9	5.3	2.5
Great Britain	197.5	0.4	100.0	100.0	100.0	100.0	100.0

Source: OPCS/GRO(S) (1993) Volume 2, Table A.

metropolitan counties, though the ethnic group was also strongly represented in the other regions of the south and east of England (the East Midlands and East Anglia).

The larger ethnic groups within the Other–Asian grouping displayed a similar geographical distribution, but some were even more strongly concentrated. Two thirds of East Africans, three quarters of people from Other Asia, over 85 per cent of Caribbeans and nearly 90 per cent of Sri Lankans lived in the South East region. In each case, well over half lived within Greater London, while nearly 70 per cent of Caribbeans and nearly 75 per cent of Sri Lankans lived in Greater London. The Malaysia/Singapore grouping contrasts strongly with the remainder, since only half of all people from this group lived in the South East, and just over a third lived in Greater London. The largest concentrations of East Africans outside Greater London were found in the East Midlands (mainly Leicester), the West Midlands metropolitan county, the North West and East Anglia. Outside Greater London, Caribbeans were concentrated in the Midlands and Scotland. Sri Lankans living outside Greater London were more evenly distributed, but there were local concentrations in the East Midlands, West Yorkshire and East Anglia. The largest concentrations of those from Other Asia outside Greater London were in the West Midlands and Greater Manchester metropolitan counties, East Anglia, the South West and Scotland (the latter possibly reflecting the presence of financial services and electronics companies). Those born in Malaysia and Singapore displayed a much more dispersed pattern of settlement, with the West Midlands and Tyne & Wear metropolitan counties, Wales and Scotland having the largest shares of people with these national origins.

Demographic features

The Other–Asian ethnic group has a demographic profile similar to that of the Chinese ethnic group. Both are very different to both those of other ethnic minority groups and to the White population. Figure 8.2 presents the population pyramid for all Other–Asian people in 1991 (and includes the estimated effect of census under-enumeration by age-group, indicated by the darker shading at the end of each bar). The most notable feature is the marked 'bulge' in the number of people in the younger part of the working age range. Children were much less prominent in the population than for other ethnic minority groups, while older people were less common than in the White ethnic group. Women were more numerous than men in some of the economically active age-groups.

Figure 8.3 contrasts the age structure of persons born inside and outside the UK. A very marked contrast is revealed. Nearly all people of working age and older were born outside the UK (see the darker shading), but the percentage born in the UK increased with declining age. As a result, the age distribution of UK-born Other – Asians had a strongly pyramidal shape, indicating rapid growth in the number of children born in the UK. However, the percentage born outside the UK was substantial in all but the youngest age-groups, indicating the continuing importance of immigration for the growth of this ethnic group.

Figure 8.2 Age and gender structure of Other–Asians

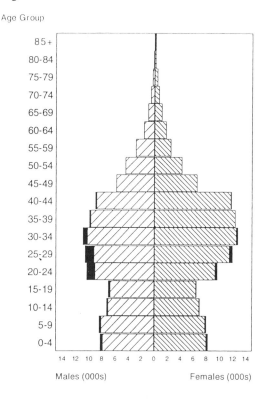

Age Group

Males (000s)   Females (000s)

Figure 8.3 Age and gender structure of Other–Asian people born within and outside the UK

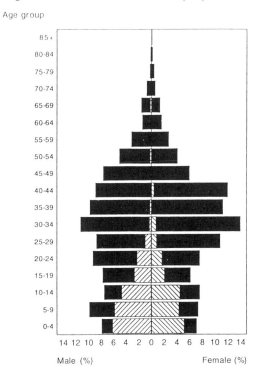

Age group

Male (%)   Female (%)

Table 8.3 also summarises the age and gender structure of the ethnic group, contrasting persons born inside and outside the UK. The contrast in age structure within the ethnic group is dramatically highlighted, with the average age of those born outside the UK being nearly three times greater than that of the UK-born. Around three quarters of people born in the UK were of school-age or less, with a quarter in the pre-school age-group. Only about 10 per cent of females and a smaller percentage of males were aged over 25. In contrast, only an eighth of males and a tenth of females born outside the UK were children. Half of males and more than half of females were in the prime economically active age range, 25–44 years. In the older age-groups, men were more numerous than women.

The contrasts in age structure strongly influenced the patterns of marital status. The percentage of UK-born men and women who were single was 2.5 to 3 times higher than that of people born outside the UK. Conversely, the percentages of UK-born men and women who were married or remarried was only a third for men and half for women of the corresponding percentages of non-UK-born people. In the foreign-born population, women were slightly more likely than men to be married, but UK-born women were much more likely than men to be married, implying a much lower mean age at marriage for women than men. Differences in the percentages widowed and divorced between those born within and outside the UK were quite small.

Differences in age and sex structure between the various ethnic groups subsumed within the Other–Asian category are illustrated in Table 8.4.

Table 8.3 *Summary demographic characteristics of the Other – Asian ethnic group contrasting those born within and outside the United Kingdom, for Great Britain ,1991*

Age group, marital status	All Other – Asians		Born in UK		Born outside UK	
	Male	Female	Male	Female	Male	Female
Population (000s)	93.6	103.9	(453)	(414)	(1495)	(1720)
% aged 0– 4	8.4	7.6	25.5	26.4	2.1	2.4
% aged 5–15	17.6	15.3	46.6	46.5	10.0	8.2
% aged 16–24	15.6	14.0	19.3	16.4	14.8	11.9
% aged 25–44	40.6	46.1	6.6	9.6	48.7	57.5
% aged 45–59/64	15.7	12.8	1.4	0.9	20.9	15.3
% pensionable age	2.1	4.2	0.6	0.2	3.4	4.7
Median age in years	29.2	30.9	12.3	12.6	33.9	34.2
Percentage of all aged 16 and over						
Single	34.7	27.0	74.4	58.8	30.0	21.0
Married/remarried	62.0	64.4	23.2	36.9	67.4	71.1
Widowed	0.8	4.4	1.6	3.7	2.2	4.0
Divorced	2.6	4.2	0.8	0.7	0.3	3.9

Sources: 1991 Census Local Base Statistics (ESRC purchase); Crown Copyright. OPCS/GRO(S) (1993) Two per cent individual SAR.

Note: Figures in brackets are numbers of people in the SAR.

Table 8.4 *Summary demographic characteristics of the individual Other – Asian ethnic groups, Great Britain, 1991*

Age group	East Africa	Carib-bean	Sri Lanka	Malaysia /Singapore	Other Asia
Males per 1000 females	1,070	444	1,380	1,094	647
% aged 0–4	-	5.4	1.3	6.6	2.7
% aged 5–15	1.7	2.9	7.5	8.6	12.1
% aged 16–24	12.1	12.5	14.0	25.2	12.4
% aged 25–44	57.6	31.6	51.5	47.3	55.9
% aged 45–59/64	25.1	39.1	18.6	11.4	14.4
% pensionable age	3.4	8.4	7.1	0.9	2.5
Mean age in years	37.4	40.4	36.0	28.6	32.2

Source: Two per cent individual SAR.

There were marked contrasts in the sex balances of the various national origins; men were strongly in the majority among Sri Lankans, but women formed the majority of Caribbeans and those born in other countries of Asia, with a broad balance in the other two categories. East Africans and Caribbeans tended to be older on average, with a quarter of the former and nearly two fifths of the latter aged from 45 to retirement age. Moreover, pensioners formed a much larger percentage of the Caribbean group than all the other groups, except Sri Lankans (echoing the more elderly age structure of Black–Caribbean people).

With the exception of Caribbeans, half or more of each national group were in the 25–44 age-group. The Malaysia/Singapore national grouping was distinctive in being much younger on average than the other four. The percentage aged 16–24 was around twice that for the other four national groupings. The percentage of pre-school-age children in the Malaysia/Singapore group was much higher than for the other national groupings, but the share of school-age children was highest for people from the Other Asia group of countries. This might be a reflection of workers from these countries bringing their families with them (e.g. younger managers in Japanese car companies; but this average figure may conceal considerable differences between, say, those born in Japan and the Philippines). Unfortunately, children born in the UK to people from these national origins cannot be identified from the 2 per cent individual SAR (the one per cent household SAR does provide this information, but sample sizes are very small).

8.3   Families, household structure and housing

Families

The Other–Asian ethnic group as a whole had a relatively large percentage of married couples in 1991, while cohabiting was quite rare and the percentage of lone parent families was lower than for families from both White and many other ethnic minority groups (Berrington[1996] deals with marriage patterns in greater detail). There were some notable differences between the five major national origins within the Other–Asian ethnic group (Table 8.5). Caribbean people were more likely to live in families containing a married couple, while people born in Malaysia and Singapore were least likely to live in such families. The latter were also more likely to live in families containing cohabiting couples or lone parents. Caribbean families were most likely to have dependent children, and also most likely to have non-dependent children — reflecting their relatively older age structure. Of those who lived in families containing cohabiting couples or lone parents, those born in Malaysia and Singapore were most likely to have dependent children.

Households

Other–Asian households were larger than average in 1991, but smaller than those of South Asian ethnic groups (Table 8.6). This phenomenon appears to reveal a contrast between the South and South East Asian components of the ethnic group. East African, Caribbean and Sri Lankan households were larger than the average for the ethnic group, while those for the Malaysia/ Singapore and Other Asia-born were smaller than the average. This differential was repeated for the mean number of dependent children per household. The greater average age of Caribbean-born people was responsible for this section of the ethnic group having the highest proportion of pensioner households.

Table 8.5 *Comparison of family types for the Other–Asian ethnic group and its components, 1991*

Type of family	All Other–Asians	East Africa	Carib–bean	Sri Lanka	Malyasia Singapore	Other Asia
Total families	**4,456**	**(48)**	**(9)**	**(79)**	**(18)**	**(140)**
Married couple family (%)	*82.7*	*85.4*	*100.0*	*84.8*	*66.7*	*85.0*
0 dependent children (%)	17.1	12.5	-	22.8	16.7	18.6
1+ dependent children (%)	49.0	64.6	66.7	51.9	50.0	62.1
non-dependent children (%)	8.1	8.3	33.3	10.1	-	4.3
Cohabiting couple family (%)	*3.4*	*2.1*	*0.0*	*0.0*	*11.1*	*2.8*
0 dependent children (%)	2.6	-	-	-	-	1.4
1+ dependent children (%)	2.1	2.1	-	-	11.1	1.4
non-dependent children (%)	0.2	-	-	-	-	-
Lone parent famiy (%)	*13.8*	*12.6*	-	*15.2*	*22.3*	*12.2*
1+ dependent children (%)	10.0	6.3	-	7.6	16.7	9.3
non-dependent children (%)	3.8	6.3	-	7.6	5.6	2.9

Source: One per cent household SAR. Figures in brackets are sample sizes.

Table 8.6 *Household size, housing tenure and amenities for the Other – Asian ethnic group, and its components, 1991*

Household characteristics or family type	All Other – Asians	East Africa	Carib– bean	Sri Lanka	Malaysia Singapore	Other Asia
All households (100%)	58,955	(57)	(10)	(100)	(32)	(203)
Mean household size	3.2	3.5	4.0	3.5	2.9	2.9
Mean number of dependent children	1.9	1.1	1.2	0.8	0.9	0.9
Percent pensioner households	2.6	-	10.0	4.0	6.3	2.0
Percentage of households						
Owner-occupied	53.9	71.9	70.0	76.0	34.4	29.6
Renting: private	24.5	10.5	10.0	11.0	46.9	48.8
Renting: housing association	4.4	8.8	10.0	4.0	3.1	3.0
Renting: public sector	13.6	8.8	10.0	9.0	15.6	18.7
Percentage of households living in each type of accommodation						
Detached houses	12.7	14.0	10.0	15.0	-	16.3
Semi-detached houses	17.9	19.3	40.0	19.0	28.1	13.8
Terraced houses	33.9	45.6	40.0	34.0	31.3	21.2
Flats	32.8	19.3	10.0	31.0	34.4	45.8
Rooms	0.5	-	-	-	-	1.0
Bed-sits	2.0	1.8	-	1.0	6.3	2.0
Percentage of households						
With 1+ person per room	11.0	8.8	-	23.0	6.3	9.4
Lacking/sharing bathroom/WC	3.0	1.8	-	1.0	6.3	3.0
Without a car	32.4	26.3	40.0	23.0	50.0	36.5

Source: One per cent household SAR. Figures in brackets are sample sizes.

Housing

The South East Asia/South Asia contrast was also apparent in housing tenures. Over 70 per cent of households with heads born in East Africa, the Caribbean or Sri Lanka were owner-occupiers, while a third or less of households with South East Asian-born heads were owner-occupiers. The latter were also far more likely to rent from the private sector, and were less likely to be housing association tenants than households whose heads were born in the Caribbean, East Africa or Sri Lanka. There was also some evidence of a contrast in the type of dwelling in which households resided. East African and Caribbean households were most likely to live in semi-detached and terraced houses, and less likely than other sections of the Other–Asian ethnic group to live in flats. People born in Malaysia and Singapore or Other Asia were more likely than the South Asian sections of the ethnic group to live in flats and bed-sits; probably reflecting their tenure types and relative youth. Turning to physical housing conditions, Sri Lankans were most likely to live in overcrowded conditions (at a density of more than one person per room) than the other national origins, while overcrowding was least prevalent for households with heads born in Malaysia and Singapore. However, households from the two South East Asian sections of the ethnic group were most likely to live in accommodation without the exclusive use of basic amenities (bathroom and WC); again a reflection of greater propensity to live in less spacious privately rented accommodation. Car ownership is often used as an indicator of material prosperity. On this measure, Sri Lankans and East Africans emerged as most prosperous (since only around a quarter of households did not have a car) and those born in Malaysia and Singapore as least prosperous, since half of all households did not have a car; though this might also reflect the lesser need for car ownership for students living in large urban areas. Caribbean and Other–Asian households occupied an intermediate position on this measure.

8.4 Social and economic characteristics

This section explores contrasts in health between the Other–Asian ethnic group as a whole and the rest of the population and contrasts the experience of the five components of the ethnic group in the labour market and in terms of educational qualifications.

Health differentials

The 1991 Census contains information on the number of people who suffered from a limiting long-term illness. This can be used to compare differentials in health between ethnic groups and between men and women. Table 8.7 compares Other–Asian people with White people and the average for all people from ethnic minority groups. The crude percentages of people suffering from limiting long-term illnesses show that people from ethnic minority groups were much less likely than White people to be experiencing a long-term health problem in 1991, and that Other–Asian people experienced illness rates well below the ethnic minority group average. The percentage of households containing a person with a limiting long-term illness was also strikingly low.

However, health tends to deteriorate with age, and inter-ethnic group differences are thus strongly influenced by the differences in age structure between ethnic groups. It is thus more meaningful to compare the rate of limiting long-term illness with the same rate standardised to take the age structure of an ethnic group into account, which can be calculated using the individual 2 per cent SAR. This confirms the relatively good health of the Other–Asian ethnic group (Table 8.7). The percentage of White people with limiting long-term illnesses was very close (actually marginally below) that which would be expected from the age structure of the ethnic group for both males and females, but illness rates for the Other–Asian ethnic groups were only around 80 per cent of the expected value for both males and females.

Table 8.7 *Limiting long-term illness for Other – Asian people compared to White people and all ethnic minority groups, 1991*

Long-term ill persons and illness rates	Other – Asian	White people	Ethnic minority groups
Persons suffering limiting long-term illness (000s)	10.9	6,949.7	251.8
Percent of all persons	5.5	13.4	8.4
Households containing a long-term ill person (000s)	8.2	5,227.4	182.3
Percent of all households	13.9	24.9	20.9
Mean number of ill per household	1.3	1.3	1.4
Male age standardised long-term illness rate	6.7	12.0	8.1
Female age standardised long-term illness rate	6.2	13.1	6.1
Male relative illness rate	0.79	0.99	1.15
Female relative illness rate	0.81	0.99	1.32

Sources: 1991 Census Local Base Statistics (ESRC purchase) and two per cent individual SAR; both Crown Copyright.

Labour market participation

It has already been noted that the population structure of the Other–Asian group is highly biased towards the younger end of the economically active age range (from 16 to 59 for women and 64 for men). Accordingly, patterns of economic activity and the way in which they vary between the components of the Other–Asian ethnic group are of considerable interest.

The percentages of Other–Asian men and women of economically active age who were economically active in 1991 were slightly lower than the corresponding averages for all ethnic minority groups, and substantially below those for White people (Table 8.8). Just over three quarters of men and just over half of all women were participating in the labour market, and thus nearly a quarter of men and half of all women were economically inactive in 1991. However, this disguises the fact that younger people were much less likely to be working or seeking work than older people; under half of 16–24-year-old men and less than two fifths of women in the same age-group were economically active, representing a rate of economic activity well below the ethnic minority group average, and even further below the rates for White people.

Men from East Africa and the Caribbean and women from the Caribbean and Sri Lanka displayed economic activity rates of well above the average for all Other–Asians (Table 8.9). Less than half of all men born in Malaysia and Singapore were economically active, in marked contrast to the remaining Other–Asians. For women, economic activity rates were much lower for South East Asians than for South Asians. The percentage of both men and women aged 16–24 active in the labour market was much lower than those for the working age population as a whole, across all national origins, with the exception that young East African women were more likely to be

Table 8.8 *Labour market participation of Other – Asian people in Great Britain, 1991*

Economic status	White people		Ethnic minority groups		Other – Asian people	
	Male	Female	Male	Female	Male	Female
Aged 16+						
Total (000s)	19,927.7	21,918.7	1,000.6	1018.1	69.0	80.1
Economically active (000s)	14,577.7	10,897.4	761.9	539.8	52.8	43.2
Economic activity rate%	73.2	49.7	76.2	53.0	76.4	53.9
Aged 16–59/64						
Total (000s)	16,442.7	15,259.2	949.9	937.7	67.0	75.7
Economically active (000s)	14,299.4	10,422.8	755.0	530.4	52.4	42.5
Economic activity rate (%)	87.0	68.3	79.5	56.6	78.2	56.2
16–24 year olds						
Total (000s)	3,262.1	3,246.6	237.8	246.5	14.6	14.5
Economically active (000s)	2,544.2	2,169.9	138.4	120.4	6.7	5.7
Economic activity rate (%)	78.0	66.8	58.2	48.8	45.9	39.1
All in work (000s)	12,822.4	10,087.9	589.4	440.8	43.8	36.6
Unemployed (000s)	1,556.5	689.7	154.4	84.0	7.5	5.3
Unemployment rate	10.7	6.3	20.3	15.6	14.2	12.3
Economically inactive aged 16 and over						
Total (000s)	5,345.0	11,021.3	238.7	478.4	16.5	37.0
Inactivity rate (%)	26.9	50.3	23.8	47.0	23.8	46.1
Composition of the economically inactive						
Full-time students (%)	13.5	6.7	49.9	20.7	68.4	24.7
Permanently sick (%)	18.5	6.6	19.9	7.6	10.0	4.2
Retired (%)	65.2	42.9	21.9	10.9	12.2	6.9
Other inactive (%)	2.7	43.9	8.2	73.4	9.3	64.2

Source: OPCS/GRO(S) (1993), Volume 2, Table 10.

Table 8.9 *Economic activity rates for Other – Asian people by national origin and gender, Great Britain, 1991*

Ethnic group or national origin	Aged 16–59/64		Aged 16–24	
	Male	Female	Male	Female
Other – Asians	78.2	56.2	45.9	39.1
East Africa	82.7	57.7	58.3	59.0
Caribbean	86.3	69.5	-	39.6
Sri Lanka	78.1	67.5	49.3	37.6
Malaysia/Singapore	46.0	43.3	17.7	22.9
Other Asia	79.5	48.2	38.3	24.7

Source: 1991 Census two per cent individual SAR, Crown Copyright.

economically active than all women of working age. Again, those born in Malaysia, Singapore and Other Asia displayed the lowest economic activity rates, with under a fifth of men born in Malaysia and Singapore economically active.Figures 8.4 (a) and (b) illustrate how labour market participation varied with age for men and women from the Other–Asian ethnic group as a whole. Male participation rates increased much more gradually with age than for the population as a whole, reaching a peak for 40–44-year-olds, remaining high for longer as age increased, but declining rapidly after the age of 60. For women, the peak rate of labour market participation occurred for 45–49-year-olds, declining thereafter with increasing age. There was a smaller peak for women aged 25–29, suggesting that women in their early thirties may follow the pattern of White women in temporarily withdrawing from the labour force in order to look after children.

However, the main influence on this slow entry into the labour market was the relatively long time spent in full-time education. Among 16–24 -year-old men and women, full-time education was the predominant type of activity, and only when the 25–29-year-old age-group was reached did the number in employment exceed the number in full-time study. The number of students remained substantial at least up to the age of 40. For women, the number 'other inactive' (which includes people looking after a home or family full time) increased rapidly after the age of 20, and was largest for women aged

Figure 8.4a *Economic status by age-group, males*

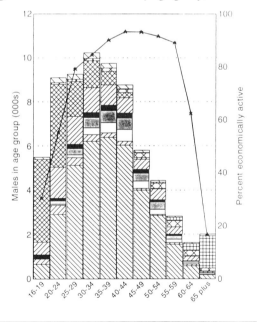

Figure 8.4b *Economic status by age-group, females*

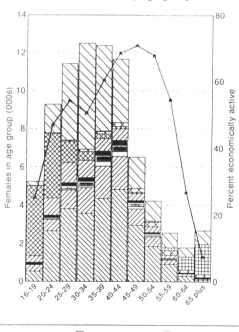

from 25 to 44. Among men, the majority were full-time employees, with part-time employment only significant for younger men. The share of the self-employed increased with age up to 45 years, with entrepreneurs (self-employed people employing others) most common in the 35–49 age range. The largest numbers of unemployed were aged 20 to 25, thereafter declining with increasing age. For women, part-time employment was more impor-tant, particularly for 30 to 45-year-olds, which was also the age range in which unemployment was most common. For both men and women, the numbers permanently sick increased with age.

For both men and women, the pattern of economic activity varies across the different national origins categories (data not shown). Turning first to males, differences in age structure between national origins were reflected in contrasts in activity; a quarter of Caribbean men were permanently sick or retired, while more than half of Malaysia and Singapore-born men were full-time students. Other–Asians, East Africans and Sri Lankans were most likely to be employees. Self-employment was most significant for East Africans and Caribbeans, and slightly less significant for the third South Asian national group, the Sri Lankans. The percentage of men aged 16 and over unemployed was highest for Sri Lankans and lowest for those born in Malaysia and Singapore. With the exception of the Caribbean group, less than half of women aged 16 and over were employees. Self-employment was most significant for East African women. A higher percentage of Sri Lankan women than women from any other national origin was unemployed. Full-time students were most common among those born in Malaysia and Singa-pore, followed by Other Asia and Sri Lanka. While a third or more of women born in East Africa, Malaysia/Singapore and Other Asia were 'other inac-tive', this category accounted for a quarter or less of Caribbean and Sri Lankan-born women.

Unemployment

Unemployment rates for Other–Asian men were a third higher than those of White men, while unemployment rates for Other–Asian women were nearly double the corresponding figure for White women in 1991 (see Table 8.10). For both men and women, unemployment rates for Sri Lankans were well above the Other–Asian average, while those for other national origins were often well below the average. Those born in Malaysia and Singapore expe-rienced particularly low unemployment rates, being the only Other–Asian ethnic group to experience an unemployment rate lower than that for White men (10.7 per cent). Female unemployment rates were lower than those for men for all national origins, and were lowest for those born in Malaysia, Singapore and the Caribbean.Young Other–Asian men appear to be more disadvantaged relative to White men than all men of working age since their unemployment rate was about 70 per cent higher than that for White men in 1991. Once again, the unemployment rate for the ethnic group as a whole was increased by the very high unemployment rate experienced by young Sri Lankan men (an unemployment rate even higher than that experienced by young Pakistani men). Unemployment rates for other national origins, though high, were well below the average. The unemployment rate for young Other–Asian women was about 90 per cent higher than that for 16–24-year-old White women. In marked contrast to Other–Asian men and women

Table 8.10 *Unemployment rates for Other – Asian people by national origin and gender, Great Britain, 1991*

Ethnic group or national origin	Aged 16–59/64		Aged 16–24	
	Male	Female	Male	Female
Other – Asians	14.2	12.3	29.4	21.6
East Africa	11.8	9.0	20.0	33.3
Caribbean	12.5	6.3	-	-
Sri Lanka	18.7	14.0	43.3	12.5
Malaysia/Singapore	9.1	2.6	-	20.0
Other Asia	12.3	11.4	26.6	40.0

Source: 1991 Census two per cent individual SAR, Crown Copyright.

as a whole, young Sri Lankan women experienced the lowest unemployment rates, and women born in Other Asia suffered the highest unemployment rates.

Employment

Some key features of employment for this ethnic group in 1991 are summarised in Table 8.11. Over the past 25 years, there has been a steady shift of employment from full-time to part-time jobs. In 1991, nearly all Other–Asian male employees were in full-time jobs, but a quarter of female employees worked part time. Men were slightly more likely than White men to work part time, while women were much less likely than White women to be part-time employees. East African-born men were most likely to be full-time employees and Caribbean-born men were least likely to work full time. Women born in Malaysia and Singapore and East Africa were most likely to be full-time employees, while Caribbean-born women were far more likely to be part-time employees than women from all other national origins.

The most dynamic feature of employment change during the 1980s was the rapid growth of self-employment, associated with increasing numbers of small businesses, and it is an important source of jobs for other South Asian and Chinese ethnic groups (Owen, 1996). Self-employment was markedly less significant for Other–Asian men than for White men in 1991, while the percentages of White and Other–Asian women self-employed were quite similar. East Africa and Caribbean-born men were most likely to be self-employed and those born in Other Asia were least likely to be self-employed. For women, self-employment was most common for those born in East Africa, but the percentage self-employed for women from all other national origins was similar to or below that for White women. In contrast to most other Asian ethnic groups, entrepreneurs — the self-employed with employees — formed a smaller percentage of all economically active men than for White men, though the corresponding percentages for women were very similar. Men born in the Caribbean and East Africa were most likely, and those born in Other Asia least likely, to be entrepreneurs. East Africa-

Table 8.11 *Key types of employment for Other – Asian people by national origin and gender, Great Britain, 1991*

Ethnic group, or national origin	% employed full-time		% of all working self-employed		Self employed with employees % of workforce	
	Male	Female	Male	Female	Male	Female
White	95.8	60.3	17.6	6.6	5.1	2.2
Other – Asians	94.8	75.3	12.2	6.9	4.6	2.3
East Africa	97.3	78.2	21.6	12.5	8.1	4.3
Caribbean	80.0	15.3	28.6	-	12.5	-
Sri Lanka	94.4	69.9	12.9	6.7	3.7	2.1
Malaysia/Singapore	93.9	85.7	12.5	5.1	4.5	2.6
Other Asia	95.5	73.5	6.9	5.0	2.7	1.2

Source: 1991 Census two per cent individual SAR, Crown Copyright.

born women were most likely to be entrepreneurs and Other Asia-born women were again least likely to be entrepreneurs.

The industries in which Other–Asian people of the five national origins worked in 1991 are presented in Table 8.12. More than a quarter of all men worked in the distribution sector (which includes restaurants, catering and retailing) with a further fifth employed in business services (which includes financial and professional services). The other main sources of employment were the health and education services, the engineering sector, transport and communications, and public administration. In contrast, the distribution sector, and health and education services together employed more than half of all women, with most of the remainder being employed by the business services and miscellaneous services (mainly private sector service activities) industries.

For all but those born in Malaysia and Singapore, the distribution sector was the largest source of employment; for this national origin, the health and education sector employed the largest share of all workers. For all except those born in the Caribbean, distribution, business services, and health and education were the main industries of employment. For the Caribbean-born, most people worked in distribution, health and education, and miscellaneous services. The percentage working in health and education was much higher for those born in Sri Lanka, Malaysia and Singapore than for those born elsewhere. Manufacturing industry employed only a small percentage of workers from all national origins. However, 9.1 per cent of the East African-born and 6.6 per cent of those born in Other Asia worked in the engineering industry.

Reflecting their employment mainly in the service sector, Other–Asian men had an occupational structure oriented towards white collar and profes-

Table 8.12 *The industrial structure of work for Other – Asian people ,Great Britain, 1991*

Industrial category	Other – Asian		East Africa (%)	Carib–bean (%)	Sri Lanka (%)	Malaysia /Singapore (%)	Other Asia (%)
	Male (%)	Female (%)					
Agriculture, etc	0.2	0.0	-	-	-	-	0.2
Mining	0.2	0.3	-	-	-	2.1	0.4
Utilities	0.5	0.3	0.6	-	0.6	2.1	0.2
Metals and minerals	0.2	0.1	1.3	-	-	-	0.5
Chemicals	0.7	0.4	1.8	2.3	0.4	-	1.1
Engineering	8.7	2.5	9.1	3.9	3.9	2.4	6.6
Food, drink, tobacco	1.0	1.0	1.7	3.9	1.1		0.9
Textiles and clothing	0.7	2.7	1.5	-	0.3	3.3	1.6
Other manufacturing	3.3	1.8	5.4	-	2.1	3.5	1.8
Construction	2.8	1.0	3.2	4.4	3.0	4.5	2.2
Distribution	27.5	26.5	26.2	31.8	28.8	19.2	34.2
Transport/communications	8.7	4.4	10.0	12.2	4.2	3.4	6.6
Business services	19.2	11.3	18.9	-	15.1	19.8	16.7
Miscellaneous services	5.6	13.7	5.6	18.1	7.7	7.1	9.5
Health and education	12.7	26.3	11.6	19.1	21.9	23.4	16.2
Public administration	7.8	7.7	3.0	4.4	10.9	9.2	1.5
	(1,001)	(929)	(190)	(32)	(357)	(88)	(730)

Source: 1991 Census two per cent individual SAR; Crown Copyright. Figures in brackets are sample sizes.

sional occupations (Table 8.13). The largest single occupational category was corporate managers and administrators, followed by managers and proprietors in agriculture and services, and clerical occupations. Most of the professional occupations contained around 5 per cent of Other–Asian men in work, the largest category of employment being science and engineering professionals, followed by health professionals. Skilled and unskilled manual workers were less common than among White men, but personal service occupations were more important. There was a marked gender division of labour, with the most common occupations for women being clerical occupations, personal service occupations and health associate professions.

The occupational structure of employment for all persons born in each of the national origins obscures this gender division in the type of jobs held, but the size of the SAR sample is too small to permit further disaggregation. There were clear differences in the skill structures of Other–Asian people, on the basis of their countries of birth. For East Africans, the largest occupations were clerical occupations, managers and proprietors in agriculture and services, and industrial plant and machine operators. This represents the existence of small businessmen, mainly in the distribution industry, the importance of the engineering industry for employment and probably also reflects a larger share of women in the workforce. East Africans were more likely to be managers and proprietors than people from other national origins. The occupational structure of Caribbean-born people was biased towards more routine occupations, with the largest occupations being health associate professions, other elementary occupations (unskilled jobs), industrial plant and machine operators, other sales occupations and secretarial occupations.

Table 8.13 *The occupational structure of work for the Other – Asian ethnic group*

Standard Occupational Classification sub-major group	Other – Asian		East Africa	Carib– bean	Sri Lanka	Malaysia /Singapore	Other Asia
	Male (%)	Female (%)	(%)	(%)	(%)	(%)	(%)
Corporate managers and administrators	14.2	3.8	6.0	7.9	8.1	9.7	10.8
Managers and proprietors in agriculture and services	10.0	4.9	12.2	7.2	6.1	2.6	5.6
Science and engineering professionals	6.4	0.8	3.0	3.3	6.0	3.7	3.3
Health professionals	5.1	3.7	3.3	-	11.8	4.3	1.7
Teaching professionals	1.5	3.2	4.7	2.7	1.8	6.8	2.4
Other professionals	4.3	2.3	4.0	3.3	4.4	2.1	1.9
Science and engineering associate professionals	3.0	1.5	1.5	7.0	3.2	4.5	2.0
Health associate professionals	4.4	12.1	1.1	13.0	5.0	13.9	5.7
Other associate professionals	4.9	3.4	5.0	5.6	1.7	7.5	5.3
Clerical occupations	9.2	16.5	17.9	2.6	20.2	19.1	10.6
Secretarial occupations	0.4	5.4	2.3	8.4	1.7	4.2	3.3
Skilled construction trades	0.5	0.1	0.7	-	-	-	0.4
Skilled engineering trades	4.4	0.3	7.2	-	1.1	2.1	1.4
Other skilled trades	4.7	3.0	4.6	-	1.4	1.8	3.8
Protective service occupations	1.3	0.0	-	-	0.7	-	0.4
Personal service occupations	6.4	15.6	4.4	7.6	3.4	4.1	15.8
Buyers, brokers, sales reps	3.0	0.4	0.5	-	2.3	1.1	2.6
Other sales occupations	3.9	8.0	5.4	9.1	13.2	4.5	6.9
Industrial plant and machine operators, assemblers	4.0	4.4	9.8	9.4	3.4	5.0	3.4
Drivers and mobile machine operators	2.8	0.0	1.7	2.5	1.9	-	0.7
Other occupations in agriculture, forestry and fishing	0.0	0.0	-	-	-	-	-
Other elementary occupations	5.5	10.6	4.9	10.2	2.6	3.0	12.0
Armed forces	0.7	-	-	-	0.2	0.8	0.4
	(1,055)	(982)	(190)	(32)	(378)	(104)	(781)

Source: 1991 Census two per cent individual SAR; Crown Copyright. Figures in brackets are sample sizes.

In marked contrast, Sri Lankan people were more strongly concentrated into clerical occupations, health professions and other sales occupations. Science and engineering professionals were more common for Sri Lankans than for people with other national origins. The percentages of people working as corporate managers and in professional occupations were also relatively high. People born in Malaysia, Singapore and Other Asia were more likely than other people from this ethnic group to work as corporate managers and administrators, possibly working for South East Asian multinational companies which located in the UK during the 1980s in order to gain access to the Single European Market. The other major occupations for people born in Malaysia and Singapore were clerical occupations and health associate professions, while the teaching professions accounted for a greater share of employment than for the other national origins. For people born in Other

Asia, the largest single category of work was personal service occupations, followed by other elementary occupations, corporate managers and administrators, and clerical occupations, revealing a polarisation between senior and more routine occupations, which might reflect differences in the types of work undertaken by men and women. The armed forces employ a very small percentage of the ethnic group, mainly composed of men born in Malaysia, Singapore and Other Asia.

Higher education qualifications

The percentage of Other–Asian people holding post-school educational qualifications as their highest qualifications in 1991 was strikingly high (Table 8.14). The percentage of men highly qualified was nearly twice the corresponding rate for White men, at 29.7 per cent, while nearly a fifth of women were highly qualified, over 70 per cent above the rate for White women. About an eighth of both men and women had nursing, teaching or HNC qualifications, and the percentage of men holding first degrees as their highest qualification was even higher. The percentage of women holding first degrees was lower, but still more than twice the corresponding percentage for White women. The differential in the percentage holding higher degrees as their highest qualification was even wider, for both men and women.

While the percentage of 16–24-year-olds with higher education qualifications was similar to that for the White population, the percentage of the Other–Asian population who were highly qualified increased up to the age of 45 for men. Nearly two fifths of men and nearly a quarter of women aged 30–44 held such qualifications, and while the percentage highly qualified then declined with increasing age, the differentials in the percentages of men and women highly qualified relative to both White people and the averages for all ethnic minority groups was maintained. However, while the Other–Asian population was much better qualified than the White population, it was still less successful in the labour market than the White population, with 4.9 per cent of highly qualified people unemployed in 1991, well above the corresponding figure for the White population, but substantially lower than the average for all highly qualified people from ethnic minority groups. Nevertheless, this unemployment rate was still well below the overall unemployment rate for all Other–Asian people.

Contrasts between national origins in the percentages of people holding higher education qualifications are presented in Table 8.15. For men, first degrees were the most common type of highest qualification held, while vocational qualifications were most common for women, but there were variations around this pattern. Among highly qualified men born in Other Asia countries, most held vocational qualifications as their highest qualification, while highly qualified East African-born and Sri Lankan-born women were most likely to have been educated to first degree level. The percentage of both men and women holding first degrees was highest for those born in Sri Lanka, and Malaysia and Singapore. Caribbean-born women and those born in Malaysia and Singapore were most likely to hold vocational qualifications as their highest qualification, reflecting their relatively high likelihood of working in health-related and teaching occupations.

Table 8.14 *Higher education qualifications for Other – Asian people, compared with White people and the average for all people from ethnic minority groups, 1991*

	Other – Asian		White people		Ethnic minority groups	
	Male	Female	Male	Female	Male	Female
All persons aged 18+	6,509	7,596	1,893,853	2,097,438	91,212	93,324
All qualified	1,931	1,510	292,137	240,882	16,262	12,207
Per cent qualified	29.7	19.9	15.4	11.5	17.8	13.1
Per cent with highest qualification:						
Nursing, teaching, HNC or equivalent	12.3	11.8	5.9	6.7	5.5	6.7
First degree	13.6	9.7	8.1	4.4	9.6	5.3
Higher degree	3.8	2.1	1.4	0.5	2.7	0.9
Percent of age-group qualified:						
18–24	7.9	7.2	7.7	7.4	11.3	7.1
25–29	30.5	24.4	19.5	18.4	30.5	17.6
30–44	38.7	23.8	21.5	17.9	30.4	16.7
45–59	33.7	21.1	16.5	11.8	21.5	12.4
60–64	17.8	10.1	12.8	8.1	13.4	6.3
65+	15.4	5.3	8.9	4.7	15.8	3.4
Qualified aged 18 to pensionable age	3,377		466,985		27,839	
Economically active	2,643		414,121		23,305	
Economic activity rate	78.3		88.7		83.7	
Percent in work	71.1		85.2		75.1	
Unemployed	165		14,710		1,913	
Unemployment rate	4.9		3.6		8.2	

Source: OPCS/GRO(S) (1993), Volume 2, Table 17.

Table 8.15 *Percentage of persons aged 18 and over with higher education qualifications for Other – Asian people by national origin, 1991*

Ethnic group or national origin	Higher degrees		First degrees		Vocational etc	
	Male	Female	Male	Female	Male	Female
Other – Asian	3.8	2.1	13.6	9.7	12.3	11.8
East Africa	3.8	2.4	16.5	7.3	6.8	4.9
Caribbean	8.3	-	8.3	4.2	-	25.0
Sri Lanka	4.5	4.5	24.4	18.8	11.3	8.0
Malaysia/Singapore	3.2	1.1	29.5	15.2	14.7	23.9
Other Asia	2.4	0.7	9.3	5.0	15.7	10.8

Source: 1991 Census two per cent individual SAR; Crown Copyright.

8.5 Conclusion

This chapter has examined the information available on the Other–Asian ethnic group from a range of census-related data sets in order to provide an insight into the diversity of the people covered by this grouping, and also to try to identify the features of the smaller ethnic groups aggregated together under this heading. The properties of the data make the latter objective very difficult to achieve, and the results presented depend upon an implied association between country of birth and ethnic group for these smaller ethnic groups. Indeed, it has not proved possible to further analyse some of the important components of this ethnic group, such as the Japanese.

The analysis has demonstrated that the overall averages for the Other–Asian category conceal considerable differences between the ethnic groups subsumed within it. For example, while most sections of the ethnic group tended to live in Greater London and the other major centres of population, those people born in Malaysia and Singapore had a much more widespread geographical distribution, and East African Asians had an important secondary concentration in the East Midlands. It also showed that on a number of dimensions, there was a clear distinction between people of South Asian and South East Asian extraction. For example, the former tended to have larger households and were more likely to own their own houses than the latter, who experienced a poorer standard of accommodation. Those of South Asian extraction were also more likely to be economically active than those of South East Asian origin.

Clearly, the census yields only limited information on the characteristics of the Asian ethnic groups mentioned in the introduction, and the strength of the conclusions which can be drawn is limited by the small numbers of people in the SAR. Indo-Caribbeans and East African Asians form a small percentage of all Other–Asians, because the majority of people from these ethnic groups will probably have selected the Black–Caribbean or Indian box in the ethnic group question. However, analysis of their characteristics from the 1991 Census two per cent individual SAR confirmed some of the evidence of other studies. East African Asians had a household structure similar to other South Asian people, were more likely to be entrepreneurs than most Other–Asians and contained a relatively high proportion of highly qualified people in the professions but also skilled workers in manufacturing industry. While their household structures were similar to other South Asians, Indo-Caribbeans showed more similarities to other West Indians in employment, and being predominantly female, the health associate professions and other low status service occupations were particularly significant for this ethnic group, though their relatively high rate of self-employment was untypical of people from the Caribbean.

Sri Lankan-born people were rather more numerous in the SAR. As might be expected for a refugee group, Sri Lankan people experienced unemployment rates well above the average for the ethnic group. However, they were a highly skilled and well qualified population, nearly a quarter of men and a fifth of women having first degrees or better. Many Sri Lankans thus work in health-related jobs, but the distribution sector is the largest single source of employment. The skills of this section of the population thus seem to be under-utilised, with many Sri Lankans unemployed or forced into routine restaurant and catering occupations in order to find work.

People born in Malaysia and Singapore were the most likely of all the Other–Asians to be full-time students, confirming the expectation that most people born in these countries have come to the UK in order to participate in courses of further and higher education. Their economic activity rates were much lower than the ethnic group average, and their unemployment rates were very low. Being a transient population, they were much more dependent than other Asian ethnic groups on privately rented accommodation, mostly in terraced houses, flats and bed-sits and thus experienced a higher incidence of physical housing problems. This section of the Other–Asian ethnic group was relatively youthful and was unusual in experiencing a higher rate of cohabitation and lone parenthood than the remainder of the ethnic group. Those who were working were most likely to be in health associate professions or clerical occupations. Because the labour market participation rates of women were as high or higher than those of men, the implication is that many female partners of male students were helping support them through working in health, education and other clerical jobs.

The most problematical section of the Other–Asian ethnic group remains those born in the very broad range of countries covered by the category Other Asia. People born in these countries were most likely to be corporate managers and administrators, supporting the expectation that most Japanese people would have come to the UK to work in Japanese multinationals. However, this group of countries also includes the Vietnamese, who arrived as refugees, and the Filipinos who came to work in domestic service and fill other service sector jobs, both of which would have very different characteristics. The two latter groups are probably responsible for the high percentage of people from Other Asia working in the distribution sector, while Japanese people would be more likely to be employed in the engineering (e.g. Nissan, Toyota) and business services industries. The occupational profile is polarised between the high status managers and professionals (probably Japanese) and people in personal service occupations and unskilled occupations (Filipino and Vietnamese). Other average characteristics are more difficult to interpret, though the Vietnamese might be responsible for the relative higher percentage of people living in public sector rented accommodation, but both Japanese and Filipino people may live in privately rented accommodation (of a different standard) and all may have a preference for flats.

In summary, the further analysis of the Other–Asian ethnic group using the SAR has yielded extra information on some of the ethnic groups which make up this broad category. However, the problems of small sample size and condensed categorisation of variables is a major constraint on the analysis. Moreover, it is not possible to examine the characteristics of Other–Asian people born in the UK in greater depth because many people who should be included will have fallen into one of the other ethnic groups. Overall, this chapter has highlighted the problems of disaggregating this catch-all group. Since a number of Asian ethnic groups are continuing to grow in size quite rapidly, there is a strong case for including groups such as the Japanese as separate ethnic groups in the 2001 Census ethnic classification.

References

Berrington, A. (1996) Marriage patterns and inter-ethnic marriage. In: Coleman, D. and Salt, J. (eds), *Demographic Characteristics of the Ethnic Minority Populations*. Ethnicity in the 1991 Census series, Volume 1 London: HMSO.

Brown, C. (1984) *Black and white Britain: the third PSI survey*. London: Policy Studies Institute.

Bulmer, M. (1996) The ethnic question in the 1991 Census of Population. In: Coleman, D. and Salt, J. (eds), *Demographic Characteristics of the Ethnic Minority Populations*. Ethnicity in the 1991 Census series, Volume 1 London: HMSO.

Jones, T. (1993) *Britain's ethnic minorities: An analysis of the Labour Force Survey*. London: Policy Studies Institute.

Marsh, C. and Teague, A. (1992) Samples of anonymised records from the 1991 Census. *Population Trends*, 69, 17–26.

OPCS/GRO (Scotland) (1993) 1991 *Census of Population: Ethnic Group and Country of Birth Report*. London: HMSO.

Owen, D.W. (1993) Country of Birth: Settlement Patterns. National Ethnic Minority Data Archive 1991 Census Statistical Paper no. 5, Centre for Research in Ethnic Relations, University of Warwick.

Owen, D.W. (1996) Labour force participation rates, self-employment and unemployment. In: Karn, V. (ed.), *Employment, education and housing among the ethnic minority populations of Britain*. Ethnicity in the 1991 Census, Volume 4. To be published by HMSO, 1996

Robinson, V. and Hale, S. (1989) The Geography of Vietnamese Secondary Migration in the UK. Research Paper in Ethic Relations no. 10, Centre for Research in Ethnic Relations, University of Warwick.

Sillitoe, K. and White, P.H. (1992) Ethnic group and the British census: the search for a question. *Journal of the Royal Statistical Society* A, 155, part 1, 141-163.

Chapter 9
The Other–Others: hidden Arabs?

Madawi Al-Rasheed

9.1 Introduction

The 1991 Census enumerated nearly 300,000 persons who recorded their ethnicity as Other–Other. They are the fourth largest of the enumerated ethnic groups (see Table 9.1), but the category is one of desperation. It is a problematic, residual category that does not correspond to any 'real' ethnic identity, in the way in which, Bangladeshi, for example, may be thought to do so. It is also a category for which birthplace data offer little guidance. Nearly 60 per cent of the Other–Other population was born in the United Kingdom, but if it is assumed that their origin reflects that of their parental origins, it appears that the largest single group within this total, amounting to nearly half, is of Arab or Middle Eastern descent. Taking the Arab world, in the very broadest sense, to include North Africa, Turkey and Iran, as well as the more core areas, suggests that about 47 per cent of the Other–Other population not born in the United Kingdom, originated in these countries. A further 20 per cent of the non-UK-born originate in South Asia and may include groups such as the Parsis, originating historically from Iran, while some 8 per cent originate in the Americas, largely Latin America. All in all, it suggests that the Other–Other population is the nearest approximation that is available for the Arab population, but that it is very much more heterogeneous than such a title would suggest.

Although the largest group within the Other–Other category originates in the very widely drawn Arab world, it is clear that only a minority of those born in these countries recorded themselves in this ethnic category. The majority is recorded as White. There are two main contributory causes for this situation. The first is that many people of Middle Eastern origin, recorded themselves as White. The second is that there are many European Whites born in such countries through parental connections with oil, military bases or colonial administrations. It is difficult to unravel the relative importance of each of these contributory factors. Racial categories such as White and Black are confusing especially for people whose skin colour is neither. The Arab population of Britain is one of those groups. During field work among one Arab community in 1990–91 (Al-Rasheed, 1991 and 1993), which coincided with the time when the census forms were being distributed, informants commented on the difficulties they encountered in answering the ethnic group question. The majority of Arabs regard themselves as Whites and many did tick the box 'White'. Those who are aware of the meaning this word implies in Britain, moved to the category Other–Other and wrote Arab while still convinced that they were Whites.

Table 9.1 Ethnic population, total persons, Great Britain, 1991

Ethnic group	Great Britain	Per cent of Great Britain total
Total persons	54,888,844	100.0
White	51,873,794	94.51
Black – Caribbean	499,964	0.91
Black – African	212,362	0.39
Black – Other	178,401	0.33
Indian	840,255	1.53
Pakistani	476,555	0.87
Bangladeshi	162,835	0.30
Chinese	156,938	0.29
Other – Asian	197,534	0.36
Other – Other	290,206	0.53
Total minorities	2,910,865	5.49
Persons born in Ireland	836,934	1.52

Source: OPCS/GRO(S) (1993) 1991 Census Ethnic Group and Country of Birth Report Great Britain, Volume 2, Table 6.

This problem can be illustrated by examining a cross tabulation of country of birth by ethnic group. Whereas 14,707 of the Iranian-born classified themselves as Other–Other and 7,979 of the 15,536 born in Iraq did so, only 1,680 of the 26,597 Turkish-born did so. Out of almost 23,000 Egyptian-born residents in Great Britain, approximately 17,000 said they were White and just over 5,000 chose the Other–Other category. It is unlikely that all the 17,000 Whites are of European ethnic origin. However, Britain had military bases in Egypt until the mid-1950s and many children were born to British service families in Egypt. The 1951 Census shows that 68 per cent of the 12,180 persons born in Egypt and living in England and Wales at that time, were thought to be the children of British service personnel (Registrar General, 1958). This means that in 1951, there were 8,200 or so British born in Egypt. If they were young at that time, there should be a high survival rate of this cohort in 1991. Quite a few more would have been born between 1951 and British withdrawal. It would be unwise, therefore, to assume that all 17,000 who said that they were White were ethnic Egyptians. A similar story is possibly true of Libya. Of the total of 6,604 individuals born in Libya, over 4,000 chose the White category.

Nevertheless, it is also probable that many ethnic Arabs born in Egypt or Libya recorded themselves as White on the census form. I myself encountered problems when answering the ethnic group question. I was totally aware of the meanings of the category White in the British context of the nineties. I knew that it referred solely to White people of European origin. Because of this awareness, coupled with my desire to be counted as ethnically Arab, I decided not to tick the White box. It is only after hesitation that I moved on to the Other–Other ethnic group and specified my ethnic origin. However, this does not exclude me from regarding myself as White in skin colour but not so in cultural terms. Like all racial categories that rely on colour or any other physical features, the census classifications are based on controversial, fluid and slippery assumptions.

The confusion regarding the category White applies not only to the Arab population but also to the minorities who come from the Arab world and are resident in Britain. During my fieldwork among the Iraqi Assyrian Christian community in West London, I encountered many Assyrians, some born in Iraq and others in Britain, who asserted their Whiteness. Community leaders resented the fact that as an immigrant community they had been classified as Blacks by their local authority when they tried to get Council funds in the process of establishing a community centre in the 1980s (Al-Rasheed, 1994 and 1995). Many Assyrians are in fact White, some have natural blond hair and blue eyes. This also applies to the Kurds, especially those who have been living in the mountains of Kurdistan.

What this boils down to is that perhaps half of the population that is recorded as Other–Other is of Arab or Middle Eastern origin, but that many Arabs and Middle Easterners are recorded as White. Thus, the Other–Other category probably fails to capture the whole of the Arab population, but at the same time includes significant proportions of non-Arabs among its number. It is therefore a residual category of groups excluded by the main named ethnic categories of the census and thus not easily susceptible to analysis.

Having pointed out some of the shortcomings of the census classifications, the Other–Other numbered 290,206 persons of whom 60 per cent were born in the UK and 40 per cent were born outside the country (Table 9.2). Of the 116,688 individuals born outside the UK, just under half were born in the Middle East and North Africa.

History of Arab migration

Contact between Britain and the Middle East can be traced to ancient times. This contact was motivated by the importance of trade to Britain and the people of the southern shores of the Mediterranean, the most famous of which were the Phoenicians, whose merchant vessels ventured to areas as far as the Atlantic Ocean (Halliday, 1992b). However, in modern times, trading relations were intensified from the 19th century as a result of the expansion of British commercial interests in the territories of the Ottoman Empire. There is a general dearth of research on Arabs in Britain, discussed by El-Solh (1992 and 1993a) and Al-Rasheed (1991).

It is only in the 19th century that there is a record of the settlement of Arab merchants in Britain. These early settlers constituted the first nucleus of what can be called an Arab community. They were attracted by the cotton goods produced in Lancashire and sold to the rest of the world through the commercial houses of Manchester. The city attracted foreign traders who acted as middlemen between their countries of origin and the British cotton industry. These foreign traders established their own trading houses for the export of cotton goods to their countries or to third countries in which they

Table 9.2   Birthplaces of those classified as Other – Other in the 1991 Census, Great Britain

Country of birth	Total	Per cent of total	Per cent of those born outside British Isles
Total persons	290,206	100.0	
United Kingdom	173,518	59.8	
Rest of British Isles	960		
Outside United Kingdom	116,688	40.2	100.0
Old Commonwealth	1,556		1.3
New Commonwealth	39,234		33.4
European Community (not included above)	2,357	2.0	
Remainder of Europe	703		
USSR	181		
Republic of South Africa	1,108		
Other Africa (not included above)	1,671		
America (not included above)	9,573		8.2
Turkey	1,680		1.4
Algeria	1,176		1.0
Egypt	5,151		4.4
Libya	1,980		1.7
Morocco	3,883		3.3
Tunisia	611		0.5
Iran	14,707		12.6
Iraq	7,979		6.8
Israel	1,666		1.4
Jordan	1,173		1.0
Lebanon	2,390		2.0
Saudi Arabia	1,557		1.3
Syria	1,149		1.0
Other Middle East	8,525		7.3
Remainder Asia	5,139		4.4
Rest of World	381		

Source: OPCS/GRO(S) (1993) Volume 1, Table 5.

had trading connections (Halliday, 1992a). It is estimated that by the end of the last century up to 150 merchant houses had been established in Manchester.

This commercial link with Britain eventually led to the settlement of families of Arab origin in Manchester. Lebanese and Syrian Christian traders were the first to settle in the city around the 1860s, perhaps even earlier. This migration was driven by the desire of non-Muslim minorities in the Ottoman Empire to seek economic opportunities abroad. Consequently, Arab Christians, Armenians and Jews were the first to try their fortunes outside the boundaries of the Ottoman Empire. The newly established communities in Manchester, however, tried to preserve their customs, language and dress. They established houses for worship and small schools for language instruction.

These early settlers were followed by a small community of traders from Fez in Morocco, a city renowned for the commercial activities of its citizens since the 17th century (Halliday, 1992a). While the Syrian and Lebanese merchant families were predominantly Christians, the Fasi families were Muslims with a small Jewish component. It seems that the Manchester Muslim Fasis were equally keen to preserve their Islamic way of life, especially the taboo regarding the consumption of meat butchered by non-Muslims. Historical records show that the majority of the Fasis seem to have returned to Morocco in the 1930s with the decline in the export of Lancashire textiles to Morocco as a result of competition from Japanese goods (Halliday, 1992a).

While the Fasis, the Lebanese and the Syrian merchants were the first groups to start the chain of migration from the Arab world to Britain in the middle of the 19th century, they were followed towards the end of the century by the Yemenis. The migration of the Yemenis and their settlement in Britain was, however, not caused directly by trade but related to the activities of British vessels which called at Yemeni ports, such as Aden. The first Yemenis in Britain were men who took up employment as stokers and donkeymen on British vessels calling at Aden and other Red Sea ports. Upon arrival in Britain, these men settled down, married locally and formed communities at places like Liverpool, Manchester, South Shields, Hull, Cardiff and London (Little, 1948; Collins, 1957; Serjeant, 1944; Dahya, 1964; Searle and Shaif, 1991; Halliday, 1992a and 1992b). By the 1960s, the Yemeni community consisted of no more than 10,000 individuals (Dahya, 1964); their number is believed to have risen to 15,000 in the 1990s (Halliday, 1992b). Apparently, this predominantly Muslim community organised itself along religious lines, hence providing the matrix for dense social relations and contacts between the scattered Yemeni seamen in the ports and industrial cities of this country (Dahya, 1964). With the decline of the importance of their employment in the ports, most of the Yemenis moved to cities such as Manchester, Birmingham, Sheffield, and London's East End where they sought employment in factories as unskilled and semi-skilled workers.

In addition to the Syria-Lebanese Christians, and the Fasi and Yemeni Muslims, the 19th century witnessed the beginning of the settlement of a fourth community, the Somalis. Somalia's Arab identity is a recent phenomenon, dating back to the time when Somalia joined the Arab League. Some would forcefully argue that this Arab identity is controversial and hardly worth discussing as an established form of identification, given the predominance in the country of sub-Clan and tribal identities on the one hand and the flourishing discourse related to the emergence of an African identity option on the other hand. Nevertheless, Somalia is a member of an overarching regional organisation, The Arab League, thus providing some sort of rationale behind the community's consideration among the groups constituting the Arab community in Britain.

Somalis are believed to have reached the shores of Britain during the second half of the 19th century. They were almost exclusively employed in seafaring forming transient communities in the docklands of London's East End and in Cardiff, and smaller enclaves in such ports as Bristol, Hull, Liverpool and South Shields (Little, 1948; Banton, 1955; Collins, 1957). Some sources claim that in the 1940s and 1950s, the Somalis were numerically the second largest Muslim group after the Yemenis in a number of British ports. The Somalis were reputed to be particularly independent and not to have affiliated completely with any other section (Little, 1948). A recent study of the community in London's East End shows that up to the 1950s, Somalis exhibited typical traits of a predominantly male transient seafaring community. Restricted shore leave, and to some extent racism, encouraged a pattern of social segregation centred on seamen's boarding houses and cafes (El-Solh, 1991).

This pattern began to change in the late 1980s as a result of civil strife in the country of origin. Increasing numbers of urban Somalis began to flee from political persecution and arrive in London to seek asylum. Some held British citizenship, which they had not relinquished when Somalia became independent in 1960; some came to join kin settled here; others were political asylum seekers. They were eventually joined by increasing numbers of Somali youths, whose parents' residence rights as expatriates in Saudi Arabia and other Gulf states ceases to apply to them when they come of age. In the 1990s, the East End Somali community is perhaps the second largest immigrant group after the Bangladeshis. The community grew as a result of the civil war in the home country, which led to the flight of many single mothers with school-age children, more Somali youth including a substantial number of unmarried women, men with physical handicaps incurred during the fighting and elderly refugees (El-Solh, 1993b).

However, compared with migration from the Commonwealth countries, Arab migration to Britain remained a small-scale operation until the post-second world war period. The post-war phase consists of two independent and quite different types of migration (Al-Rasheed, 1991). The first type is labour migration, predominantly from countries such as Egypt, Morocco and Lebanon. This migration resembles that of other immigrants in this country who came as migrant workers in the 1950s and 1960s and later settled and established ethnic minority groups, mainly in the South East, London and the Midlands. The Moroccan community of North Kensington is the archetype of this Arab labour migration. While the Moroccan community in this country remains very small compared with its counterpart in France, where the majority of labour immigrants come from North Africa as a result of previous colonial links, it is a substantial sub-ethnic minority group within the overall Arab community. It consists of unskilled and semi-skilled workers who found jobs in the service sector of the local economy. The majority of Moroccans work in hotels in the West End of London and restaurants as chefs, cleaners, waiters, receptionists and porters (Karmi, no date).

Involuntary migration

The second type of migration is of an involuntary (forced) character resulting from political upheavals and instability that have been dominant in the region since the 1950s. Perhaps the classical case of this involuntary migration is that of the Palestinians who fled their country after the establishment of the state of Israel in 1948 and the Arab Israeli war of 1967. The Palestinian community consists of both Muslims and Christians. The first to arrive in Britain were carriers of the British Subject Document, issued by the British mandate authority in Palestine and people who worked for British organisations and institutions during the mandate period. The Iraqis are also a good example of this involuntary migration. They have been arriving in Britain as asylum seekers and refugees since the establishment of an independent Iraqi state (Al-Rasheed, 1992 and 1993). Iraqis here are ethnically and religiously heterogeneous. In addition to the Arab majority which belongs to the Shia and Sunni Muslim sects, the community includes Kurds, Assyrians, Chaldeans and Armenians. All are ethnic and religious minorities, whose continuous flight from the country is related to various economic and political pressures.

While it is difficult to estimate the number of Arab ethnic minorities in general, it is almost impossible to arrive at a conclusive figure relating to the number of those minorities who, if born in Arab countries would have been included with the Arab majority. The question on ethnic origin is equally unsatisfactory in estimating their numbers. It can never be established how many of those people ticked the White category and how many moved on to the Other–Other category and specified their ethnic origin or group. My guess here is that a substantial number of people of Arab origin or of Middle Eastern minority group origin (e.g. Kurds, Assyrians, Armenians, Copts and Berbers) ticked the White category because they do regard themselves to be racially Whites. The majority are unaware of the fact that this category is reserved for the indigenous White population of Britain, Europe and other parts of the world where European Whites have been settled, such as Australia, New Zealand, the USA and South Africa.

The above mentioned two types of migration in the post-second world war period create heterogeneous subgroups within the Arab community. Labour migrants tend to be either unskilled or highly skilled. According to a recent health authority survey on the welfare of ethnic minorities in north west London, Moroccans emerged as one group of immigrants with low educational achievement and qualifications (Karmi, no date). The survey shows how they are concentrated in unskilled and semi-skilled occupations. Labour migration from other Arab countries includes people with advanced educational qualifications who are concentrated in highly skilled professions. This results from the migration of Arab skilled workers who search for better economic opportunities outside their country of origin. The Egyptian and Lebanese communities include people of this category. (The famous London-based heart transplant surgeon, Dr Magda Yacoub, is of Egyptian origin and is a good example of this kind of skilled migration from the Arab world.) Many of these migrants came as students seeking higher education and advanced qualifications. After finishing their graduate degrees many opt for settlement, dependent on finding employment and changing their immigration status from students to residents. These comments on the socio-economic status of Arab immigrants and their educational level are derived from previous qualitative research using fieldwork techniques conducted among a number of Arab communities carried out under the auspices of the London School of Oriental and African Studies Centre for Near and Middle Eastern Studies.

9.2 Geographical distribution

Similar to other ethnic groups, the main regional concentration of the Other–Other population is in England (94 per cent), with inner and outer London attracting just over 40 per cent. This is followed by the rest of the South East (16.7 per cent), West Midlands (8.68 per cent) and the North West (7.86 per cent) (see Table 9.3). Inner and outer London seem to attract almost the same proportion of the Other–Other population.

Unlike other ethnic groups, the areas of highest concentration in inner London are generally in the most affluent parts of the capital, such as in the City of Westminster and the Borough of Kensington and Chelsea. However, a major exception to this generalisation is Cardiff, where the second highest concentration in the country is found. This is one of the oldest places of settlement for the Somali and Yemeni seamen. Similarly, Hackney, a poor part of the East End of London contains a rather different group from the Westminster and Kensington pattern. None of these areas of concentration is very dense, none reaching above 12 per cent of the total population (see Table 9.4).

Table 9.3 Region by ethnic group

Region	% Other – Other
Greater London	40.98
Rest of South East	16.70
West Midland	8.68
North West	7.86
Rest of UK	25.78
Total	100.0

Source: 1991 Census. Two per cent individual SAR, region by ethnic group.

Table 9.4 Highest concentration of Other – Other population by ward, 1991 Census

Area	Ward	Other – Other	Total	Per cent of ward
Westminster, City of	APFD	574	4,956	11.58
Cardiff	TNFB	329	3,663	8.98
Kensington and Chelsea	AGFK	674	7,873	8.56
Westminster, City of	APFK	715	8,609	8.31
Westminster, City of	APFM	741	10,242	7.23
Westminster, City of	APFA	322	4,472	7.20
Westminster, City of	APFT	642	9,517	6.75
Hackney	ACFT	542	9,294	5.83
Westminster, City of	APFL	258	4,927	5.24
Kensington and Chelsea	AGFM	431	8,377	5.15

Source: 1991 Census Local Base Statistics, Table 6. Crown Copyright.

9.3 Demographic characteristics

Sex and age

The Other–Other population does not have a balanced sex distribution similar to that of Whites or some of the ethnic groups (e.g. the Chinese). Of the total 290,206 Other–Others, 150,097 are males and 140,109 females. This is equivalent to 93 women to every 100 men, a ratio comparable only to the Bangladeshis (100:92) and Pakistanis (100:94) (see Table 9.5).

Among the Arab component of the Other–Other category, cultural restrictions on single female migration and over-representation of males in involuntary migration explain why generally there are more males than females among this migrant community. The sex imbalance seems to be exaggerated among people born in Algeria and Jordan where males represent roughly 65 per cent and 64 per cent of the total population born in the two countries respectively (Table 9.6). Among people born in Saudi Arabia, the percentage of males (roughly 53 per cent) is much lower than that among people born in those two countries. The fact that the majority of the Saudis in Britain tend to be married and living within family-based households is perhaps one of the reasons behind the relatively narrow gap between the number of males and females.

Table 9.5 Sex ratio by ethnic group, Great Britain, 1991

Some ethnic groups	Sex ratio
Whites	100:100
Indian	100: 98
Pakistani	100: 94
Bangladeshi	100: 92
Chinese	100:102
Other – Other	100: 93

Source: OPCS/GRO(S) (1993), Volume 2, Table 7, pp. 636–7.

Table 9.6 Country of birth by sex

Country of birth	% Male	% Female
Algeria	65.4	34.6
Egypt	53.0	47.0
Libya	57.4	42.6
Morocco	57.8	42.2
Tunisia	60.7	39.3
Iraq	60.3	39.7
Jordan	63.6	36.4
Lebanon	58.7	41.3
Saudi Arabia	52.8	47.2
Syria	59.6	40.4
Other Middle East	55.9	44.1

Source: OPCS/GRO(S) (1993) Volume 1, pp. 403–6.

The age structure of the Other–Other population tends to be similar to that of other immigrant groups, especially those who do not have a long history of settlement in Britain (Figure 9.1). It is a relatively young community with a wide base of under fives (just under 8 per cent). In this respect, the age structure stands in between the extreme young of the Black—Other (under fives are just over 10 per cent) and the Bangladeshis (around 7 per cent). The 20–40 age-group is also wide, which indicates that the presence of the Other–Other population is very much linked to the fact that this is a predominantly labour migration of a recent history.

9.4   Social and economic characteristics

Household and family structure

Some 33 per cent of the Other–Other households have no families, that is, households with one or two person. Almost 66 per cent have one family, and married couple families (that is, nuclear families) represent 46 per cent. There is a very low number of cohabiting couples (5.8 per cent) and lone parent families (13.4 per cent) (see Table 9.7).

The number of Other–Other households with more than two families is very small (1.1 per cent), thus indicating the predominant orientation towards nuclear family households (see Table 9.7). Statistics regarding the family composition of the Other–Other ethnic group indicate that the majority are married (70 per cent). Only 9 per cent are cohabiting and 21 per cent are lone parents (see Table 9.8).

Figure 9.1 *Comparison of the age/sex structure of the Other–Other population and total population*

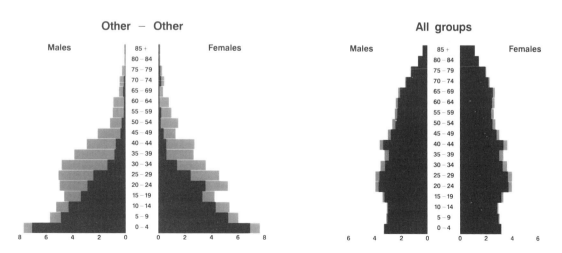

Dark shading represents UK-born population: light shading represents overseas-born

Table 9.7 Other – Other: household type

Type	Other – Other %	White
Households with no family	33.3	29.8
Households with one family	65.6	69.4
Married couple family	(46.5)	(55.4)
Cohabiting couple family	(5.8)	(5.4)
Lone parent family	(13.4)	(8.7)
Households with >two families	1.1	0.8
Total	100.0	100.0

Source: OPCS/GRO(S) (1993) Volume 2, Table 18, pp. 828.

Table 9.8 Other – Other: family composition of residents

Family composition	Other – Other	White
Married couple family	70.2	79.2
Cohabiting couple family	8.6	7.7
Lone parent family	21.2	13.1

Source: OPCS/GRO(S) (1993) Volume 2, Table 19, pp. 829.

Housing characteristics

Table 9.9 shows that a smaller proportion of the Other–Other population are owner-occupiers than is the case for the total population (54 per cent against 64 per cent). This is because a smaller proportion own their homes outright (11 per cent versus 24 per cent) even though the same proportion are buying their homes with a mortgage (43 per cent versus 42 per cent). A significantly higher proportion of the Other–Other population is in privately rented accommodation (14 per cent compared with 4 per cent). This picture is in line with what might be expected for a population with a significant proportion of recent migrants.

Education

Data from the 1991 Census bears out some of the findings from qualitative analysis on the educational level of the Other–Other population, discussed above. Table 9.10 demonstrates that the proportion of educationally qualified in the Other–Other population is double that for the population as a whole (26.0 per cent versus 13.4 per cent). The proportion of those qualified who hold advanced degrees is more than double that of the total population (16.6 per cent compared with 7.0 per cent). The figures for those with first degrees or lower qualifications appear very close to the total population. However, because these figures are expressed as percentages of those with qualifications, they are, in effect twice as high as those of the total population.

Table 9.9   Other – Other: housing characteristics

Household tenure	Other – Other	Total
Owner occupier–outright	10.9	23.9
Owner occupier–buying	43.0	42.4
Rented private furnished	14.1	3.5
Rented private unfurnished	4.0	3.6
Rented job business	2.3	1.9
Rented housing association	6.1	3.3
Rented local authority/New town	19.3	21.4
Lacking/sharing baths or shower	3.0	1.3
No central heating	16.7	18.9

Source: OPCS/GRO(S) (1993) Volume 2, Table 11, p. 769.

Table 9.10 Comparison of Other–Other and total population for persons aged 18 and over by educational qualifications

Qualifications	Other – Other	White
Percentage qualified	26.0	13.4
Of whom:		
Higher degree	16.6	6.7
First degree	46.2	46.0
A-level	37.2	47.3
Below A-level		
Total	100.0	100.0

Source: OPCS/GRO(S) (1993) Table 17.

Economic activity, employment and socio-economic class

Some 75.4 per cent of Other–Other males are economically active, a percentage higher than that among White males. And the percentage of Other–Other females who are economically activity is also slightly higher than that among White females, roughly 54 per cent compared with 50 per cent among White females (Tables 9.11 and 9.12).

Male Other–Other economic activity rate is higher than that among Bangladeshis, Pakistanis, Chinese and those born in Ireland, but slightly lower than that among Black–Caribbeans, Black–Others and Indians. Female economic activity rate seems to be in line with those of the Indians, Chinese and Asians, which are much higher than comparable rates among the Pakistani and Bangladeshi populations. It is much lower than those for the Black–Caribbean, Black–African and Black–Other groups.

Male unemployment for the Other–Other group is substantially above that for the total population (19.7 per cent compared with 10.7 per cent for Whites). It is on a par with that for the Black–Caribbean population, but much lower than that for the Pakistanis and Bangladeshis (28.5 and 30.9 per cent respectively).

Table 9.11 Ethnic group for men, aged 16+, by socio-economic class, Great Britain, 1991

	Econo-mically active	In employ-ment	I	II	II Non-manual	III Manual	IV	V
Total	73.3	87.4	6.8	27.4	11.5	32.2	16.4	5.7
White	73.2	88.0	6.7	27.6	11.3	32.4	16.3	5.7
Black–Carribbean	80.1	73.8	2.4	14.2	12.2	38.9	23.6	8.7
Black–African	69.0	66.8	14.3	24.5	17.5	17.6	17.3	8.9
Black–Other	81.9	70.5	3.2	24.8	17.2	30.2	17.6	7.1
Indian	78.1	84.9	11.4	27.2	14.4	23.8	18.1	4.0
Pakistani	73.3	68.9	5.9	20.3	13.5	29.9	24.1	6.3
Bangladeshi	72.4	67.3	5.2	8.5	12.9	31.5	35.0	6.8
Chinese	70.1	88.1	17.6	23.3	19.3	29.5	8.0	2.4
Other–Asian	76.2	83.0	15.9	34.3	18.2	16.0	12.3	3.3
Other–Other	**75.4**	**77.7**	**14.5**	**30.5**	**16.1**	**19.8**	**14.0**	**5.1**
Irish–born	70.1	84.3	6.9	23.3	7.7	34.3	16.9	10.9

Source: GB Local Base Statistics, Table 9 and two per cent SAR. See also OPCS/GRO(S) (1993) Volume 2, Table 10.

Table 9.12 Ethnic group for women, aged 16+, by socio-economic class, Great Britain, 1991

	Econo-mically active	In employ-ment	I	II	III Non-manual	III Manual	IV	V
Total	49.9	92.1	1.7	25.9	38.8	7.6	18.0	7.9
White	49.7	92.6	1.7	25.9	39.0	7.6	17.8	8.0
Black–Carribbean	66.9	84.1	1.0	30.3	33.7	6.9	19.5	8.5
Black–African	60.1	71.0	3.0	31.8	30.8	5.6	16.9	12.0
Black–Other	62.9	77.9	1.3	25.2	40.6	9.3	19.1	4.6
Indian	55.4	85.3	4.4	20.9	34.9	6.4	29.2	4.1
Pakistani	27.1	65.5	2.7	22.3	34.2	6.5	31.7	2.6
Bangladeshi	21.8	57.6	1.8	22.9	35.8	6.4	26.6	6.4
Chinese	53.1	90.0	7.6	28.5	31.6	13.0	13.9	5.4
Other–Asian	53.9	84.9	6.0	30.7	33.8	7.0	16.6	6.0
Other–Other	**53.9**	**82.5**	**4.5**	**30.8**	**38.4**	**6.2**	**15.1**	**4.9**
Irish–born	49.9	92.4	2.6	33.2	26.8	6.3	18.5	12.6

Source: GB Local Base Statistics, Table 9 and two per cent SAR. See also OPCS/GRO(S) (1993) Volume 2, Table 10.

Paradoxically, although male unemployment is higher than that for the White population, the socio-economic structure is much more favourable. Other–Other males have a significantly higher representation in the white collar groups than the White population and a correspondingly lower representation in the manual occupations. Table 9.11 shows that 14.5 per cent of Other–Other males are in Class I, compared with 6.7 per cent of Whites, while the percentages in Class II and III Non-manual are 30.5 and 16.1 compared with 27.6 and 11.3 per cent for Whites.

Female employment in the Other–Other population shows a similar pattern to that for men, with a higher representation in Classes I and II than for the White population and a lower proportion in the manual groups: 4.5 per cent of Other–Other women were in Class I compared with 1.7 per cent of the equivalent White population and 30.8 per cent were in Class II compared with 25.9 per cent (see Table 9.12).

9.5   Conclusion

The Other–Other ethnic category is one of the least satisfactory of the 1991 Census groupings. It is essentially a heterogeneous collection of people defined more by exclusion from other categories, than for any intrinsic qualities of its own. It is a matter of regret that the census did not follow the example of the Labour Force Survey in using the Arab category, as the most substantial identifiable group within the group originates in the Middle East and North Africa.

From the evidence of ethnographic studies and from its geographical areas of prominence (Table 9.4) it seems that three main subgroups, with contrasting characteristics, may be present. The first is the Arab population from the oil-rich Middle Eastern countries. Areas of concentration in affluent boroughs such as Westminster, and Kensington and Chelsea suggest this possibility. The second is the long-established Somali and Yemeni populations of the old dockland communities discussed by Halliday (1992b) and others. The Tiger Bay concentration found in Cardiff is also indicative of this community. Finally, a third group, possibly comprising poorer, but well educated, asylum seekers and refugees, is suggested by the concentration in the poor borough of Hackney (Al-Rasheed, 1992). The Other–Other population has a much higher level of educational qualification than the total population and this is most marked in the higher degree level.

This combination of new, affluent groups and poorer old-established and more recent refugee groups might explain the contradictory nature of the employment statistics. On the one hand, Tables 9.11 and 9.12 suggest high unemployment and on the other, high socio-economic structure. Similarly, the housing tenure figures (Table 9.9) suggest a higher than average dependence on social housing, while at the same time showing a much higher representation in the private rental sector, associated, perhaps, with an affluent visiting population. The marginally higher (though small) proportion of households lacking or sharing a bathroom or a shower, may also indicate the presence of a disadvantaged subgroup within the broader population (Table 9.9).

All in all, the Other–Other population remains something of an enigma on which much more work needs to be done, particularly on its SARs, to tease out the myriad of threads that are tangled together in this group.

References

Al-Rasheed, M. (1991) Invisible and divided communities: Arabs in Britain. In: *Arab Communities in Britain Concerns and Prospects*. London: Riyad El-Rayyes Books, pp. 1–13.

Al-Rasheed, M. (1992) Political migration and downward socio-economic mobility: the Iraqi community in London. *New Community*, 18, 537–50.

Al-Rasheed, M. (1993) The meaning of marriage and status in exile: the experience of Iraqi women. *Journal of Refugee Studies*, 6, 89–104.

Al-Rasheed, M. (1994) The myth of return: Iraqi Arabs and Assyrian refugees in London. *Journal of Refugee Studies,* no2/3, Volume 7 pp. 199-219.

Al-Rasheed, M. (1995) In search of ethnic visibility: Iraqi Assyrian Christians in London. In: Baumann, G. and Sunier, T. (eds), *Post-Migration Ethnicity.* Amsterdam The Hague, Martinns Nijhoff, pp. 10-35.

Banton, M. (1955) *The Coloured Quarter: Negro Immigrants in an English City. London*: Cape.

British Refugee Council, UK Asylum Statistics 1982-1992. London

Collins, S. (1957) *Coloured Minorities in Britain*. London: Lutterworth Press.

Dahya, B. (1964) Yemenis in Britain: an Arab migrant community. *Race*, 6, 177–90.

El-Solh, C. (1991) Somalis in London's East End: a community striving for recognition. *New Community*, 17, 539–52.

El-Solh, C. (1992) Arab communities in Britain: cleavages and commonalities. *Islam and Christian Muslim Relations*, 3, pp. 236–58.

El-Solh, C. (1993a) Arabs in London. In: Merriman, N. (ed.), *The Peopling of London*. London: Museum of London.

El-Solh, C. (1993b) Be true to your culture: gender tensions among Somali Muslims in Britain. *Immigrants and Minorities*, 12, 21–46.

Halliday, F. (1992a) The millet of Manchester: Arab merchants and the cotton trade. *British Journal of Middle Eastern Studies,* 19, 159–76.

Halliday, F. (1992b) *Arabs in Exile: Yemeni Migrants in Urban Britain*. London: I.B. Tauris.

Karmi, G. (1988) *The Moroccan Health Survey 1987–1988*. Unpublished report. Department of Public Health Medicine, North West Thames Regional Health Authority.

Little, K. (1948) *Negroes in Britain*. Kegan Paul: London.

OPCS/GRO(S) (1993) *1991 Census Ethnic Group and Country of Birth, Great Britain*. vol. 1 & 2. London, HMSO.

Registrar General (1958) *Census 1951 England and Wales: General Report*. London: HMSO.

Searle, C. and Shaif, A. (1991) Drinking from one pot: Yemeni unity at home and overseas. *Race and Class*, 32. 65–81.

Serjeant, R.B. (1944) Yemeni Arabs in Britain. *The Geographical Magazine*, 17. (4), 143-147.

Chapter 10
The Irish: invisible settlers

Judith Chance

10.1   Introduction

The Irish have been migrating to Britain in substantial numbers for at least 150 years, and now form the largest single ethnic minority group in the country. This chapter, however, starts from a rather different basis than most of the others in this volume, as there was no clear provision to record one's ethnic identity as Irish in the 1991 Census. The data used are drawn from country of birth records.

There are two rather different Irish communities, from North and South Ireland, whose identities are imperfectly captured by birthplace. None the less, in some ethnic tables in the 1991 Census the category 'Born in Ireland' occurs as a surrogate Irish ethnic group. It is only possible in some tables to distinguish between those born in the North and the South, and, in any case, these categories exclude those of Irish descent. This seems a significant omission, given the long history of Irish migration to Britain.

For any respondent who chose to ignore the White category and to use the 'Any other ethnic group' option, describing themselves as Irish, or as a mixture of Irish with any other group, there were higher level codes available. Unfortunately, as a result of a processing error, those who chose to record their ethnicity as Irish have not been included in Table A of the *Ethnic Group and Country of Birth* report (OPCS/GRO(S), 1993a and 1994b). A revised version of Table A estimates that 11,000 people, of whom 10,000 live in Greater London, recorded their ethnicity only as Irish, while a further 20,000 ticked the White box and also recorded their ethnicity as Irish. The latter group were simply coded as White. The revised report also estimates that 60 per cent of the 10,000 living in Greater London and recording their ethnicity as Irish were born in Ireland, and 40 per cent were born elsewhere. Since the figures do not make a significant difference to the tables used in the main census returns (and since the revisions are based on small samples and are therefore subject to relatively large sampling errors), the analysis below is confined to the 'Born in Ireland' category.

On the basis of this rather flawed data set, the Irish-born population living in Britain in 1991 consisted of 836,934 people. Of this total, 592,550 or 71 per cent, were born in the Republic of Ireland (including 'Ireland, part not stated') and the remaining 244,914 (29 per cent) in the North. Taking a slightly different measure, those living in households where the head was born in Ireland number 1,000,510 (OPCS/GRO(S), 1993a, Table 11). Of these, 780,476 (78 per cent) lived in households where the head was born in the

Republic of Ireland. This gives a very crude estimate of at least 800,000 first and second generation Southern Irish. It can only be seen as a major under-estimate, however, as it excludes those households in which an Irish-born woman with a non-Irish-born partner is not listed as head of household. It thus seems clear that the Irish ethnic group, using first and second genera-tions, is larger than the Indian population (840,000), which is the largest ethnic minority group recorded in the 1991 Census. If the Northern Irish are added, then the Irish, even using only the head of household data, exceed the Indian population.

The whole issue of Irish ethnicity in Britain is contentious: surveys used to design the ethnicity question for the 1991 Census showed that a majority of the Irish people approached did not want to record their identity as Irish. There are, however, three main problems in using birthplace data as a synonym for ethnic identity. First, Irish birthplace excludes all those born in Britain but with one or more Irish-born parent or grandparent (most of these people have statutory rights to claim Irish nationality). Second, there are particular problems when referring to those born in the North of Ireland. Political allegiance is likely to influence their choice of ethnic label, but the census offers no way of identifying nationalist or unionist responses. Third, a very small number of those born in Ireland fall into one of the main ethnic minority categories used in the census (see Table 10.1).

For the purposes of this chapter, the term Irish will refer to those born in any of the 32 counties; Southern Irish will refer to those born in the Republic and, where appropriate, to those who did not record in which part of the country they were born, and Northern Irish to those born in the six counties. For the most part reference will be made simply to the Irish, but there are interesting variations in the spatial concentrations of the two groups which will be explored in relation to their age structure, as it is likely that the relatively greater concentrations of the Northern Irish in the west and their absolute superiority in numbers in the north are a product of different cycles of labour migration.

Table 10.1 Ethnicity of the Irish-born population in Great Britain, 1991

	Total	White	Black–Carib-	Black–African	Black–Other	Indian	Pakis-tani	Bangla-deshi	Chinese	Other–Asian	Other–Other
Northern Ireland	244,914	242,915	236	460	261	290	170	23	161	100	298
Irish Rep.	592,020	586,508	1,058	637	908	974	351	124	237	324	899
Ireland (pt not stated)	530	503	2	1	5	6	1	1	2	4	5
Total Irish–born	837,464	829,926	1,296	1,098	1,174	1,270	522	148	400	428	1202

Source: OPCS/GRO(S) (1993a) Volume 1, Table 5.

Irish migration to Britain is unusual in that females are just as likely as males to be primary labour migrants. Several factors have contributed to this: the long history of migration means that most Irish people have relatives in Britain, so information flows are good; high universal education standards in Ireland coupled with a very young population structure mean that school leavers find it hard to secure appropriate job (Sexton, 1986); in the past the stem family structure, designed to avoid subdivision of already small farms, put pressure on both sons and daughters to leave; it has also been suggested that emigration is now an accepted part of Irish culture (O'Toole, 1990).

The propensity of females to migrate in their own right is reflected in both their distinctive socio-economic structure and their patterns of spatial concentration when compared with Irish males. This is much more marked in the case of the Southern Irish, and in the case of younger migrants (i.e. for the purposes of the 1991 Census, those who have left Ireland since the late 1970s).

10.2   Historical background

Migration between the two countries has, with the exception of the duration of the second world war, been free from restriction. The proximity, the low cost of passage and the effective communication networks, both formal and informal, mean that migration flows have been very sensitive to changes in both countries. The peak period for emigration from Ireland was 1931 to 1961, a time of great rural poverty, and relative lack of industrial investment in the South. Until the 1930s the United States had been the most favoured destination, but the introduction of immigration quotas there led to an increased flow to Britain. The value of the Southern Irish as a replacement labour force during the second world war saw relaxation of the restrictions imposed in 1940, and even extended to direct recruitment of both men and women. In the case of Irish women the war opened up new areas of employment in Britain, with clerical and factory work replacing domestic service (Lennon et al, 1988). The huge demand for labour in the post-war period saw a massive influx: in the decade 1951–61 net emigration from Southern Ireland was 409,000.

During this period emigration from the North was relatively unimportant because the heavy industries of the North, together with the textile industry, were generating sufficient domestic employment, and politically the area was enjoying relative stability.

By the early 1970s the Southern Irish economy was booming, thanks in no small part to membership of the EEC. The period saw, for the first time since 1840, an increase in population size and, even more surprisingly, net immigration into Ireland (Mac Laughlin, 1994). The boom in Ireland was opening up new opportunities, while the British economy was already beginning to show signs of recession. Families, especially those who had bought houses in the south east of Britain, were able to realise their assets and use the capital to establish businesses in the Republic of Ireland (Sexton, 1986). In particular, expertise acquired in the building trade in Britain was valuable in the construction boom in Ireland, where EC funds were available for road building, housing programmes and commercial developments.

The same period saw an increase in emigration from the North, reflecting both growing unemployment and the rapid escalation of violence from 1969.

By the mid-1980s Southern Ireland's bubble economy had burst, and emigration was rising. The 1986 Irish Census indicated that net emigration 1981–86 was 75,300 (CSO, 1986). Not all of these emigrants would have come to Britain and the absence of any monitoring of passenger flows between the two countries makes it impossible to tell how many did come to Britain, but it is clear that Britain remains the single most common destination (Mac Laughlin, 1994). Mainland Europe has also become a favoured destination, with many cases of direct recruitment in Ireland, especially targeting university graduates (Cobbe and MacCarthaigh, undated, cited in Mac Laughlin, 1994). Interviews carried out in the west of Ireland indicate a high level of return and temporary migration among the youngest and least well prepared migrant groups: of 1,520 emigrants from 6,000 families surveyed in 1989 only 15.8 per cent had not returned home at least once in the 12 months preceding the survey (Mac Laughlin, 1994).

The occupational structure and source areas have shifted quite dramatically in this most recent wave of emigration. While migration remains a common strategy among working class and farming families it is increasingly spreading to professional and middle class urban families (Courtney, 1989, cited in Mac Laughlin, 1994).

The 1980s saw a rise in Protestant emigration from the North of Ireland, but by 1991 there was net migration from Britain to Northern Ireland, amounting to a net gain of about 3,000 (OPCS, 1993b). Estimates for the first five years of the 1990s suggest continued population loss in Southern Ireland; in

Table 10.2 Numbers of Irish-born (32 counties) in Great Britain, 1901–1991

Date	Number
1901	631,629
1911	550,040
1921	523,767
1931	505,385
1951	716,028
1961	950,978
1971	952,760
1981	850,387
1991	836,934

Source: Census Reports 1901–1991.

spite of an estimated birth rate of 14 per thousand and an estimated death rate of only nine per thousand, the projected population growth is minus 0.2 per cent (OPCS, 1994a). Table 10.2 shows the numbers of Irish-born residents in Britain 1901–91.

10.3   Demographic, social and economic characteristics

Demographic patterns

Two age and sex pyramids are shown in Figure 10.1. The first represents all of the Irish-born, with the Northern Irish shown in darker shading. The second pyramid shows the population living in households headed by a person born in the South of Ireland. The dark shading represents those born in the Republic, while the light shading represents those born in Britain living in such households.

In the first pyramid, both the Northern and the Southern Irish show a slight preponderance of women. It is also clear that very few of the children have been born in Ireland, while both populations show a very marked increase in numbers between the 15–19 and the 20–24 age bands, reflecting the arrival of primary migrants, often within a couple of years of leaving full-time education, be it secondary or tertiary level. It is also clear that the Northern Irish form a higher proportion of the Irish born in the age bands 0–39. This is shown more clearly in Table 10.3.

In the second pyramid the lower age bands are dominated by young people born in Britain, typical of the pattern found in other migrant communities. The apparently sharp gender disparity among the older age bands of those born in Britain, showing large excesses of females born in Britain reflects the marriages of Irish-born men to women born in Britain. It is impossible to tell from the census data what proportion of these women might be ethnically Irish (i.e. the children or grandchildren of Irish immigrants). Caulfield and Bhat (1981) estimated that only 26 per cent of second generation Irish people in Britain are born into families where both parents are Irish-born, and argue that Irish women are more likely to marry out than Irish men.

The relatively high proportions of the Northern Irish in the age bands 0–39, and especially in the band 10–19, are somewhat hard to explain given the recent estimates of annual emigration from the North and the South; Courtney estimates a quarter of a million emigrants from Ireland between 1982 and 1988, and a national survey of emigrants in 1988 found that about 67 per cent were going to Britain (Courtney, 1989, cited in Mac Laughlin, 1994 and NESC, 1991). Conversely, Nagle (1994) reports annual figures of 20,000 net emigrants from the North of Ireland between 1981 and 1991, while by 1991 OPCS was estimating net immigration from Britain to the North of Ireland. If the figures for the South are in any way accurate, then the 1991 Census figures suggest that large numbers of younger Irish immigrants must have

Figure 10.1 *Age-sex pyramids of the Irish population Great Britain 1991*

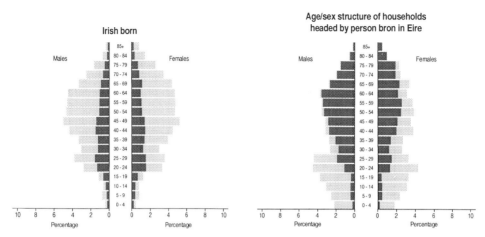

Irish born

Dark shading refers to those born in
Northern Ireland

Age/sex structure of households
headed by person bron in Eire

Dark shading refers to those born in Eire;
Light shading refers to those born in UK

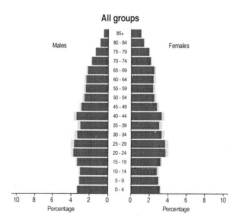

All groups

Dark shading refers to those born in UK;
Light shading to those born overseas.

Table 10.3 *Northern and Southern Irish-born population by proportion in each age band, Great Britain, 1991*

Age	Northern Irish		Southern Irish	
	Number	Per cent	Number	Per cent
0-9	6,876	38.3	11,062	61.7
10-19	12,655	45.3	15,289	54.7
20-29	49,614	38.3	65,478	61.7
30-39	41,963	37.3	70,566	62.7
40-49	46,093	29.2	111,781	70.8
50-59	35,308	22.3	123.301	77.8
60-69	32,767	23.3	108,140	76.8
70-79	21.229	24.0	67,228	76.0
80+	7,630	27.2	19,705	72.8

Source: OPCS/GRO(S) (1993a) Volume 1, Table 2.

moved on to other destinations. One possibility is that survey returns showing migration to Britain may be masking illegal Irish migration to the United States; the estimates for Irish illegal migrants in New York City alone range from 40,000 to over 100,000 (Corcoran,1991).

Socio-economic patterns

The socio-economic class of Irish males aged 16 and over is broadly similar to that of the total male population in that age bracket, but is somewhat skewed towards blue collar work. Table 10.4 and Figure 10.2 show that there is a general under-representation in white collar work and over-representation in manual work. This difference is most marked for Class V (unskilled manual workers) which employs 8.8 per cent of Irish male workers, double the national average. Percentages in other groups are generally similar except for Class IIIN (skilled non-manual white collar work) which provided 7.6 per cent of Irish male employment as opposed to 11.1 per cent of total male employment. Class II (managerial and technical) accounts for 25.2 per cent of the Irish compared with 28.6 per cent of the total male workforce. There is, however, a slight excess of Irish males in Class I (professional), with a figure of 7.6 per cent as against 7.2 per cent for the total male working population.

Irish female employment contrasts significantly with that of Irish men. In the first place, over 60 per cent of women are in white collar jobs, compared to only 40 per cent of men. Second, Irish women are over-represented in Classes I and II in comparison with the total female workforce (see Table 10.5 and Figure 10.3). On the other hand, Irish women, like Irish men, are over represented in Class V (11.3 per cent, compared with 7.3 per cent for total female employment). They are significantly under represented in Class IIIN, which includes secretarial and clerical work.

Table 10.4 Comparison of total and Irish-born males aged 16 and over by socio-economic group (per cent), Great Britain, 1991

Socio-economic class	All males 16+	Irish–born males, 16+
I	7.2	7.8
II	28.6	25.2
IIIN	11,1	7.6
IIIM	31.5	31.7
IV	14.6	15.9
V	4.5	8.8
Armed forces	1.4	1.6
Not stated	1.1	1.3
Total	100	100

Source: OPCS /GRO(S) (1993a) Volume 2, Table 16.

Figure 10.2 *Comparison of socio economic group of total male population age 16 and over with that of the Irish born males, Great Britain, 1991*

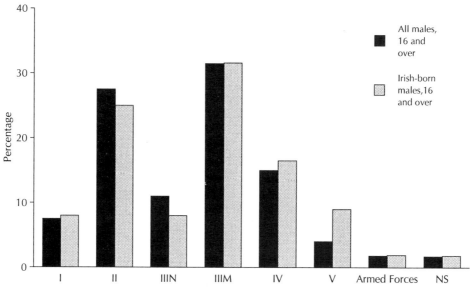

Source: OPCS (1993) Volume 2, Table 16

Table 10.5 Comparison of total and Irish–born females aged 16 and over by socio-economic group (per cent), Great Britain, 1991

Socio-economic class	All females 16+	Irish–born females 16+
I	1.92	2.66
II	28.07	34.84
IIIN	38.63	26.29
IIIM	6.97	6.42
IV	16.19	17.33
V	7.25	11.31
Armed forces	0.15	0.12
Not stated	0.83	1.04
Total	100.00	100.00

Source: OPCS /GRO(S) (1993a) Volume 2, Table 16.

Figure 10.3 *Comparison between the socio economic structure of the total female population aged 16 and over and women born in Ireland, Great Britain 1991*

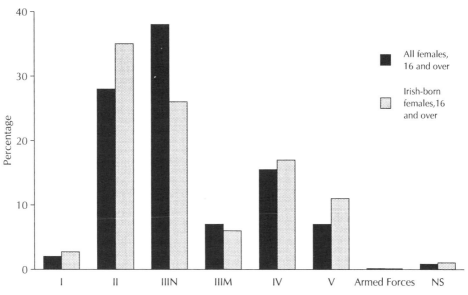

Source: OPCS (1993) Volume 2, Table 16

If one disaggregates the employment data by industry, then the Irish male pattern shows high employment in the construction industry, which accounts for 32.1 per cent of Southern Irish males, 16.5 per cent of Northern Irish, and only 12.5 per cent of the White male population (Owen, 1995). Irish female employment by industry is less distinctive, but there is over-representation in the health and education category, at 26 per cent, compared with 20.5 per cent for White females (Owen, 1995).Disaggregation by both industrial division and by country within Britain (i.e. England, Wales, Scotland), reveals clear differences. Table 10.6 is based on the 'Born in Ireland' category, so it does not distinguish between Northern and Southern Irish directly, but the different pattern in male employment, especially in division 5 (construction) reflects the over concentration of the Northern Irish in Scotland and Wales, and the Southern Irish in England. In both Wales and Scotland the largest male employment is in division 9 (other services, which includes health and education), whereas in England it is construction.

Again, Irish women show less clear regional differences, with division 9 the majority employment in all three countries, followed in each case by division 6 (distribution, hotel and catering).

Irish male unemployment levels are significantly higher than those for the total population. Unemployment for men aged 16 years and over was 15 per cent, compared with 11 per cent for the total population. These levels are nevertheless much lower than for most ethnic minority groups. Black–Caribbean male unemployment was 23 per cent, for both Black–Africans and Pakistanis the rate was 29 per cent, while for Bangladeshis the level was 31 per cent. Conversely, Indian male unemployment was only 13 per cent, and the figure for the Chinese was as low as 11 per cent (OPCS, 1993a, Table 10).

Irish females are once again in a better position than Irish men, with an unemployment rate of 7 per cent, virtually identical with the level for the

Table 10.6 Employment by industrial division of the Irish in Great Britain, 1991

Industrial division	England per cent		Wales per cent		Scotland per cent	
	Males	Females	Males	Females	Males	Females
0	1	0	3	1	4	1
1	2	1	4	1	4	1
2	3	1	3	1	2	1
3	10	4	8	4	9	3
4	7	6	7	7	6	5
5	26	1	22	2	18	1
6	13	21	15	25	13	19
7	9	3	6	1	6	3
8	10	11	6	6	11	9
9	19	50	23	52	27	57
Not stated	1	1	1	1	0	0
Outside UK	0	0	1	0	0	0

Source: OPCS (1994b) Table 19.

total population. Rates for other ethnic minority groups were all higher: 8 per cent for the Chinese; 13 per cent for Indians; 14 per cent for Black–Caribbeans; 30 per cent for Pakistanis and 35 per cent for Bangladeshis (OPCS/GRO(S), 1993a, Table 10).

Housing tenure

Comparing the tenure pattern of all household heads with those for households whose head was born in Ireland reveals a slightly more working class pattern than is the case for the population as a whole (see Table 10.7 and Figure 10.4). While 66 per cent of all households owned their property, for the Irish the figure was 55 per cent. And while 21 per cent of all households were in council housing (or its Scottish counterpart) the equivalent figure for the Irish is 26 per cent. Similarly, a somewhat higher proportion of the Irish headed households were in private rentals of various kinds than was the case for the total population (OPCS/GRO(S), 1993a, Table 11). This is to be expected from the occupational structure in which hospitals and hotels feature strongly for women and mobile employment in the construction industry for men.

The apparently more working class structure of Irish headed households is in part a product of the differential employment structures of Irish men and women, since head of household is normally taken to refer to the male partner.

There is also information available about those who live in communal establishments and those who have no home (OPCS/GRO(S), 1993a, Table 8). The Irish are very significantly over-represented in all three categories which relate to homelessness (sleeping rough, hostels and common lodging

Table 10.7 *Housing tenure for total households compared with that for households with head born in Ireland*

	All household heads	Household head born in Ireland
Owner occupied		
Owned outright	23.92	19.63
Buying with mortgage	42.44	35.75
Privately rented		
Furnished	3.52	7.26
Unfurnished	3.63	3.65
Rented with work	1.93	2.39
Rented from housing association	3.13	5.06
Rented from local authority, new town or Scot homes	21.43	26.26
Total	100	100

Source: OPCS /GRO(s) (1993a) Volume 2, Table 11.

Figure 10.4 *Comparison of household tenure, all households and household head born in Ireland*

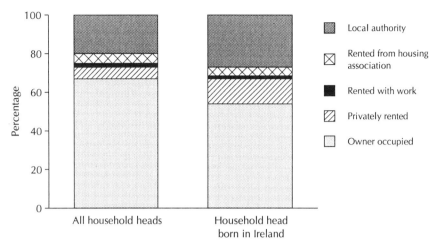

Source: OPCS (1993a) Volume 2, Table 11

houses, and other miscellaneous establishments) and are also over-represented in hospital staff residences (see Table 10.8). The over-representation of the Irish among the homeless supports claims made by a number of pressure groups that young Irish immigrants arriving in London are especially vulnerable. A survey of young Irish migrants carried out in 1985 in London found that 27 per cent had spent at least some time sleeping rough since arriving in London, and that 74 per cent had arrived in London with less than £100 (AGIY, 1985).

The over-representation in hospital accommodation reflects the concentration of both Irish men and, more notably, Irish women in the health care sector.

Table 10.8 Residents in communal establishments and sleeping rough, Great Britain, 1991

Type of accommodation	Total persons	Born in Ireland (number)	Born in Ireland (per cent) of total
Effectively homeless			
Sleeping rough	2,827	422	14.9
Hostel & common lodging house	23,009	1,643	7.1
other miscellaneous establishments	40,255	4,217	10.5
Hospital staff residents			
NHS psychiatric	3,268	295	9
NHS other	22,007	2,168	9.8
Non NHS psychiatric	270	29	10.7
Non NHS other	855	95	11.1

Source: OPCS/GRO(S) (1993a) Volume 2, Table 8.

Educational qualifications

The Irish-born population resident in Britain has a higher level of educational qualification than the White population for qualifications attained which are beyond GCE A-level standard. Of the eligible population (i.e. those aged 18 or more) 16.4 per cent of Irish females hold higher qualifications compared to 11.5 per cent of White females. On the other hand, only 13.2 per cent of Irish males hold such qualifications, compared with 15.4 per cent of White males.

When the figures are subdivided by level of qualification it becomes clear that Irish males are mainly holders of graduate and postgraduate level qualifications, whereas Irish females mainly hold qualifications below the level of a first degree. This reflects the high concentration of Irish females in the nursing and health care sectors of employment.

Looking at the comparison of qualifications by age, the picture becomes a little more confused (see Table 10.9). In the case of higher degrees (Band A), Irish males of all ages are more likely to possess these qualifications than White men, while Irish females are more likely to possess them than White females for every age band except 45–59.

Table 10.9 Comparison of education qualifications of White and Irish-born populations, aged 18+, by age and gender (per cent) in Great Britain, 1991 (10 per cent sample)

	White male	Irish male	White female	Irish female
Total number	1,893,853	36,454	2,097,438	41,729
With higher qualification	15.4	13	11.5	16.4
A: higher degree, UK standard	9	15.5	4	4.8
B: first degree, UK standard	52.5	56.1	38	28.8
C: over GCE A–Level but under first degree	38.5	28.4	58	66.4

Qualification level	White male			Irish male		
Age group	A	B	C	A	B	C
18–24	2.2	56.3	41.5	4.6	67.7	27.6
25–29	6.7	57.9	35.4	11.4	66.5	22.1
30–44	10.8	53.1	36.1	18.7	55	26.3
45–59	10.3	46.7	42.9	16.3	45.1	38.6
60 plus	7	54.1	38.9	17.7	53.9	28.4

Qualification level	White female			Irish female		
Age group	A	B	C	A	B	C
18–24	1.3	55.1	43.6	2.9	55.3	41.8
25–29	3.8	52.6	43.6	6.7	54.2	39.1
30–44	5.4	41.1	53.5	6.6	32.6	60.7
45–59	3.8	25.8	70.4	3.6	15.2	81.2
60 plus	2.2	22.7	75.1	2.5	12.3	85.2

OPCS/GRO(S) (1993a), Table 17.

Irish females in the age bands 18–29 are more likely to have UK standard first degrees (Band B) than their White counterparts, but for those aged 30 and over the position is reversed. Irish males aged 18–44 are more likely to have degrees than their White counterparts, but from the age of 45 up they are marginally less likely to have degrees than their White counterparts.

In the case of qualifications higher than A-level but lower than UK standard first degrees (Band C), Irish males are less likely to hold these for all age-groups than White men. Irish women are less likely to hold them in the age range 18–29, but more likely in the older age range.

10.4 Geographical distribution

Spatial distribution of the Irish in Britain in 1991

The major concentrations of Irish people are in the metropolitan counties, with outer London being the single largest centre. If a comparison is made between the standard statistical regions of England, and Wales and Scotland, significant differences between the Northern and Southern Irish patterns are immediately apparent. The percentage figures show the proportion of the Northern, Southern or total Irish population living in each region.

The most obvious differences in the patterns of the two Irish populations are in Scotland and the North, both regions showing an absolute majority of Northern Irish, and in the South East, which shows a major over-concentration of the Southern Irish. The South East and the West Midlands are the only two regions in which the proportion of Southern Irish exceeds that of the Northern Irish, indicating a markedly more restricted pattern of settlement. This impression is strengthened when looking at the distributions within these regions: the Southern Irish are more heavily concentrated in the metropolitan counties (see Table 10.11). In England 60.1 per cent of the Southern Irish live in the metropolitan counties, compared to only 41.9 per cent of the Northern Irish.

This pattern of urban over-concentration persists even in those shire counties which contain major Southern Irish clusters. The highest shire county concentration is in Bedfordshire, with 12,154. A closer look at the figures for Bedfordshire shows that 7,853 of the Southern Irish are in Luton, accounting for 62.7 per cent of the total, whereas the corresponding figure for the Northern Irish is only 1,413 out of a total of 3,155, only 44.8 per cent (SCAMP, 1993). This pattern of relative over-concentration of the Southern Irish in major urban areas is very consistent.

When the figures are further broken down by gender, it becomes apparent that the Southern Irish males are more concentrated in the cities than their female counterparts. Overall, the Irish-born population is predominantly female, but Table 10.12 shows how the male:female ratio differs.

Table 10.10 Irish population in Great Britain, 1991, by standard regions

Region	Northern Irish		Southern Irish (including part not stated)		All Irish	
	Number	Per cent	Number	Per cent	Number	Per cent
North	8,883	3.6	7,418	1.2	16,301	1.9
Yorkshire & Humberside	15,426	6.3	25,264	4.2	40,690	4.9
East Midlands	14,597	6.0	27,892	4.7	42,489	5.1
East Anglia	7,573	3.1	10,869	1.8	18,442	2.2
South East	89,552	36.6	323,311	54.3	412,863	49.3
South West	18,802	7.7	28,473	4.8	47,275	5.6
West Midlands	24,237	9.9	67,131	11.3	91,368	10.9
North West	32,063	13.1	65,948	11.1	98,011	11.7
Wales	7,388	3.0	13,453	2.3	20,841	2.5
Scotland	26,392	10.8	22,791	3.8	49,184	5.9
Great Britain	244,914	100	592,550	100	837,464	100

Source: OPCS/GRO(S) (1993a) Volume 1, Table 2.

Table 10.11 Comparison of the proportion of the Irish-born and total population living in the main urban centres of Great Britain, 1991

Urban area	Total population	Northern Ireland-born	Born in Republic	Part not stated	Total Irish-born
Greater London	6,679,699	42,243	214,033	194	256,470
South Yorkshire metropolitan county	1,262,630	2,746	5,086	4	7,836
West Yorkshire metropolitan county	2,013,693	7,303	14,876	14	22,193
West Midlands metropolitan county	2,551,671	14,503	50,891	35	65,429
Greater Manchester metropolitan county	2,499,441	13,205	37,825	14	51,044
Merseyside metropolitan county	1,403,642	5,815	11,431	17	17,263
Total in named urban areas	16,410,776	85,815	334,142	278	420,235
Great Britain	54,888,844	244,914	592,020	530	837,464
Per cent	**29.9**	**35.0**	**56.4**	**52.5**	**50.2**

Source: OPCS/GRO(S), (1993a), Volume1, Table 1.

Table 10.12 Male: female ratios of Irish-born in Great Britain, 1991

Area	Northern Irish	Southern Irish	Total Irish
Britain	95:100	86:100	89:100
Metropolitan counties	99:100	88:100	90:100
Rest of England	94:100	84:100	87:100
Wales	89:100	92:100	91:100
Scotland	88:100	77:100	83:100

Source: OPCS/GRO(S) (1993a), Volume 1, Table 2.

Once again, Scotland stands out as anomalous, having a very low ratio, especially in the case of the Southern Irish. Both groups show higher male proportions in the metropolitan counties. They diverge, however, in Wales, which has the highest Southern Irish male:female ratio, but almost the lowest for the Northern Irish. If the scale of analysis of gender differences in residential locations is at the county level, some areas of unusually high gender concentrations can be identified. There are only two counties in England which show an absolute surplus of males in both the Northern and the Southern populations: South Yorkshire and Derbyshire. The neighbouring counties of Humberside and Nottinghamshire also show absolute surpluses of Southern Irish men; the other cases of absolute surplus male populations are rather scattered, making it difficult to identify any clear pattern or causal factor.

In the case of female surpluses, most counties show an absolute surplus, reflecting the dominance of females in the Irish-born population. This analysis concentrates on the Southern Irish female population, which is more markedly variable in concentration than the Northern Irish females. For instance, in only two counties does the Northern male:female ratio fall below 80:100 (Clwyd and Powys), whereas, for the Southern Irish, this is true for 16 counties. Table 10.13 shows these clusters, ordered by the degree of female superabundance.

This list shows some quite clear trends: Southern Irish females seem to cluster in four distinct areas: the south coast and the South West; North Wales and Merseyside; the Home Counties (Buckinghamshire has a score of 80.7); and the rural upland counties of north eastern England.

Table 10.13 Clustering of Southern Irish females in Great Britain, 1991

County	Male: 100 female
Surrey	66.5
East Sussex	67.0
Isle of Wight	67.8
Dorset	69.3
West Sussex	70.8
Merseyside	71.8
Cornwall and Scilly	72.8
Somerset	73.0
Essex	73.8
Clwyd	75.5
Northumberland	75.8
Devon	78.1
Kent	78.6
North Yorkshire	79.0
Hertfordshire	79.0
Gwynedd	79.5

Source: SCAMP (1993).

A number of possible explanations exist. Caulfield and Bhat suggest that Irish females are more likely to marry into the British population (Caulfield and Bhat, 1981), which might lead to a greater degree of spatial assimilation than for Irish males. The south coast focus might also reflect the different age structures of the male and female populations, with the female population forming an increasing majority in the older age bands. It may also reflect the different employment patterns of males and females, in particular the female concentration in both health care, and hotel and catering services.

Microscale concentration

The highest proportion of a ward's population formed by the Irish-born in England and Wales is 17.7 per cent in Cricklewood ward, in Brent. By comparison, the highest percentage that Black–Caribbeans form is 30.1 per cent in Roundwood, also in Brent. The Black–African population reaches 26.6 per cent in Liddle ward, Southwark. For the Indian population, the highest percentage at ward level is 67.2 in Northcote, Ealing, although there are several almost as high in Leicester. The most highly concentrated Bangladeshi ward is Spitalfields, Tower Hamlets, at 60.7 per cent. The Pakistani population's most concentrated ward is University, in Bradford, where they form 52.8 per cent of the population.

10.5 Conclusion

This chapter reveals the anomalous nature of the Irish-born population in Britain. All of the categories of ethnic minority group revealed by the census ethnic group question are non-European. The Irish-born are included in the 1991 Census volumes dealing with ethnicity, but are included solely as a birthplace group, though in such a way as to invite comparison with other ethnic groups. The loss of even those few responses which chose to record Irish as an ethnic identity rather than a birthplace makes it even more difficult to draw such comparisons. For example, it is not possible to use the 1991 Census data directly to prove whether or not the Irish form the largest single ethnic minority group in Britain.

A commonly used model suggests that there are two main trajectories for ethnic minorities in Britain: the Jewish model and the Irish model. This is particularly ironic, because little as is actually known about the Irish, far less is known about the Jewish population in Britain. Nevertheless, in the absence of adequate quantitative data, the pattern has been presumed to be as follows: the Irish pattern is working class, blue collar, council housed and with limited educational qualifications; conversely, the Jewish pattern is self-employed, professional, owner occupying and with high educational qualifications.

While this chapter cannot throw any light on the Jewish reality, the Irish reality (insofar as the census can be said to reveal it) differs a good deal from the stereotype. Irish men have a socio-economic profile very close to that of the total population (see Figure 10.2), though within these broad bandings there remains a significant concentration in the construction industry, especially for the Southern Irish. Irish women, on the other hand, are over-represented in the two highest and the two lowest classes, with their most significant occupational cluster being nursing.

Younger Irish migrants, both male and female, have higher than average levels of educational qualification, reflecting the spread of migration to the professional and middle classes in urban Ireland in the 1980s. Conversely, housing tenure does seem to support the more traditional working class image, while the problem of homelessness among the young Irish in London suggests a much more disturbing pattern.

However, when compared to other ethnic minority groups, and bearing in mind the fact that the 1991 Census really only shows the first generation Irish in Britain, the pattern is far closer to that of the country as a whole. Analysis of the level of geographical concentration shows that the Irish are fairly dispersed and have low levels of segregation from the White population. The highest level of concentration which they form in any ward is less than one fifth. Indices of dissimilarity for the Irish against the White population at ward and even enumeration district level in London and Birmingham are in the 20s or low 30s. All in all, the Irish profile is one with few large differences from that of the White population of Britain and one which appears highly integrated into the population as a whole.

What must not be overlooked in this apparently satisfactory picture, however, is the huge diversity within the Irish population (as within all other ethnic minority groups). The gender differences are clear from the 1991 Census, with Irish women being in a relatively better position than Irish men, at least with regard to employment. The Northern/Southern differences are a good deal harder to pinpoint, especially given the problems with treating the Northern Irish as a homogeneous ethnic group. Two recent successful cases alleging racial discrimination against Irish men (Trevor McAuley in 1994, Independent 1994; and Alan Bryans in 1995, Independent, 1995) show an increasing awareness of what has too often been a more or less hidden form of discrimination. Not until we have access to more accurate data sources, not just on the Irish, but on other European ethnic minority groups, including the Jewish population, can we hope to obtain a full picture of the diversity of the British population.

References

AGIY (1985) Survey report presented to Irish Youth in London Conference by Action Group for Irish Youth. Unpublished.

Caulfield, B. and Bhat, A. (1981) The Irish in Britain. *New Community*, 9, 73–83

CSO(1986) *Preliminary Report on the 1986 Census*. Dublin: Central Statistics Office.

Cobbe, E. and MacCarthaigh, S. (undated) *Living and Working in Europe* Dublin: Gill and Macmillan.

Corcoran, M. (1991) Informalization of metropolitan labour forces. *Irish Journal of Sociology*, 1, 31–51.

Courtney, D. (1989) *Recent Trends in Emigration from Ireland*. Cork: Department of Social Science, Regional Technical College.

Independent (1994) 'Irish Victim of Racist jokes Awarded £6,000'. Wednesday 8 June 1994.

Independent (1995) 'Lecturer awarded £29,000'. Saturday 23 September 1995.

Lennon, M., et al. (1988) *Across the Water*. London: Virago.

Mac Laughlin, J. (1994) *Ireland: the emigrant nursery and the world economy*. Cork: Cork University Press.

Nagle, G. (1994) Bombs, bullets and banners. *Geography Review*, 8, 31–51.

NESC (1991) *NESC Report 1991*. Dublin: National Economic and Social Council.

OPCS/GRO(S) (1993a) *1991 Census Ethnic Group and Country of Birth, Great Britain*. London: HMSO.

OPCS (1993b) *Social Trends* 23. London: HMSO.

OPCS (1994a) *Social Trends* 24. London: HMSO.

OPCS (1994b) *1991 Census. Supplement to Report on Ethnic Group and Country of Birth*. London: HMSO.

O'Toole, F. (1990) *A Mass for Jesse James*. Dublin: New Island Books.

Owen, David (1995) *Irish-born People in Great Britain*, Centre for Research in Ethnic Relations, 1991 Census Statistical Paper No 9, University of Warwick.

SCAMP (1993) SCAMP CD-ROM containing 1991 100 per cent and 10 per cent census tables.

Sexton, J (1986) 'Employment, Unemployment and Emigration' in Kennedy, K (ed) *Ireland in Transition*. Cork: Mercier Press.

Index

Where the word *population* occurs, this refers to the population in the UK, not in the country of birth.
Page numbers in *italics* and **bold** represent a figure or table appearing away from its text respectively.

Index 241